Planning *growth* in Your Church

Planning *growth* in Your Church

- Evangelism
- Caring
- Worship
- Education
- Service
- Administration

Duncan McIntosh • Richard E. Rusbuldt

Judson Press® Valley Forge

PLANNING GROWTH IN YOUR CHURCH

Copyright © 1983
Judson Press, Valley Forge, PA 19482-0851

Second Printing 1986

Scripture quotations are from the *Good News Bible*, the Bible in Today's English
Version. Copyright © American Bible Society, 1976. Used by permission.

Library of Congress Cataloging in Publication Data

McIntosh, Duncan.
  Planning growth in your church.

  Includes bibliographical references.
  1. Church growth. I. Rusbuldt, Richard E. II. Title.
BV652.25.M317 1983   254'.5   83-9412
ISBN 0-8170-1007-6

Acknowledgments

"When will the book on church growth be published?"

How many times that question was asked! It came from the students of a class on church growth taught by Dr. Duncan McIntosh in 1978 at Northern Baptist Theological Seminary in Lombard, Illinois. It came from pastors in Wisconsin, Michigan, Kansas, Iowa, New York, Pennsylvania, and several other states. They all had a part in building this book. But it was the persistence of Dr. Emmett Johnson and the support of other colleagues that finally brought this book into being. The Evangelism Staff of the Personal and Public Witness Unit of National Ministries and the American Baptist Evangelism Team gave constant encouragement.

Among the many who helped are some who stretched their time to the limit. Drs. Orlando E. Costas, David O. Moberg, Robert H. Roberts, and John Douhan read and reread the manuscript, scrutinizing it for theological and sociological content which would be practical for the church. Drs. Marshall Schirer, William D. Scott, and Rev. Floyd E. Welton worked diligently at testing the handbook among the churches of their regions. We thank the many pastors who gave time from busy schedules to study and respond to this process for planning growth. Some of their stories are told in these pages.

While many helped to work on the content, others helped give it form. The patient, competent typing of Joanne Powers makes this partly her book. She was assisted by Melody Garrell. Among the many readers were Mary Anne Forehand, Pat Schell, and Laura Alden, whose comments helped make complicated details readable. And through many long nights there was the loving, understanding waiting of our families and wives. Now that the pens have been laid aside and the typewriters have stilled for a while, it is our desire that our families get more time and our prayer that churches will be helped to grow for the glory of God.

Duncan McIntosh
Richard E. Rusbuldt

Preface

This is a practical book, written by practitioners of the art of church growth. It is one of the few books one sees, in an avalanche of books on church growth, which targets the work of a local church growth planning committee. In fact, its major presupposition is that the locus of power for growth is the lay membership of the congregation. Its aim is to bring the laity on board as *owners* of, and hence, workers in, the program for a growing church.

It clearly says, in contrast to so much church growth material, that the pastor is not *the* key to growth for the church. The whole church must be part of planning and implementation.

In no way, however, does it minimize the minister. He or she is seen as a vital link in the whole process, a link without which the dream is doomed to failure.

One of the strengths of the book is its clear insistence that a biblical base be sought for the church's ministry. Chapter 3 is especially rich in biblical and theological foundation material for the whole undertaking of the church as the people of God, the body of Christ, the fellowship of the Spirit. It provides a rich mine of material for pastors to use in preaching to the congregation for the emphasis of church growth.

Chapter 3 is also unique in the literature today because it demands that a church define its reason for being before making a single plan for growth. Further, this important book shows carefully and in detail how the church can move from vision to action. Many churches have aborted their efforts to grow by not moving to *action!*

Finally, what is unique about this book in the whole field of church growth is that it perceives that growth is holistic. A church, to be fully the church (and not merely parachurch) must plan and act for growth in these areas: evangelism, care, worship, education, service to the world, administration—all in the context of the total ministry of that church.

I commend the book, but only to pastors and people willing to do the hard work and spend the long hours in this kingdom enterprise, never promised as easy.

Emmett V. Johnson
Director of Evangelism
American Baptist Churches, USA

Contents

Preparation Stage

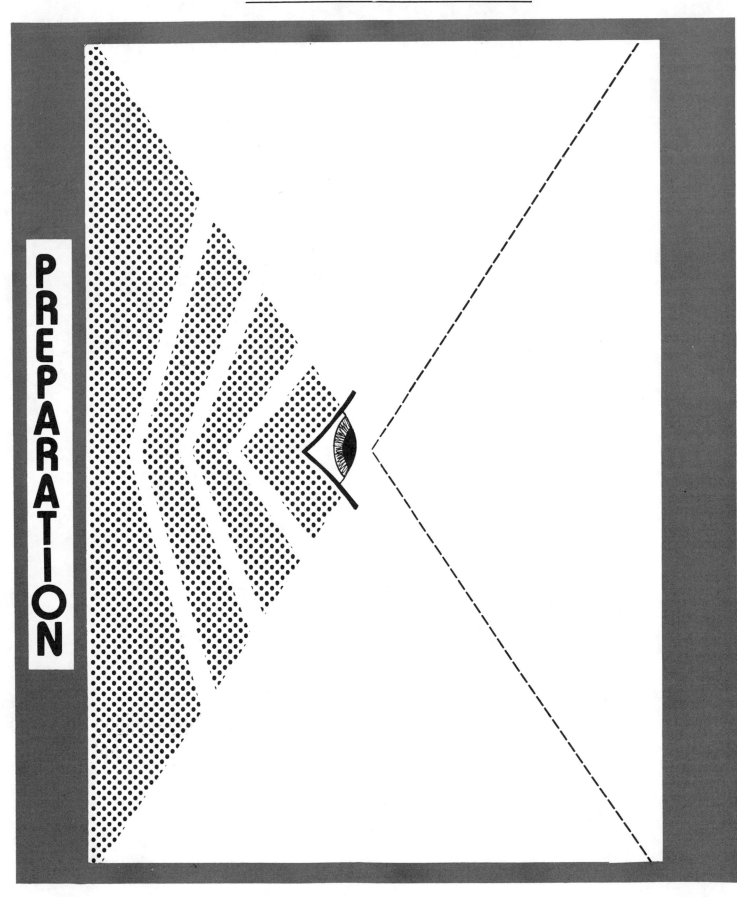

Calendar for Growth

Alongside each step in the following calendar are two columns: one for the dates when a step or an activity is planned to be done, the other for the date when it is done. On the right-hand side is space for notes. Use this space to list any additional activities you will use to complete a step, information about those responsible for doing a task, or methods for doing a task. The pastor and/ or lay leader will complete Steps 1 and 2; the Church Growth Committee will set the rest of the dates at its first meeting. You will be able to mark your progress by filling in the dates as work is completed.

DATES		STEP	ACTIVITIES	NOTES
TO BE DONE BY	**WAS DONE BY**			
			PREPARATION STAGE	
_____ _____ _____ _____ _____ _____	_____ _____ _____ _____ _____ _____	1	**Build Awareness of Growth Emphasis** (pages 17-18, 35-37) Read the book carefully. Discuss the growth emphasis with the church's primary board. Discuss it with other boards and committees. Preach _____ sermons on growth. Do small group Bible studies on growth emphasis. Other: _____ _____	
_____ _____ _____	_____ _____ _____	2	When the church is committed to growth, **Form Church Growth Committee** (pages 18-20, 38) Select members and chairperson. Commission members. Meet and discuss "First Steps," pages 17-20, 197.	
			PURPOSE STAGE	
_____ _____	_____ _____	3	**The Church Purpose** Committee studies chapter 1 (pages 23-31, 198). Invite others to work on statement of purpose (Steps 5 and 6 below).	

DATES		STEP	ACTIVITIES	NOTES
TO BE DONE BY	**WAS DONE BY**			
———— ————	———— ————		Do the "Church Member Perception Questionnaire," page 115. Pastor preaches on purpose and mission of the church.	
———— ————	———— ————	4	**The Agents of God's Purpose** Committee meets to study chapter 2 (pages 33-42, 199). Form prayer support group (pages 38-39). Delegate work on Appendix B (pages 135-174) to be done by Step 8 below.	
————	————	5	**The Church and God's Purpose** Committee meets to study chapter 3 (pages 43-54, 200).	
———— ———— ————	———— ———— ————	6	**Our Church's Purpose** Write the statement of purpose (pages 52-54, especially Step 4 on page 54). Present the statement of purpose to the board (Step 5, page 54). Church adopts the statement (Step 6, page 54).	
			VISION STAGE	
———— ————	———— ————	7	**The Arenas for Our Church's Vision** Committee meets to study chapter 4 (pages 57-64, 200-201). Invite program leaders who will work with you on Steps 10, 11, and 12 below.	
————	————	8	**Starting to Build Our Vision** Committee meets to analyze the data collected (pages 65-66, 175-181, 201).	
————	————	9	**Our Church's Vision** The committee completes the analytical work (pages 66-69, 183-185, 202).	

DATES		STEP	ACTIVITIES	NOTES
TO BE DONE BY	**WAS DONE BY**			

PROGRAM STAGE

10   **Setting Growth Goals**

Committee and program leaders meet to study chapter 6 (pages 73-78, 187, 203-204).
Congregation approves the goals before moving to Step 11.

11   **Developing Growth Objectives**

Committee and program leaders meet to study chapter 7 (pages 79-82, 189, 204).
Program boards and committees submit their objectives to the committee.

12   **Creating Growth Program Plans**

Committee and program leaders meet to study chapter 8 (pages 83-102, 191, 204-205).
Program boards and committees submit their program plans to the committee.

EVALUATION STAGE

13   **Continuing to Grow**

Committee meets to review plans, to study chapters 9 and 10, and to make a calendar for the monitoring, celebrating, evaluating activities.

First Steps

Organizing for Growth in Your Church

The key objective of this manual is to help your church grow in every way possible. This will not be an easy task, but you are not alone. During the past decade many churches have worked hard to try to grow. Many studies have searched for clues to church growth. This manual brings together findings from some of those studies, as well as some experiences of churches that tried to grow.

Growth of any kind is mysterious, yet it usually has predictable elements. When a seed is planted, there is always potential for life. But if growth is to take place, someone must prepare the ground, plant the seed, and care for the young plant. This requires commitment, time, and effort. If certain steps are taken in correct sequence and circumstances are favorable, the results are predictable. But when all is done, the mystery of growth remains. We continue to marvel at how a tiny seed becomes a multicolored flower or a fruit-laden vine.

Just like a seed, each church is packed with potential for life, beauty, and service to others. Church growth is the result of combining two important factors: the mysterious working of the Holy Spirit and certain prescribed steps.

As you consider your church's history, its present problems, and its potential, you wonder about its future. If you had stood in the shadow of the cross that Friday afternoon, you probably would have wondered about the future of Christianity, too. But the empty tomb declares that God is still powerful. The tiny seeds of life which Jesus had carefully sown began to spring into life, producing a young church which the forces of death could not overcome . . . even today (Matthew 16:18)!

Part of the mystery of church growth is that when you stop struggling to survive and to preserve the past, you will begin to grow. If you look ahead with anticipation, rather than look back with longing, you can grow. This is a lesson Jesus taught when he talked about bearing the cross and risking life itself for his sake (Mark 8:34-38). Jesus later referred to his own death when he spoke of a grain of wheat that becomes part of the harvest only after it dies in the ground (John 12:24-26). Part of the mystery of church growth is that God can make something new and meaningful

out of a church that allows its past to become seeds for its future. Your church's past should *not* be its future; however, it can be one of the keys to your church's future.

While there is a mystery to church growth, one thing is very predictable: when growth is strongly desired and certain correct steps are taken, growth almost always happens. Most of the studies of how churches grow conclude by saying very simply, "Churches that want to grow, grow. Churches that don't want to grow, don't grow." One professor was so impressed by supporting evidence that he titled a review of an extensive study of growth and decline in the United Church of Christ "Small by Design." [1]

To wish, hope for, or even pray sincerely for church growth without an equal commitment to planning and hard work will produce few results. Daydreams, good intentions, or heavy dependence on a successful past will not bring about a successful future ministry.

God has a purpose for your church. When your membership becomes excited about that mission (purpose), there will be great potential for your church to grow. When you have identified your church's true "reason for being" and become enthusiastic about it, you will begin to catch a vision—one which will excite your people. It will describe your church's potential as the body of Christ, the fellowship of the Spirit, and the people of God. It will be dynamic because it is God's will for your church at this time and in this particular place.

This manual will help your church discover a vision and then act to fulfill that vision. It deals with some of the mysteries of church growth. It will take you through the stages that make growth possible.

The Preparation Stage (First Steps) tells how to start.

The Purpose Stage (Chapters 1, 2, 3) deals with the kind of growth God seeks in the church, who can make it happen, and the foundation for that growth.

The Vision Stage (Chapters 4 and 5) helps you describe what the church and community are and discover a vision for a renewed church in its community.

[1]Theodore H. Erickson, *Consultation on the Small Church,* Lancaster Theological Seminary, April 26, 1977.

The Program Stage (Chapters 6, 7, 8) takes you through steps for turning the vision into action.

The Evaluation Stage (Chapters 9 and 10) suggests ways to nurture the vision into reality.

There is no established pattern for church growth which tells you exactly how to begin. Sometimes the desire to grow begins with key lay leaders in a congregation; at other times it begins with pastors. There are also situations in which the desire for a church to grow permeates the whole congregation, eventually breaking forth at different levels of ministry and administration. In a thriving, healthy church, the desire to grow may emerge from its strength and a greater vision for expanding the kingdom. A declining church may reach the point where it must grow—"or else." If closing the church's doors is unacceptable, this congregation must begin the search for ways to grow.

Any church that is serious about church growth, however defined, will need many dedicated workers and leaders. Some members will study, while others collect data; some will pray, while others plan; some will catch a vision, while others carry out that vision.

Many frustrated, discouraged lay leaders and pastors echo the question, "How can we grow?" How does a church grow when it has been resting on a plateau for the past decade, with few complaints or accomplishments, and nothing in the future but more of the same? How does a church grow when it has been struggling to hang on to a thin thread of life for many years, when few people are available to do anything other than "keep the doors open"? How can any church break out of a pattern of decline? How can a church whose leaders have become tired from overwork, as well as the aging process, enlist the attention and commitment of a younger generation? How can a church that is experiencing numerical growth deal with the difficult task of assimilating new members? How can a church change from simply "repeating the past" to an attitude expressed by the statement "We are God's church with a mission to carry out in this decade"?

There is no magic formula or simple solution for church growth. But we do believe that there are some helpful, specific steps which must be taken by your church in order to become involved in a significant church growth effort. Here are six steps which will help your church organize for new growth.

Step 1

The church's lay and pastoral leadership must *make a commitment to grow*. They must become aware of *who* God has called your congregation *to be, and what you should be doing* as a result of that call. This type of awareness begins when key leaders say: "We are not all that God wants us to be. We want to discover the fullness of who

God is calling us to be. We are ready to do whatever is necessary to help our church grow."

This type of awareness and attitude can come from many sources. Here are a few:

- discontentment with things the way they are, things such as declining attendance, resting on a plateau, few new ideas, tired leaders, and difficulty reaching budget;
- a general stirring among the church's leaders, exhibited by a positive feeling about the future;
- the discovery of interesting, exciting, or even bothersome challenges or opportunities within the community;
- a growing awareness of the feeling that the Holy Spirit is seeking to challenge or lead this congregation into new ministries.

It is true that a congregation will make little progress toward understanding what church growth is unless both clergy and lay leaders share the same concern. Likewise, the work required to make a successful growth effort demands a significant commitment from all the church's leaders, both lay and clergy. One cannot do it without the other.

Step 2

Next, there is a need to *interpret meanings and possibilities for growth to the membership* so that they can "buy in" to the process. If only a few of the leaders share hopes or visions for the church's future, they must seek the commitment of many more persons within the congregation. The pastor can use the pulpit and various teaching roles to help the membership understand what is happening, or what needs to happen. Church leaders can share thoughts and ideas in board and committee meetings, as well as in individual contacts. Before a congregation launches into a concerted effort to grow, there needs to be consensus and affirmation by the congregation.

Step 3

Now the congregation should *officially delegate the planning responsibility to an appointed group*. If church growth is to be a priority for your congregation, *one* group should have the responsibility for study and implementation of the findings from the study of this manual. We recommend that you create a *Church Growth Committee* to assume these responsibilities. If the diaconate or the church board has the responsibility for planning for church growth, it would be best to form a subcommittee. The members of this committee should have planning skills and be freed from other work to undertake this important task.

The size of the committee is determined by the size of your congregation. A committee of three persons and the pastor can do the work in a small membership congregation. Larger congregations should consider five or more persons, plus the pastor. A key to the committee's effectiveness is to have full representation of the various aspects of the congregation's life and ministry.

Because the work of the committee demands specific administrative and leadership skills, as well as a deep spiritual commitment, members of this committee should be:

● committed to God's calling for themselves and their church;
● understanding and supportive of the pastoral leadership;
● committed to the future of the congregation;
● eager for the church to grow;
● willing to pray regularly for the work of the committee and the church; and
● open to accept the Bible for guidance, wisdom, and support.

The people selected for the committee should be released, if at all possible, from all other responsibilities for at least one year. (A two-year term would be preferable.) This will permit them to be invested fully in this important task and also will indicate clearly to the congregation the importance being placed on the church growth emphasis.

Just as care must be taken in selecting members for the committee, so also must great discretion be exercised in selecting its leader. That person must be competent at working with details of analysis and planning, and excited about putting all the pieces together to make the church grow in as broad a way as possible. But more important, this leader must be able to motivate and guide the committee and to enlist people to do specific tasks. He or she should be highly respected by the church and have a very positive outlook about its future. A contagious enthusiasm, sense of humor, and flexibility are needed to bring the committee and the church through the long and difficult parts of the process without getting lost in unimportant details and questions. If the key to planning is the committee, the key to the committee's success is the chairperson. It is, therefore, imperative that this person be able to work closely with the pastor throughout the entire planning process.

Step 4

The Church Growth Committee needs to *make a significant commitment of time and energy* in using this manual. It is difficult to say how many hours will be needed. Study, collection of data, analysis, planning, and evaluation must be done. When visions of new ministries and goals emerge, detailed plans will need to be developed to make them happen. Some churches may already have data on hand that is recent enough to be valuable. If so, the work of planning will move much more rapidly. Some committees will want to invest a great amount of time discussing and analyzing data, while others will rapidly draw conclusions and move ahead.

Each committee member will need to commit himself or herself to reading the manual and completing all of the assignments for each chapter in advance of each committee meeting. The meetings are outlined in the Leader's Guide at the end of this manual. The first meeting, designed to last one hour and thirty minutes, deals with introductory matters and organization of the committee. The remaining nine meetings are planned to last approximately two and one-half hours each. Chapter 5 will require two sessions to complete. If a committee chooses to do so, and could do a lot of work between sessions, it could meet weekly and move to program plans (the programs, projects, and activities) within three months. Although you may not be able to work at that pace, you should be able to complete the process within six months by having meetings every other week.

Step 5

A key role of the committee is to *maintain communication between the congregation and itself.* From time to time the committee will share the results of studies and analyses with the congregation. At other times the congregation will speak to the committee by responding to questionnaires, making reports, or sharing information and ideas. Sometimes the committee and congregation will listen together and respond to God's word for their church as it is proclaimed by the pastor.

The church growth committee needs to work with other boards and committees to develop programs which will help to fulfill God's purpose for their church. Newsletters, bulletins, and worship services can continually tell the story of what is being planned and, later, what is happening.

Step 6

Eventually there will be a need to *evaluate what has been done* and to *prepare for the next phase of church growth.* This is discussed in chapter 9 and will happen after the program plans and growth objectives have been completed.

Administration—A Gift for Ministry

In conclusion, our God is the Lord of what was, what is, and what shall be. In each church there are those persons who help preserve and celebrate the past. There are also those persons who are doing today's ministry and work. They visit the sick, feed the hungry, and introduce the Good News of new life in Christ to those who are unchurched. Although they are few in number, there are also persons who point to the future. These are the persons who can plan and organize. Through their work, God, who is the Lord of tomorrow, can guide a church into the existing possibilities for tomorrow's ministries.

Administrators and leaders are gifted by the Spirit of God

to direct the affairs of the church (Romans 12:7; 1 Corinthians 12:28). All that is represented by surveys and graphs, questionnaires and reports should be considered as the work of God. They describe what the church has done for the Lord in the past and contain vital information from which possibilities for the future ministry of the church can be drawn. When those gifted by the Spirit for the administration of the church search and discover God's will for the church and set it down in a plan, God speaks to your church. This is the ministry of administration.[2] When those gifted by the Spirit for leadership build programs for the church's out-reach and guide the church workers in those directions, they are fulfilling their ministry.

Launch into this manual with confidence that this is the work of God! The growth which you seek is not measured at its beginning or ending only by the numbers of those who have responded to God's call for salvation and service; it is measured primarily and ultimately by the faithfulness of the church to the proclamation and demonstration of a new life in Jesus Christ. Not all evangelizing churches will double their membership in a year. But all growing churches will be obedient to God's will by being lights in the midst of the world's darkness and by offering the Word of life to the world (Philippians 2:14-16a).

Start to pray and plan so that your church may grow and demonstrate the presence of God in all that you do.

---

[2] If you are going to use the book *Discover Your Gifts* (see page 125 for bibliographical information) as a resource for the growth emphasis in your church, be aware that what we call administration in this book is covered by the term leadership in *Discover Your Gifts*. The element in administration that we are highlighting is the ability to think futuristically and analytically.

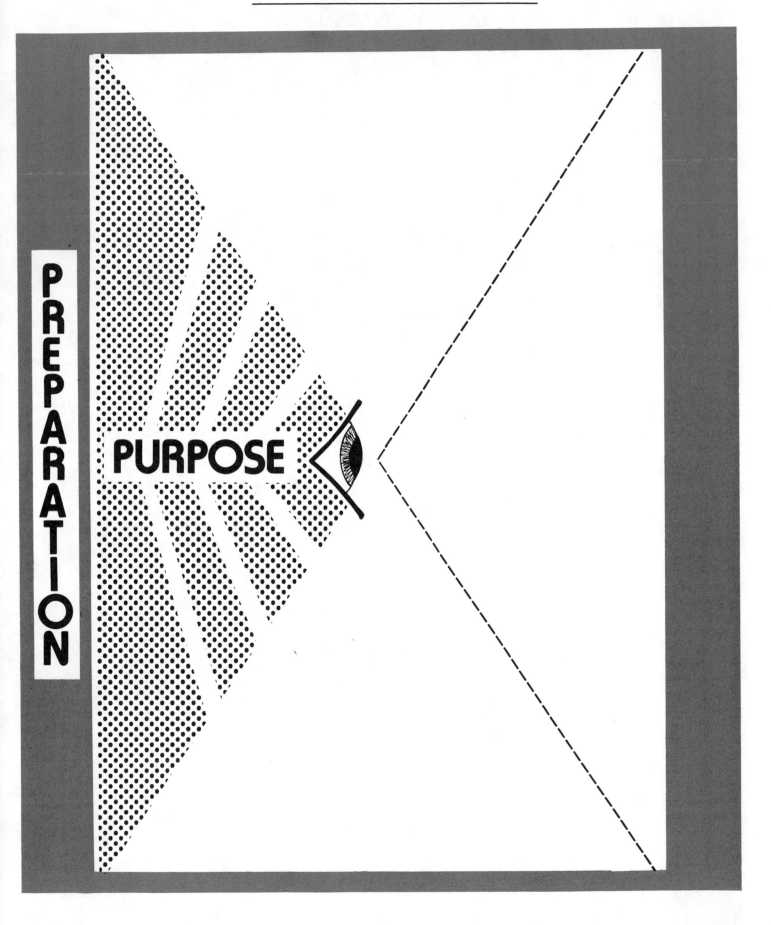

1

And God Said . . . Grow?

Many exciting events are recorded in the book of Acts. Perhaps the most exciting, and most difficult to understand in the twentieth century, is the story recorded in the second chapter.

There are three sections in the second chapter of Acts. Each addresses a phase of church growth which you need to consider. Verses 1 through 13 describe the coming of the Holy Spirit to the believers. From that moment on, things began to happen in exciting ways for the early Christian movement. After you have read these verses, describe in your own words what happened in that room. What are the implications for your church today?

Verses 14 through 36 contain Peter's sermon. The Word of God is proclaimed with authority by a converted fisherman! In a growing church today, proclamation of the Word and individual and group Bible study are given high priority. Read Peter's sermon. What was the heart of the message? How much of that message can be used in today's churches?

From verse 41 to the end of the chapter we read about what happened through the enabling of the Holy Spirit and the preaching of the Word of God. The results were quite outstanding!

Read the chapter in its entirety. Then think about the period of time you have been related to a local church. Remember some of the key events you have experienced. Make a list of some of the times when you were keenly aware of the presence, movement, or working of the Holy Spirit in either your personal life or the life of your church.

Moments of awareness:

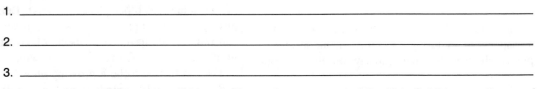

1. _____

2. _____

3. _____

Now, pray that you and others will be sensitive to the movement of the Holy Spirit in your lives and in the life of your church.

There are *two basic questions* which your church must consider if it is serious about its growth and development. They are:

Does God want your church to grow?

Do the members of the congregation want your church to grow?

It is easier to answer the first question than the second. The expansion of the kingdom through the addition of new Christians is something God wants very much. The gift of Jesus Christ demonstrates the extent of God's commitment to the growth and expansion of the kingdom. You can safely assume, with few exceptions, that God wants your church to grow in every way!

It is unthinkable for a parent to bring a child into the world and not yearn for the fullest, most comprehensive development of that child into meaningful adulthood. No farmer plants a fruit tree without desiring that it reach full growth and produce as much fruit as possible. Two persons who have just fallen in love become starry-eyed as they dream of possibilities for the continued growth of their love for each other. It is no different with God and the church. God wants your church to grow and develop to the fullest extent possible.

Not only are new additions to the kingdom expected and wanted, but God also desires that each Christian grow into spiritual maturity. And whenever Christians come together,

God desires full maturity in their relationships and experiences.

God was the source of energy and power for all that happened to the early church. Early in the book of Acts, Peter addressed 120 disciples (Acts 1:15). After the miracle of Pentecost, the number of believers grew to 3,000 (2:41), and continued to grow (2:47; 5:14; 11:24).

The church followed Christ's last instructions and moved from Jerusalem and Judea into Samaria and to the ends of the earth: Ethiopia (Acts 8:4-39), Caesarea (Acts 8:40; 10:1-48), Antioch (Acts 11:19-26), Greece (Acts 16:9-10), and Rome (Acts 28:16). The church grew in the midst of persecution (4:4), internal conflict (5:14; 6:1-7), risk (9:22-31), and through opening up new areas for new churches (11:19-24; 13:48-49). It also grew through the nurturing of its internal spiritual life and as a vivid, living demonstration of a new way of life (Acts 2:41-47; 16:5).

The New Testament does not limit the growth and spread of the Christian faith to the first generation of Christians. The apostle Paul urged *all* of the churches to which he wrote letters to continue to grow. He reminded them that it is God who desires and enables growth to take place when churches are faithful in planting, cultivating, and harvesting. To the church at Corinth, Paul wrote:

> I planted the seed, Apollos watered the plant, but it was God who made the plant grow. The one who plants and the one who waters really do not matter. It is God who matters, for he makes the plant grow. . . . For we are partners working together for God, and you are God's field (I Corinthians 3:6-9).

Paul teaches that the growth of the Christian and the church has aspects of maturing and reproducing similar to growing plants. He uses this picture to say four things about growth:

- Growth has a mysterious element in it that is explained only by saying, "It is of God."
- Growth demands a partnership of people working with God.
- God anticipates fruit and new growth.
- Growth calls for sowing and cultivating before there is harvest.

Thus, in answer to the first question "Does God want your church to grow?" we state clearly that it is God's desire for every church to grow in every way possible. But the answer to the second question "Do the members of *your* congregation *want your church* to grow?" is more difficult. Growth will not occur if this question is not answered with a strong, committed "yes." The urgency and importance of this question is clear in this editorial from a denominational executive to churches in his region:

It is obvious that if our churches are to survive in our Region that we need to be reaching new people for Christ and the church. With a high proportion of people past fifty in membership, and with a net loss of one to two percent per year in many churches, it is obvious that without replacement of members many churches will close by the end of the century.

The clue to the future lies in *whether or not we really want new members*. First of all, we will not seriously attempt to reach new people *unless we really want them to be a part of our local church fellowship*. It takes too much effort to call upon people and to try to help them make a Christian decision *unless we really want them* to share our lives in the church. It requires too much initiative to devise attractive church programs that will lead people into our churches *unless we really care*.[1] (Italics added.)

One of the reasons why it is difficult to answer the question about *your* church wanting to grow is because there are two contradictory ideas about church growth. One says that God desires numerical growth of the church. The other says that in biblical history God depended on a faithful few, not on large numbers. In fact, what God desires is the continuous numerical increase of the church until it becomes the fullness of the kingdom, gathered from the corners of the earth (Luke 13:29), *as well as* the continuous maturing of individual Christians in their personal faith, in their fellowship with other Christians, and in their service for the kingdom of God in the world. These two aspects of growth cannot be separated without destroying what God intends.

This comprehensive and normal growth was modeled by Jesus (Luke 2:40, 52) and by the early church (Acts 2:46-47 and numerous other places in Acts). Luke compiled the history of the church as if it were a repetition of the life and ministry of Jesus. All aspects of growth were evident in the life of Jesus Christ. So it was with the early church.

The motivation to be a growing church must be evident within the church's members and pastor. Without a strong desire to grow, your church probably cannot grow. Much preaching, teaching, listening, and dialogue need to take place in order to discern a congregation's desire to grow.

A growing congregation will never make itself the end product. It knows it is commissioned by God to bear witness in life and word to the love, justice, peace, and salvation of the kingdom. A growing church will follow Jesus by being of service to others without expecting something in return. It is even ready to die for that faith (Mark 10:45). A growing church will follow Jesus by inviting others to enter the kingdom and live out the new life daily. A growing church will strive for the fullness of faith: testing and being tested, praying and trusting, witnessing and serving. That church, "by speaking the truth in a spirit of love," will

[1]R. Eugene Crow, *Newsletter*, American Baptist Churches of Pennsylvania and Delaware, vol. 6, no. 3 (March, 1981).

"grow up in every way to Christ, who is the head" (Ephesians 4:15).

Describing Church Growth

When the words "church growth" are mentioned, some people think only in terms of numbers and size. Others immediately think of improved quality. Because American Baptists are committed to the fullness of the gospel and to a comprehensive approach to church growth, its national team of evangelism leaders adopted the following definition of church growth: *Church growth is the comprehensive and natural expansion that can and should be expected from the life and mission of the church as the people of God, the body of Christ, and the fellowship of the Spirit.*[2]

Church growth is comprehensive because:

- God desires the addition of new believers to the church.
- God calls all believers into discipleship.
- God seeks more vitality in the worship and nurture of the church.
- God expects a church to make a difference in its community by confronting the forces and forms of evil with the truth and power of the gospel lived out by those who claim salvation through faith.

Church growth is natural because:

- God wants, expects, and makes possible the growth of the church.

A growing church identifies with and reflects New Testament concepts of the church as a living organism. Christ is head of the church and the church is the body. Together they are the living, growing church. The church is both witness and servant. The church is a witness to God's presence, to the reality of the new life in Jesus Christ, and to the hope of the new creation. At the same time, the church is a servant, *for* others and *to* others.

Attitude Is the Key

It is not unusual for persons to see the same situation differently. In as diverse a society as ours, we can expect many different perceptions within the life of our churches.

An amusing newspaper article appeared in the *Toronto Sun*, July 27, 1977, in which drivers who had accidents recounted "exactly what happened" in a few words on insurance or accident report forms. One of the drivers reported: "The pedestrian had no idea which direction to go, so I ran over him."

While the newspaper doesn't say so, we can imagine that

[2] Adapted from Orlando E. Costas, "A Wholistic Concept of Church Growth," in *Exploring Church Growth*, Wilbert R. Shenk, ed. (Grand Rapids: Eerdmans, 1983).

the pedestrian had an entirely different viewpoint about that accident. Each witness to the accident may have seen something completely different from that which the driver and the pedestrian saw.

Whether describing automobile accidents or why churches don't grow, what we see and feel (or at least *think* we do) is often very different from what others see, and often different from reality itself. Consider these imaginary conversations which reflect attitudes that block growth in a church:

Church to pastor:	"This is *your* church because you are our pastor. We need to grow, so bring in some new people."
Pastor to church:	"This is *your* church. It is your responsibility to reach new people for Christ."

or . . . .

Church to visitors:	"We are a very friendly church."
Visitors to church:	"They say they are friendly, but they're only friendly to each other."

or . . . .

Church to Community:	"We are declining because there are no new persons to invite to our church."
Community to church:	"Sixty-eight percent of our community is currently unchurched."

or . . . .

Church to community:	"We care for you and pray for you."
Community to church:	"Many of us hurt and are lonely; you don't show that you care for us."

or . . . .

Church members pray:	"O God, we need to grow. Help our pastor find the keys to church growth."
Pastor prays:	"O God, we need to grow. Help our members find the keys to church growth."

or . . . .

Some members pray:	"O God, we need to grow. Send us some new people."
Other members pray:	"O God, we need to grow. But don't make us change."

or . . . .

Successful church to struggling church:	"Why don't you grow up? God wants all churches to be big and influential."
Struggling church to successful church:	"It's a shame you're so big; God wants us to be small. You just can't get close to people in a church your size. We are part of God's remnant."

There are often different perceptions and ideas about church growth within a congregation. Some pastors, for instance, are challenged by talk about growth possibilities, while others see neither the need for nor the possibility of growth in their congregations. Some lay leaders are open to talking about growth possibilities. Others do not want to hear about it because they fear it will bring change to their church.

Differences in perceptions most often emerge from attitudes. Attitude is probably the **key** to your response to any definition, description, or approach to church growth. If you don't want to grow, you won't. *If you want to grow,* numerically as well as in the quality of your spiritual life and Christian fellowship, *your church can grow.*

When perceptions and attitudes of lay leaders and pastors are similar, they provide a healthy climate for church growth. Consider several:

Members pray:	"God, encourage our pastor as well as us to be serious about our church's growth."
Pastor prays:	"God, guide me so that I may help your people to have a common vision about our church's growth."
	or . . . .
Community to church:	"We have many hurts, and need help. Come and help us."
Church to God:	"God, our community needs a lot of help. Please guide us in this ministry."

Ingredients Are Important

A bride of a few months was baking her first pie, using the wild blackberries her husband had picked and brought home. Not having a recipe but remembering her childhood baking efforts, she put the pie together and placed it in the oven. When it came out, it was beautiful to look at and had a mouth-watering aroma.

As they sat together at their little kitchen table, her husband was most eager to take the first bite of the pie. She watched anxiously, but with satisfaction, as her husband put the first bite of pie in his mouth. To her dismay, his face immediately puckered as he struggled to swallow. She cried out, "What's wrong?" He sputtered back, half choking, "Something's missing!" Then she remembered, "I forgot to put the sugar in!"

Though they didn't laugh then, the experience provided many laughs later. However, in some situations it is not humorous when all the ingredients appear to be there but something is missing.

Even when all of the ingredients are present, but not in the right proportions, it is difficult for a pie to taste the way it should. The anticipated pleasure of a tasty piece of pie quickly turns to disappointment when something is missing. It does not satisfy.

So it is with your church. If one ingredient for growth is missing, or present in the wrong proportion, this may prevent the growth and development of your church. Satisfaction with worship experiences, church programs, and interpersonal relationships often hinges on one ingredient, or on the proper mix of all the ingredients which make up the life of your church.

Just as wanting to bake a pie is not enough to guarantee success, just "wanting" your church to grow does not guarantee that it will happen. You need to discover the ingredients that are essential for your church to grow. If one ingredient is missing, or present in the wrong proportion, growth may not happen.

Why Churches Fail to Grow

Significant declines in attendance and membership have been experienced by many churches during the past fifteen years. Since some churches *are* growing numerically in most communities, the comparison of growing and declining churches easily becomes the topic of conversation.

Current polls indicate a lessening of impact and importance of the church. Many view organized religion as a social institution of declining importance on the American scene. In general, Protestantism no longer has the dominance it once enjoyed.

Many studies have been made about the causes of membership losses and the resultant decline of churches. Much of the cause for decline is related to external causes such as location, population shifts, and changing social and economic conditions.

In seeking to identify internal causes, conclusions have not been as easy to come by, though some general observations can be made. Richard G. Hutcheson states:

> Numerical growth or decline is not attributable to any single or simple formula, but is rather the result of a complex combination of factors. . . .[3]

He indicates that almost all studies of church growth and decline have affirmed the importance of several factors: (1) member satisfaction with worship, fellowship, and congregational life, (2) involvement in evangelism and other programs of outreach and enlistment, (3) a growing Sunday church school.

Factors which have not received unanimous support, but which most studies affirm include: (1) pastoral competence, (2) relationship to and identification of the church with the community, and (3) a declining Sunday church school, which is a direct predictor of the future decline of the congregation.

A 1978 Gallup study of backgrounds, values, and interests of unchurched Americans gave reasons why persons became less involved with their church. They included:

[3]Richard G. Hutcheson, Jr., *Mainline Churches and the Evangelicals,* (Atlanta: John Knox Press, 1981), pp. 111-112.

competing activities; objections to the church (its teaching or members); making decisions on one's own; moving to a different community; the belief that the church was no longer helping in the search for meaning or purpose in life; a different life-style; illness; work schedules.

The unchurched were asked why they had problems with the church or found it unhelpful. Narrow teachings about beliefs were cited by 37 percent and too much breadth by 7 percent of those queried. Moral teachings were considered too narrow by 28 percent but too loose by 3 percent. Traditional forms of worship were disliked by 23 percent, though 9 percent wanted no change in the form. While 16 percent wanted the church to work seriously to change society, 12 percent disliked involvement in social or political issues. One out of five wanted a deeper spiritual meaning than they found in the church. The same number had personal disputes with members or felt no care from others and were dissatisfied with the leadership.[4]

This study highlighted the fact that people drop out of church because spiritual meaning, personal relationships, and mission activity are lacking. These same people expressed a deep interest to be involved if these needs were being met. Churches can grow if they have a sense of purpose and reach out to the people around them. No congregation will reach all, but every congregation with clear vision and people-centered programs can reach some.

However, there are other factors that affect growth over which a church does not necessarily have much control. They are:

- church membership changes that are directly related to population changes;
- the declining American birthrate, which accounts for at least a part of the significant decline in our church schools;
- the increasing over-sixty-five age group which is reflected in many churches;
- the fact that the large increase in young adults is not reflected in churches; and
- changing family patterns, directly related to a changing value system.

A "Church Member Perception Questionnaire" is included in Appendix A, page 115. Complete the exercise in anticipation of your next meeting. Your committee will decide whether to use this questionnaire with your congregation to confirm or correct your perceptions. If you do, save the results for reference and later use.

The Costs of Church Growth

Church growth is not easy. In his book *Your Church Can Grow*, Peter Wagner states:

. . . we recognize that we still have a great deal to learn about why some churches grow and some don't. Simply put, *church growth is complex*. There is no way it can be reduced to a simple formula or a canned program.[5]

Because church growth is complex, you must be prepared to invest whatever is necessary to get to the heart of the matter. Since no two churches are alike, you must engage in a significant effort to understand your own particular church and community. Whether you are interested in an increase in the size of your congregation or in discovering a new formula for creating congregational caring, you must fully understand what your church and community are, as well as what they have been in the past. Then you can take that information and forge your way into an unknown future, a future which you can help to design.

One pastor, reading an early draft of this manual, remarked:

The one thing that strikes me most about church growth is the *COST* which must be paid by pastor and people who are sincerely committed to growth. It is a cost that exhibits itself in terms of priorities, time, dollars, and willingness to give up the comfortable "status quo" of "our church" to allow others to enter and share in ministry.[6]

Lyle Schaller states that churches that have a low self-image generally overestimate the cost of growth, and at the same time underestimate their potentialities for growth. You need to discover both *your most realistic potential for growth* and the *"real" costs of growth*. Later in this manual you will work on the potential of your congregation, but now it is time to look at some of the costs of church growth.

The Cost of Commitment

In order to deal effectively with your concern for growth, whether in numbers or in quality, your congregation may need to invest one to two years of intense efforts in getting started. Meaningful results from church growth efforts do not happen overnight. "Business as usual" must be set aside for a period of time. Key leaders need to be released from other responsibilities to function in the growth effort. Church growth must be the priority of your leaders and

[4]*The Unchurched American* (Princeton, New Jersey: The Princeton Religion Research Center and The Gallup Organization, Inc., 1978).

[5]C. Peter Wagner, *Your Church Can Grow* (Ventura: Regal Books, 1976) p. 29.

[6]Rev. Robert Bouder, pastor of First Baptist Church, Bethlehem, Pennsylvania.

people for several years. It should become a basic style of life for your congregation.

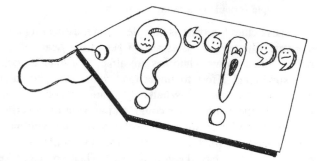

The Cost of Attitudinal Change

If there is to be meaningful movement into the future, some attitudes must change. In some cases, pastors' attitudes will need to be changed; in others, lay leaders will need to examine theirs and make some adjustments. In most cases, both pastor and people will need to change attitudes. Many attitudes will be involved, such as those about:

- the past vs. attitudes about the future;
- who is responsible for what;
- new people, new programs, new ideas;
- the community;
- enthusiasm, participation, excitement;
- prayer;
- the question ''Who are we as the people of God?''; and
- the question ''What does God wish to do *through* our congregation?''

The Cost of Becoming Biblically Literate

The Bible has much to say about the growth of the kingdom of God. It also refers to the growth of local churches. It is through the Bible that a church discovers its purpose, its mission, and its potential for growth. The Bible needs to come alive for both pastor and people. Many pastors need to rediscover its freshness as well as new insights into preaching. Church members need to be willing to study the Word of God in a variety of settings, not just hear it proclaimed on Sunday morning.

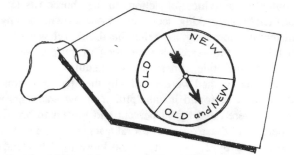

The Cost of New Ideas and New Ways

Giving up the phrase ''We've never done it that way before'' may be costly. Longtime members of churches are almost always faithful and committed, but they *can* be a hindrance to the freshness that new ideas bring, as well as to the freshness of the leading of the Holy Spirit.

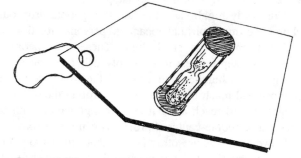

The Cost of Time

A selected group of people needs to invest significant hours and days in the use and implementation of this manual. Boards and committees must also be prepared, at certain points, to invest additional time in processes suggested in this manual.

The Cost of Deciding What It Means to Evangelize

Many churches have nothing more than a general and vague idea about commitment to evangelism. Any congregation that wishes to become involved in a comprehensive approach to church growth must consider the meanings and implications of evangelism. Evangelism must be clearly defined and the pastor and congregation must make a commitment to the meaning of the definition of evangelism which they accept. Whatever you mean by evangelism, you must be *intentional* about doing it. For the sake of discussion, your congregation may want to consider this definition of evangelism prepared by the American Baptist Evangelism Team:

Evangelism is
    the joyous witness of the People of God
        to the redeeming love of God
    urging all to repent
    and to be reconciled to God and each other
    through faith in Jesus Christ
        who lived, died, and was raised from the dead,

so that
    being made new
    and empowered by the Holy Spirit
    believers are incorporated as disciples into the church
    for worship, fellowship, nurture, and
        engagement in God's mission
            of evangelization and liberation within
            society and creation,
        signifying the Kingdom which is present and yet to come.[7]

The Cost of Risk

It is risky to "give up the past" when you don't know what the future holds. Actually, no church has to give up its past, but new opportunities often demand new ways. Those who hold on to "old ways" often lose new opportunities. A growing church knows how to unshackle itself from its past while at the same time celebrating its mission and thrusting out in new ways. There is always risk when a new program, ministry, project, or way of doing things is attempted. Sometimes the price tag for risk is failure; however, failures often provide valuable insights into the future and need not be ends in themselves.

[7] Adopted by the American Baptist Evangelism Team on February 5, 1982.

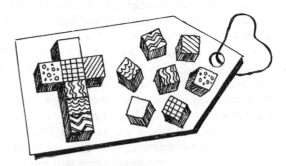

The Cost of the Assimilation Process

There are factors within every church which tend to discourage, if not exclude, new people. Some are easily identifiable. Others are unintentional and more difficult to discover. Sometimes without realizing it is doing so, a congregation can exclude people by its building, its schedule, or the way it organizes groups and programs. There is no question that "outsiders" bring changes with them. To add new people to a group means to change the relationships within the group. It may mean giving up a place of leadership to newcomers. It may mean that oldtimers will have attention shifted from themselves in order to make newcomers feel welcomed and loved. One pastor recently stated: "I am convinced that churches will grow only to the extent that the congregation is able to assimilate new people into its inner circle of *fellowship and ministry*." Are *all* of the members of your congregation open to new people? Are new people welcomed and brought into the community? Are you aware of current barriers to the assimilation of new people into the life of your church? Keep your answers in mind for use later in this process.

The Cost of Forgiveness

A wound left unattended takes a long time to heal and, depending on the circumstances, may never heal. Some of the greatest barriers to church growth are wounds and scars from past or present disagreement, tension, sparring, and open conflict. In some churches the assumption is made that "time will heal all wounds." This is not necessarily true.

When long-standing tension and conflict exist in a church,

there is a need for understanding and forgiveness. Applying biblical teaching can ease the hurt and misunderstanding. Ephesians 4:32 asks us to "be kind and tender-hearted to one another and forgive one another as God has forgiven you through Christ." Colossians 3:13 says: "Be tolerant with one another and forgive one another whenever any of you has a complaint against someone else. You must forgive one another just as the Lord has forgiven you."

The health and subsequent growth of the people of God must be seen as important enough to follow scriptural teachings to forgive. For some churches that will mean discovering how to live together in harmony and learning how to manage conflict when it does occur.

It is almost impossible for any church growth to take place when the church is involved in continuous bickering and fighting. New people, as well as present members who dislike the tension that goes with fighting, will not be persuaded to remain in such a congregation. For many churches that wish to grow, there is an expensive price tag attached. It is the price tag of forgiveness.

The Cost of Wounded Pride

Some church members and pastors may need to admit that past efforts were not as intensive, well-planned, or fruitful as were anticipated. They may need to "turn around" in their attitude toward, or their approaches to, church growth.

You have considered many important concerns in chapter 1. The work of your Church Growth Committee is just getting under way. What you do in the weeks and months which lie ahead will have an important bearing on the future of your church.

Some committees may wish to make a formal covenant with each other regarding their task. On page 31 is a type of formal covenant for the committee to consider at its next meeting. You may wish to modify it in some way to fit your particular situation.

If the committee decides not to use the formal covenant, you may take some time at the conclusion of your first meeting to pray for each other and the task at hand. This time of prayer can be a prayer covenant to undergird your effort, enlist God's guidance and power, and start the team-building process.

Covenant for
Church Growth Committee Members

I covenant with God, my church _____,
and the other members of this Church Growth Committee to give the necessary time and energy to complete our task. I will strive to listen to God and to the other members of the committee in an effort to determine God's leading for the future of our congregation.

Signed: _____

Date: _____

Witnessed by: (other members of the committee)

_____

_____

_____

_____

_____

_____

_____

_____

2

The Laborers and Their Tasks

As a member of the Church Growth Committee, part of your task is to be a person of vision. You are being asked to look into the future, to discover, to listen attentively for the voice of God speaking to you and your church. This is, indeed, an exciting, yet difficult task. Yours is a key role in your church's efforts to grow.

Vision comes in many ways. The Bible contains different accounts of persons receiving vision. In the Old Testament the sixth chapter of Isaiah is an account of his vision. Here Isaiah gave us, as well as could be done, a description of God's glory. It is an awesome vision, a revelation of the God we worship and turn to for guidance, wisdom, and support for the future. Isaiah played a key role in getting God's message to Israel.

Read Isaiah 6:1-8 twice. Pause briefly between each reading and reflect on God and the future. Think about God's call for Isaiah. What is God calling your church to be and to do today?

In the New Testament, Acts 16:9-12 records a vision of Paul. "Come over to Macedonia and help us!" was the plea. Read these verses and consider the key role Paul played in the expansion of the kingdom of God.

Because you are a member of the Church Growth Committee, you take your stand alongside other significant persons throughout the history of Christianity. Other leaders in your church also have important roles to play. Together you stand side by side with Isaiah, Paul, and other key leaders in God's work to redeem the world. Pray that God will strengthen and guide each person who has a role in the task of planning growth in your church.

This chapter presents six roles, each of which is a necessary ingredient for a growing church. They are the roles of the:

- Holy Spirit;
- pastor;
- lay leaders of the congregation;
- congregation;
- Church Growth Committee; and
- prayer support group.

When you have completed this session, your Church Growth Committee should understand these roles and be able to help select persons for prayer support groups.

The Key Role of the Holy Spirit

There they stood . . . she in her prettiest dress and he in his finest suit. They stood beside the shiniest of new cars, one which had been carefully cleaned, brushed, waxed, and polished. They had the keys, as well as the directions to the place where they were going. They anticipated what this brightest of evenings would mean to each of them.

But they didn't go anywhere! In spite of all their finery, the automobile's looks and equipment, they could not move because they were *powerless*. An empty gas tank, in spite of the best equipment and the finest intentions, will get one nowhere.

Churches today are better equipped with buildings, budgets, and trained leaders than the first-century churches. Yet too many seem to lack direction, vitality, and power. An empty power tank, regardless of the best equipment, the most capable leaders, and the finest intentions will get a church nowhere.

Jesus' last recorded words were: "But, when the Holy Spirit comes upon you, you will be filled with power, and you will be witnesses for me in Jerusalem, in all of Judea and Samaria, and to the ends of the earth" (Acts 1:8). Jesus was announcing to the world that upon his departure, the role of the Holy Spirit was to be that of the "energizer," the one who provides power. The rest of the book of Acts describes what took place because of that power.

It appears, however, that many of today's churches consider Acts 1:8 to be a piece of church history, that the Holy Spirit was promised to the early Christians, and the promise was fulfilled when the necessary power to establish the early church was forthcoming. Since that happened almost two thousand years ago, Acts 1:8 seems to have little meaning for many of today's churches. Despite the appearance, this is *not* true! The role of the Holy Spirit in providing power for the church is as valid today as it was for the early Christian movement. Whether we are talking about inviting new persons to find faith in Jesus Christ, discovering new meaning and worth in our worship experience, or providing services to the needy, the energizing presence of the Holy Spirit makes a difference in what happens.

A recurring phrase in the New Testament is: "They were all filled with the Holy Spirit" (Acts 4:31). Again and again we read this statement before a great event in the life of an individual or a group of Christians (Acts 2:4; 4:8; 4:31; 7:55; 8:17, 18; 10:44; 11:15, 24; 13:9; 19:6). To many churches today, it serves as a haunting reminder of a missing ingredient for ministry.

What do you believe about the Holy Spirit? Do you believe that the Holy Spirit of God was the force or power that "started" the early Christian church? Do you think the Holy Spirit has vanished from the face of the earth? If not, do you believe that the Holy Spirit is, or can be, a real, vital, and supportive leader of your congregation? What evidence is there in the life of your church to indicate the presence and activity of the Spirit? Consider these points:

● The power of Pentecost (Acts 2:1-13) was a reminder of the Spirit of God who blew across the barrenness of chaos to bring about a new creation (Genesis 1:1-2).

● The mysterious renewing strength of the Spirit of God brought back to life the graveyard of dry bones (Ezekiel 37).

● The Spirit is the only source of new life (John 3).

● The Spirit is the only source of power for Christians (Acts 2). Since power is the ability to effect change, it can be demonstrated either by the most quiet word or act, or in the noisiest, most visible action or deed.

● The Spirit is the only source of unity (Ephesians 4).

● The Spirit is the only source of spiritual gifts for Christians (Romans 12; 1 Corinthians 12; Ephesians 4).

● The Spirit is the only source of wisdom for the churches of the entire Christian era, including the twentieth century (John 16:7-15; 1 Corinthians 2:10-15).

You are likely to agree with the first six statements; you may hesitate to agree with the last statement. These are the issues for today's churches: Is the promise contained in Acts 1:8 as significant to today's church as it was prior to Pentecost? Is the Holy Spirit your key leader? Do you depend heavily on the leadership and motivation of the Spirit of God for your witness and ministry?

The power of the Holy Spirit is described throughout the New Testament. The Spirit breaks through human rebellion to convince us of sin and righteousness. The power of the Spirit is the key factor in the moment of conversion. The Spirit leads the Christian into maturity and is the Christian's constant guide in worship and in mission. The Holy Spirit also provides all that the church needs for its service in the world.

Even though the Spirit is able to do all of these things, and many more, the Spirit is not always an uninvited intruder into our lives. The Spirit's power may be resisted and the Spirit's ministry frustrated (Ephesians 4:30; 1 Thessalonians 5:19).

Because the ministry of the Holy Spirit is much neglected in churches today, it seems that the Spirit is powerless. Most American church members have been influenced greatly by their predominately materialistic society. They reject myths and fairy tales about spirits. Magic is considered as entertainment alone. Mysticism is not a common part of the religious practices. Many church members would fear that talk about the Holy Spirit only opens the door of the Christian faith to emotionalism.

The Holy Spirit is not myth, fairy tale, or magic. Speaking in tongues is not the only thing that may happen when we talk about the Holy Spirit. Nor is the Spirit only a still, small voice that comforts us all the time or leads us in very safe and predictable directions. Michael Green reminds us that:

> The Holy Spirit is not always a gentle zephyr; sometimes the Spirit is like a raging fire consuming all the rubbish in our lives, or a gale sweeping it away. When [the Spirit] is allowed to have control in a church, in an individual life, then the possibilities for evangelism are unbounded. But only then.[1]

As your church growth committee proceeds with its study

---

[1]Michael Green, *First Things Last,* (Nashville: Discipleship Resources, 1979), p. 13. Used by permission of Michael Green.

of growth possibilities, you must decide about the role of the Holy Spirit in the life of your church—what it is, or what you want it to be. Answer the "Questions Regarding the Role of the Holy Spirit in Your Church," on page 117, Appendix A, in preparation for your next meeting. For additional study resources on the Holy Spirit, see page 41.

The Role of the Pastor

The torrid July sun seemed to burn everything it touched. Sweat poured from the brows of twenty-five teens and fourteen adults as they struggled to complete five significant work projects in three days in Johnstown, Pennsylvania. Five years earlier a July flood had brought great destruction to the city. Five years later a group of thirty-nine American Baptists returned to assist five struggling, hurting, handicapped families.

Most of the group worked very hard and there were many opportunities to witness to the reason for their being in Johnstown. "We come in the name of Jesus Christ," was a frequent response. Carpenters, painters, electricians, and a host of general workers made major repairs to two porches, completed siding a house, painted six rooms on two floors of another home, and tore out ten large windows and replaced them with new double-hung windows—all at no cost to any of the families or individuals.

It was interesting to observe the group working. Most of the youth came with a high level of motivation, but the hot July sun and the dirty, sometimes boring work soon took its toll on personal motivation. It was at this point that the leader's role became significant. The leaders in each group

provided the spark of life when energy or vision failed. It wasn't anything they said. It was easy for the young people to see and experience the enthusiastic attitude of each leader, especially when the going was "tough." The attitude of the leaders guaranteed the success of each of the five projects.

As the groups worked, it was almost as if the words of the apostle Paul were being echoed across the centuries:

> You yourselves know very well that you should do just what we did. We were not lazy when we were with you. . . . we worked and toiled; we kept working day and night. . . . we did it to be an example for you to follow (2 Thessalonians 3:7-9).

Much has been written about the role of the pastor in growing and declining churches. In the eyes of many members, if the church is growing numerically, they have a "good" pastor. If attendance or membership is declining, it is the fault of the pastor. The church growth movement, in general, has identified the pastor as the primary factor in the growth or decline of churches. For instance, Peter Wagner, in his book *Your Church Can Grow,* states:

> Vital Sign Number One of a healthy, growing church is a pastor who is a possibility thinker and whose dynamic leadership has been used to catalyze the entire church into action for growth.[2]

Since this claim and others like it were made, continuing studies of mainline churches that are both growing and declining indicate that the charisma of the pastor is *not* the dominant factor in church growth. Even the most gifted pastors can be captive to conditions that are not suitable for any kind of growth. Conversely, some of the most promising situations for church growth and congregational development can be negated by pastoral leadership which is not appropriate. There is general agreement today, however, that *the pastor does have a key, critical role to carry out in a growing church.*

Carl Dudley states:

> The pastor's attitude and approach to the congregation permeates every study of congregational growth and decline. Although professional competence is not unimportant, *skills do not make the impact that attitude does.* Membership satisfaction in worship and program has the strongest correlation with numerical growth or decline. *The most consistent contribution to program satisfaction is the attitude of the pastor.*[3] (Italics added.)

Enthusiasm is not so much stated as observed and experienced. Pastors (and other leaders) wear their feelings "on their sleeves," visible for all to see. It takes a congre-

---

[2]C. Peter Wagner, *Your Church Can Grow* (Ventura: Regal Books, 1976), p. 57.
[3]Carl S. Dudley, *Where Have All Our People Gone?* (New York: Pilgrim Press, 1979), p. 106.

gation little time to detect the attitude of a pastor toward worship experiences, church growth, program development, planning, visitation, and evangelism.

The attitude of the pastor sets the stage for most of what happens in gathered experiences. Without a doubt it plays the most significant role in building the interest to continue participating.

The Pastor Helps Develop a Common Vision

A key role for every pastor, in the midst of the diversity found in most congregations, is to help in the development of a vision which can be understood and shared by most of the membership. Different ages, life-styles, vocations, family groups, backgrounds, and levels of knowledge exist in most congregations. The pastor can see the total picture of the life and needs of the church and, with other leaders, initiate and carry through a process of envisioning and planning that will produce a ministry which is shared by the congregation.

The Pastor Shares a Vital Faith

The pastor needs to share a personal faith with the congregation as well as the community. What the pastor believes is important to those who worship. A contagious, vital faith can stretch the imagination of those who listen and observe and can encourage those who are growing in their faith to take steps they have never taken. This is not an easy task; it often takes years to accomplish, not merely weeks or months. Pastors who articulate and live their Christian experience become models for their members.

It is important for members of growing churches to have pastors with a confident, dynamic faith who, whether the day brings laughter or tears, are seen as close to God as well as close to the people.

The Pastor Feeds the Flock

A frequently used illustration throughout the Bible is that of the sheep and the shepherd. The shepherd had the task of providing for the sheep; he determined what, where, and when the animals would eat. The shepherd chose the feeding spot and located the fold. The shepherd also doctored the sheep and provided for their security (Psalm 23, John 10).

The pastor, more so than any other person or group, determines the "diet" of the congregation. The selection of sermons and Bible studies usually rests with the pastor and greatly affects the health and overall condition of the congregation. The role of the Holy Spirit was discussed earlier in this chapter. How much your congregation understands about the role and the ministry of the Holy Spirit is largely the result of the spiritual food provided by the former and present pastors.

Even when good, nutritious food is available to people,

they sometimes prefer "junk" food. More than one pastor has been frustrated by a congregation that did not or could not eat the "solid meat" that it needed (1 Corinthians 3:2). However, most congregations are responsive to good food presented in an appetizing manner. Good food is a necessary ingredient to a growing church. One of the pastor's key roles is preparation of an adequate diet which will sustain and encourage that growth.

The Pastor Communicates

A great deal of communication takes place in a growing church. At the center of these efforts to communicate is the pastor. Pastor and people communicate facts and feelings, using a wide variety of methods to do so. Many are effective, but some do not communicate what is intended.

Cummings and Somerville, in their book *Overcoming Communication Barriers in the Church*, summarize the functions of communication:

1. Provide information.
2. Find solutions to problems.
3. Resolve controversies.
4. Modify behaviors.[4]

The Good News is information which needs to be communicated to those inside the church as well as to those who are on the outside. Finding solutions to problems and supporting and caring for persons while they search for solutions are parts of the church's ministry. There is a pastoral and lay role in this which is not soon forgotten by those who receive this kind of support. The "word gets around" if this kind of love and care is communicated. It attracts others.

There is much stress and conflict in our technological society. The pastor and church that are sensitive to the hurts of individuals as well as groups will be noticed. Jesus was always sensitive to people who were hurt or in conflict. Today's church needs to communicate clearly this same type of sensitivity. One way it does this is to deal graciously and redemptively with conflicts among members and about its program. As God's agent of reconciliation, the church will also respond with understanding and mercy to the brokenness of society.

Paul understood that as an ambassador for Christ he was to be a persuader (2 Corinthians 5:11). Jesus, in telling the story of Lazarus and the rich man, said that people who listened to Moses and the prophets would be persuaded to believe (Luke 16:31). To persuade is to convince people of the truth of something so that they will change. Persuasive pastoral leadership in the church today is desirable and needed. It will also be recognized by the community. Ef-

[4]H. Wayland Cummings and Charles G. Somerville, Jr., *Overcoming Communication Barriers in the Church* (Valley Forge: Judson Press, 1981), p. 19.

fective persuasion is a necessary ingredient for your church to grow.

The Pastor Teaches Church Leaders

Even though the pastor is expected to teach the entire church about the Christian faith, the pastor has a special teaching role with the church's leaders. Church leaders need to be fed, challenged, inspired, and sometimes shown how to do certain tasks. Church leaders very often expect this kind of leadership from pastors and wait for it. Pastors should not deny church leaders instruction to aid their ministry. Paul's model of ministry was to teach trustworthy people so they could teach others (2 Timothy 2:2). Each pastor should examine his or her role as teacher among the church's leaders and be intentional about that role.

In summary, five aspects of the role of pastor in a growing church have been presented. They are:

1. The pastor helps develop a common vision.
2. The pastor shares a vital faith.
3. The pastor feeds the flock.
4. The pastor communicates.
5. The pastor teaches church leaders.

Vision, faith, feeding, communicating, teaching—they are all important. More important than these is *attitude*. All these roles may aid growth if the pastor wants growth. What the pastor wants is often nurtured by what a congregation seeks and allows to happen. The growth of your church is a team project and the pastor is an important part of that team.

The Role of the Lay Leaders of the Congregation

Every football team has a quarterback and a captain. They are the leaders on the field during the game and, in general, try to guide and direct the team to victory.

Think of two teams that have played the first quarter of a football game and are taking a few minutes to relax between quarters. They've worked hard, pushed and shoved, run and passed, and exerted much energy, but neither team has yet scored. At the beginning of the second quarter the team with the ball gathers in its huddle and the quarterback says, "This is hard work, gang. I'm not sure this is what we really ought to be doing. I think we should take a few minutes to talk to each other and decide if this is the game we should be playing. Personally, I wish I was sitting in the stands with my girl friend!" The captain agrees with the quarterback!

You can guess how long the quarterback would retain a leadership role. Doubtless, the captain also would be quickly replaced! Lay leaders are the quarterbacks and captains of your church team. They play an extremely important role

in every aspect of the church's ministry. Are those who lead your committees, boards, and task forces fully committed to their leadership roles? Is each committed to the overall task of the church? How committed are your "quarterbacks" to the challenge of church growth?

For lay leaders, as for the pastor, attitude is the primary factor. It is crucial to the ability of the congregation to grow. It cannot be said too strongly nor too often: *A congregation will not grow if lay leaders do not want it to grow!*

Leaders, like pastors, need other important qualities in order to encourage growth in a congregation:

- ability to handle diversity;
- vital, contagious, and visible personal faith;
- a realistic picture of the needs of the church and community;
- an ability to communicate with and facilitate the work of the committees they lead;
- an ability to communicate with the congregation;
- openness to change; and
- ability to relate to persons outside the church in the community.

Effective lay leaders are necessary if your church is to grow.

The Role of the Congregation

Sometimes to look at a congregation at worship can be a discouraging experience. Many people sit passively and placidly, apparently listening. One wonders if anything will happen to them or to others because they are there.

Whether they recognize it or not, these worshipers are the people of God . . . special . . . gifted . . . "called" . . . ministers and priests. But do they believe it? If they do, things happen. Excitement and enthusiasm grow out of the belief that they are the people of God. Their spirit is *contagious!* It is *attractive!* It provides *anticipation!* It is *compelling!* And it is a necessary ingredient in a growing church.

The prophetic role of an enthusiastic congregation will be constructive and positive. It will stand for something rather than merely be against something. The priestly ministry of this type of congregation will seek to celebrate God's presence joyously and to extend God's power of salvation and deliverance (see Luke 4:16-21).

Congregations that are enthusiastic about who they are and what they are about usually convey that enthusiasm to their pastor, to each other, and to outsiders. Their good feelings about themselves and their relationship with God tend to attract others who want to see what their enthusiasm is all about.

Congregations that are enthusiastic about their ministries usually are capable of handling differences of opinion and tensions which arise out of their numerous relationships and tasks. It is not difficult for these people to "preserve the unity which the Spirit gives by means of the peace that binds you together" (Ephesians 4:3).

A growing church offers to those within its fellowship the experience of the unconditional love of Christ, and a growing church looks for opportunities to share this same love with persons who are outside the congregation. People are deemed to be important because they are God's creation, not just for how much they can place in the offering plate or for the classes they can teach.

A well-known Christian writer told a story about his wife and her volunteer work in a mental hospital for emotionally disturbed children. It is the story of a small boy with a problem and a question. Can you find the two missed opportunities?

> There was a little . . . boy whom she had especially grown to love. He had never known his mom and dad. He had been relayed from one relative to another; now by [the] age of eight, he was schizophrenic. One day he asked her, "Do you suppose that there's anybody in the world who loves me?" She said, "Why, Jimmy, I love you, I love you very much." He asked her, somewhat unexpectedly, "Do you suppose God loves me?" She said, "I'm sure he does, I know he does, and I'll tell you what, I'll send the chaplain around so that he can explain God's love for you." And the little boy said, "Oh, I'd like that."
>
> Several days later when she returned for another volunteer day at the hospital she found the little boy crouched over in his corner, seemingly more withdrawn than before. Surprised, she asked him, "Did the chaplain come to talk to you about how God loves you?" The little boy snapped back, "Don't talk to me about him!" She asked, "Why, didn't he come to talk to you?" He replied, "Yes, but all he did was ask me to sing in the choir!" [5]

Caring congregations pour out love and concern for people, whatever their needs. They do not use people because people's relationship with God is primary. A caring church will meet people's needs in the name of Christ. Such a church will have qualities that will help it grow.

To help you focus on the qualities that will produce a growing church, look at "Questions About Your Congregation" on page 119, Appendix A. Describe how your church reflects these qualities. At your next meeting you will compare your answers with other members of the committee. If there is serious disagreement at any point, you may want to collect feedback from the congregation in order to be certain you have correctly analyzed the situation.

The Role of the Church Growth Committee

Since your committee is already at work, it is not nec-

[5] George G. Hunter III, *The Contagious Congregation* (Nashville: Abingdon Press, 1979), p. 102.

essary to dwell at length on the functions and roles you have undertaken. However, the role of the Church Growth Committee is discussed briefly here because you must not lose sight of the importance and significance of your task. No other group or committee in the life of your congregation is doing what you are doing. You are a part of a selected group of leaders willing to share with your pastor in an experience of study, analysis, envisioning, and planning for your church. You are the light (Matthew 5:14), leaven (Matthew 13:33), and salt (Matthew 5:13) through whom the biblical vision and promise for a growing church can permeate your whole congregation.

As a member of the Church Growth Committee you are an important leader in your church. Review the qualities of lay leaders in a growing church on page 37. Then turn to page 121, Appendix A, and complete "Qualities that Contribute to Growth." If time permits in your Church Growth Committee meeting, you may wish to compile the scores of all the members of the committee on the summary sheet on page 123. Some Church Growth Committees will want to ask other key lay leaders in the congregation to rate themselves. An average of those responses may also be added to the summary sheet.

After you have reflected on areas in which you may need to continue to grow personally, take a moment and renew the commitment you made when you first joined the Church Growth Committee. In your personal prayers bring the work of the committee before God regularly. In your committee meetings spend time in prayer together, asking God's guidance and blessings upon your efforts.

The Role of the Prayer Support Group

It was hot and extremely dry in Kansas, so much so that crops were threatened if rain did not come soon. A little girl was taken to a Sunday afternoon service during which special prayer was offered to God for the needed rain. When the service was over, she remarked to her father as they left the church, "No one really expected it to rain." "Why do you say that?" her father asked. "Because no one brought an umbrella," she replied. There is little reason to pray if you don't expect something to happen!

One of the classic stories of praying and not expecting anything to happen is found in Acts 12:11-16:

> Then Peter realized what had happened to him, and said, "Now I know that it is really true! The Lord sent his angel to rescue me from Herod's power and from everything the Jewish people expected to happen."
>
> Aware of his situation, he went to the home of Mary, the mother of John Mark, where many people had gathered and were praying. Peter knocked at the outside door, and a servant girl named Rhoda came to answer it. She recognized Peter's voice and was so happy that she ran back in without opening the door, and announced that Peter was standing outside.

"You are crazy!" They told her. But she insisted that it was true. So they answered, "It is his angel."

Meanwhile, Peter kept on knocking. At last they opened the door, and when they saw him, they were amazed.

If the power of the Holy Spirit is to be released through the life of your congregation, you need to select a church growth prayer support group. It will be a waste of time to study, analyze, and plan for growth if some group is not undergirding your efforts with prayer. Such a prayer support group should be made up of people who believe fully in the power of prayer.

There are Christians in every congregation who have the ability to pray with simplicity and sincerity, fully expecting God to respond. Form a church growth prayer support group of these persons. They may be retired persons who could spend much time in specific prayer for your church. Or they may be extremely busy persons who are willing to become prayer partners in this venture as long as there are no meetings to attend. Young people can also be enlisted.

These persons do not need to become involved in a regular meeting schedule unless they choose to do so. An informal network of church growth prayer support persons can be just as effective as one which meets together. However, there is much to be gained by coming together. In the gathering there will be opportunities for support, sharing, and unity in a common task.

Be specific in your requests for prayer. If you are searching for vision, enlist the group's aid in praying for that. If your church appears to be powerless, ask the group to pray for the power of the Holy Spirit. If your church has been unwilling to become involved in the needs of your community, ask the prayer support group to pray for a new sense of mission.

At your Church Growth Committee meeting make the following decisions about the enlistment of a prayer support group:

1. Who are the best people to enlist the prayer support persons (your committee, the deacons, the pastor)?
2. How many people are needed in the group?
3. Who will provide the specific prayer suggestions for the group?
4. When will the group be recruited, and for how long?

Before you make your decisions, you may want to consider these suggestions:

● If the diaconate is fully supportive of your church growth efforts, ask that board to recruit the prayer support persons.
● Consider recruiting for prayer support a total number which is at least 10 percent of your worshiping congregation. For instance, if you have fifty persons at worship on Sunday morning, recruit at least five prayer support persons.
● Your pastor and the members of your Church Growth Committee are probably best equipped to see overall needs and may be the best persons to share prayer requests with the prayer support group.
● The church growth process is extensive, so prayer support persons should be recruited for a specific period of time (three months, six months, one year). However, don't overlook some who might be willing to make a commitment for a shorter period of time. After the first period of participation, further commitments may be made.

In Preparation for Future Meetings

In order to study and plan for the growth potential of your church, it will be necessary for your Church Growth Committee to collect some data. All good data should serve one or more of the following purposes:

1. Data Can Clarify or Correct Perceptions and Possibilities

Throughout your study you will generate many "hunches" about problems and possibilities in the life of your church. Each hunch should be verified before acting on it. Consider the following examples:

Church "A" had "grown old" over the last years. Members decided to hire a young pastor or a youth minister to attract young people. But when they studied their community statistics, they realized that their neighborhood was older, too.

Church "B" had baptized an average of twenty-five adults per year for the last ten years but attendance still declined. Statistics showed that the community was very stable. However, after three years only 15 percent of the new members remained active. All the others had dropped out, even though they still lived in the neighborhood. Church B discovered it was not retaining members.

Church "C" realized that it was growing older in a community that was not. Its Sunday church school had declined, while its worship services were still well attended. However, it decided that there would be no future without younger families. So an associate pastor was called and given responsibilities for an evangelism ministry with young families. After two years, large membership growth was recorded but worship attendance did not increase. A study of the ages of the members over a three-year period showed that many of those over the age of forty-five who voted for the new ministry dropped out when young people began attending.

Data pointed each of these churches to a clearer perception of its problems and helped avoid wasting energies on incorrect goals or dreams.

2. Data Can Help Find Answers

Church A asked what it could do. Church B asked if certain ages/groups were dropping out while others were staying. Church C asked why people over forty-five were dropping out. Statistical studies opened new doors for understanding problems and pointed ways to new solutions.

3. Data Can Help Provide Measurements for Growth in the Future

Church A discovered that it had ministries to the senior citizens of its community. This church tried to live out the example of Jesus by caring for people with special needs and grew by bringing widowed adults and parents with "empty nests" into fellowship with Christ and the church.

Church B determined to reverse the trend of the past by retaining more people each year for the next ten-year period.

Church C realized that those over the age of forty-five would not sense that the church was theirs if all they heard concerned bringing in new young members. They needed their own programs and ministries rather than providing resources just for new, young families.

Possibilities for growth demand that plans and programs be prepared and put into action. Data can never take the place of those plans. But data may give birth to dreams that are realistic and exciting. Data will give your church a clearer picture of your resources and needs. Through data you will be able to see the strengths and weaknesses of past programs. But more practically, written statistics will help keep your memory current and specific.

Now is the time to begin collection so that the data will be available when you start work on chapter 5.

The Data to Be Collected

The data your committee will gather comes from three sources: observation, statistics, and listening.

1. *Observation* is the use of all our senses to discover what the facts are. Observations about your church are your personal descriptions of people, situations, programs, services, projects, or needs. They will lead to impressions of what is happening. It is important that observations not be passed over. Feelings are important and "hunches" need to be heard, even if they are not consistent with the facts.

2. *Statistics* give a quantitative view of the perceptions which have been expressed as observations. They will also give insights about trends that are not yet obvious to a casual observer. Statistical data generally represent the facts more precisely than observational data.

3. *Listening* to the congregation and community is one way of checking out assumptions which church leaders often make concerning what they do. Listening will bring to your committee's attention the thoughts and feelings of the people about your church and its ministries. What was reflected in the observations and represented in the statistics will "come to life" in interviews.

Below are some suggested methods for gathering this data. (The actual worksheets for collecting the data are in Appendix B.)

How to Collect Church and Community Statistical Data

1. Observational Data

Your perceptions about your church and its ministries are important. So are those of your pastor and other members of the Church Growth Committee. Therefore, the pastor as well as the committee members should respond to the statements about each of the church's ministries on pages 137 to 140, Appendix B.

The committee may also decide to ask the chairperson on each board or committee of your church to complete the questionnaire relating to the ministry of his or her board. These chairpersons may, in turn, request their board or committee members to respond. (The validity of the data would be greater if a sample group of about 10 percent of the church members responded to the questions as well. Try to include people of different ages and with different levels of commitment to the programs of the church.)

Community data can also be gathered by observation. One way to observe your community is through a "windshield survey." This can be done while riding through the community in a car. It is possible but very difficult for one person to drive and to observe a densely housed community. A second or third person can devote full time to observing. With two observers, each can focus on a side of the street. Your committee may want to have several teams do the survey at different times of day or in different areas of the community. Mark the area to be covered on a map and give it to the team. Ask them to follow the instructions on page 141 and complete the information sheet on page 142 of Appendix B. Be sure to specify when the survey is to be completed.

2. Statistical Data

An essential part of the statistical data of any church is its history. Written history is a "narrative statistic" as it provides the background for comparison between where a church has been and where it is going. Do not neglect this statistic. See Appendix B, page 143, for further instructions if you do not have a written church history.

If your church has a written history, it probably has maintained good records. Needed data can be gathered easily. Most churches have membership figures in each annual report. Be sure that records are accessible and that the people who work with those records have been made aware of the need for others to use them. The church secretary or treasurer can supply most of the information from well-kept records. If these persons are unable to compile the data, ask them if they will help someone else. Engage as many people as possible to collect data and give them deadlines for the work. Then enlist one or more persons who enjoy working with figures to complete the forms in Appendix B. Specific instructions for charting this information can be found on pages 144 to 149. If your church has not kept records, do not invent them but do begin keeping them.

Community data is available from several sources. Once again the "narrative statistic" of written history should be gathered. See Appendix B, page 151, for help in locating or writing your community's history. Census data for your area can be found in public libraries or may be obtained from your County Planning Commission. The list of data on page 152, "Community Survey Through Census Data," will guide you through the census reports. It can also be used to request data from a denominational office or from a statistical information service.

The data gathered on statistical sheets should then be transferred to charts or graphs. It will be more easily understood in this form for study or presentation. Once again seek out persons who enjoy this type of work and involve them. This will generate interest in the work of your committee as well as in the future of the church. When you present your report to the congregation, additional people will have had an investment in the process. Challenge one or two high school students with special math skills to take some of these responsibilities. Do not overlook retired or unemployed members of the congregation who have the ability and interest to work with figures and graphs.

Now gather information about the current membership of your church. Look over the "Membership Information Survey" in Appendix B on page 155 to see if your church's records are adequate to answer the questions. If not, or if your church has not kept its records up to date, you will want to begin keeping careful records. Start by asking every member to fill out the survey mentioned here. This may be done at a meeting of the congregation or by mail.

Transfer the personal information (name, address, phone numbers, and occupation) at the top of the Membership Information Survey to file cards in the church office. The remainder of the information on the Membership Information Survey is the raw data from which you will complete the charts and graphs in Appendix B, pages 157 to 167. Specific instructions regarding this information are in Appendix B on page 153.

3. Listening Data

The First Baptist Church of Traverse City, Michigan, is an old downtown church of 115 members that was founded in 1870. Worship and Sunday church school attendance had been suffering for several years. Church leaders made a decision that a change in approach was necessary to help revitalize these important aspects of the church family's life. They did two things. They switched worship time from 11 A.M. to 10 A.M. and Sunday church school from before worship to after worship, with a twenty-minute coffee break in between. They also worked to restructure the Sunday church school program so that it would be a natural extension of worship and would meet the needs of those who attended.

The response was phenomenal. Average worship attendance jumped from fifty to eighty. People who hardly knew each other started talking and sharing during the coffee time. And, most significantly, Sunday church school attendance went from an average of seventeen to an average of sixty! What made such a difference in the Sunday church school program? How were they able to leap from an average of seventeen to sixty in ten short months?

"First," says the pastor, "we listened. We asked people why they weren't coming to Sunday church school. We listened to what they were saying."[6]

Listening to and responding to people can help any congregation. Turn to the suggested interview questions starting on page 169 and decide how you will use them.

Using the Data

Gathering data does not weave a magic carpet to growth. What you do with the data is more important than what data you have. Inadequate data, used well, will often give better results than the best data used improperly. Information about interpreting data is given in chapter 5.

[6]*The American Baptist*, Michigan News Section, November, 1981.

FOR ADDITIONAL STUDY ON THE HOLY SPIRIT

General Books

Myron Augsburger, *Practicing the Presence of the Spirit*. Scottdale, Pa.: Herald Press, 1981.
Douglas Beyer, *Basic Beliefs of Christians*. Valley Forge: Judson Press, 1981, chapter 5.
Norman R. DePuy, *Help in Understanding Theology*. Valley Forge: Judson Press, 1980, part 3.

Michael P. Hamilton, *The Charismatic Movement*. Grand Rapids: Wm. B. Eerdmans, 1975.
Michael Green, *I Believe in the Holy Spirit*. Grand Rapids: Wm. B. Eerdmans, 1976.
Kenneth Cain Kinghorn, *Fresh Wind of the Spirit*. Nashville: Abingdon, 1975.
Ruth Schroeder, *Power for New Life (A Study of Acts)*. Valley Forge: Judson Press, 1977.

The Holy Spirit and Evangelism

Michael Green, *First Things Last: Whatever Happened to Evangelism?* Nashville: Discipleship Resources, 1979, chapter 6.
Herb Miller, *Evangelism's Open Secrets*. St. Louis: The Bethany Press, 1979, chapter 11.

For Pastors and Lay Teachers with Some Theological Training

Warren Lewis, *Witnesses to the Holy Spirit: An Anthology*. Valley Forge: Judson Press, 1978.
Helmut Thielicke, *The Evangelical Faith*, Grand Rapids: Wm. B. Eerdmans, 1974 & 1982, vol. 1, chapters 8-11; vol. 3, chapters 1-6.

3
The Church That Christ Built

No question is more important to the future of your church than "What is our purpose?" Jesus suggested a purpose when he said that we had not chosen him but he chose us to bear the kind of fruit that endures. Before you begin chapter 3, read John 15:1-17. Think about the relationship of your church (the branches) with the real vine (Christ). How strong and healthy is the relationship? Are the branches bearing fruit? How do people demonstrate love for one another?

Pray that God will make your congregation sensitive to its purpose.

A church without a clear picture of what God intends it to be and without a driving desire to live out God's purpose for it will soon cease being a source of renewal for its members, the community, and the world.

Two churches were located in the heart of a busy city. All the problems of the city affected their neighborhoods. One generation moved to the suburbs and new people moved in. Decline in attendance and in giving forced the members of both congregations to ask about the future of their churches. The first congregation said, "As long as we can go on in the manner to which we are accustomed, we will keep the doors open." The second looked at the same community and saw people that it had failed to serve. There were people of many different religious, cultural, economic, social, and national backgrounds. That church opened its doors on Friday nights so people could find a time and place for refreshment and fellowship. Among those who came were youth who needed a place to sleep. Recognizing the need, the church bought a nearby house and converted it into a dormitory. In a short time the first church closed its doors. The second church grew until several years later its sanctuary was nearly filled with people of all kinds. They shared a vital faith with one another. Some served Christ in the local community; others went to minister for Christ in other countries. They had a purpose and a mission because they found out what God intended them to do and caught hold of God's power to do it.

The Nature and the Mission of the Church

What is the church? What is the church to be and to do? The Bible uses more than a hundred word pictures to answer those questions. To describe what the church is and does, the Bible compares it to many things. At times the church is said to be like a temple or priests. At other times the biblical writers speak of it as a household, family, bride, flock, or trustworthy servant. A number of illustrations are taken from farming or business, government or military service. Others come from common things in life such as salt and yeast. We cannot deal with them all in this manual. However, among them are three that sum up the major aspects of the church's nature and mission. A brief study of the church as the people of God, the body of Christ, and the fellowship of the Spirit will help us understand better the church that Christ built. It will also help us understand the kind of church growth about which this manual speaks.

The Church as the People of God

The early Christians saw themselves as the continuation of Israel. They understood their salvation through Christ as a new exodus. They thought of their new life in Christ as a pilgrimage to a new Promised Land. Peter drew on the Old Testament picture of Israel when he described the church as the new nation, the new race, the new priesthood, the new people of God (1 Peter 2:9).

How Israel saw itself as the people of God is important for the church to understand, even today. Israel's identity began with the conviction that people had been created to be responsible servants of God's creation. However, they rebelled against God's authority and took on the names and identities of separate nations and races. Then God called Abraham out of his country to become the beginning of a new nation, a new race, a new people (Genesis 12:1-2).

When that Chosen People was oppressed in Egypt, Moses brought God's promise of rescue and redemption to the slaves. God cared for them, delivered them from slavery, and gave them a land and a mission. That story never left their tradition. At the heart of the story was God's promise: "I will make you my own people, and I will be your God" (Exodus 6:7).

God's gracious choice of Israel is echoed in many of the psalms which praise God for forgiveness and care, guidance and sustenance, protection and comfort. Israel's feeling is summed up beautifully and powerfully in Psalm 95 which praises God as the "Rock of Salvation," as superior to any other ruler, as creator, and as judge. It is no wonder that they said they were God's people, the flock which God shepherded (Psalm 95:7).

The prophets repeated the story many times. Isaiah reminded Israel that they became the people of the Covenant by God's act and will to declare the praises of God (Isaiah 43:21), but Israel abandoned God for Canaan's idols. As a result, Hosea was told to announce that the Chosen People had become "Not my people" (Hosea 1:9). When they repented he was able once more to call them "God's People" and "loved-by-the-Lord" (Hosea 2:1).

The Covenant that God had given at Sinai in the form of laws and to David in the form of promises was given again in the form of Christ's cross and empty tomb. God became like us in the person of Jesus to form out of the world a new people who would give allegiance to their Lord above all other loyalties. The God who brought into being the people of the old Covenant is the same as the God who saves and cares for the people of the new Covenant that was made in the life and death of Jesus Christ.

The church has its origin and its identity in this Covenant-making activity of God. As God's people, the church has a history, a purpose, and a future. The church that loses sight of its history is in danger of becoming self-centered and exclusive. It loses the awareness that God's people are connected through time and space. It tends to assume that God's purposes are all confined to that one group. Losing the sense of history leads also to a loss of the real purpose and mission of the church.

A church can also forget what it means to be God's people by losing sight of its future. The people of God will always be a people in formation until the end of history, when they will realize the fulfillment of God's promises.

The people of God may take many forms, but there is only *one God* to whom they owe allegiance. Our identification as the church comes directly from the fact that it is of God. Our identity does not come from our particular brand of faith, shape of church building, size of membership, or location. It comes uniquely from God, our source of being.

Recognizing the church as the people of God has important implications for church growth.

As you consider the possibilities of growth for your church, remember that in many cases a congregation's attitude about its building can be a great hindrance to church growth. When Britain wanted to rebuild its House of Commons, destroyed by German bombs in 1943, Winston Churchill remarked, "We shape our buildings, and afterward our buildings shape us." The same thing happens to churches. Our buildings tend to shape our image and ideas of God. They affect our concept of who we are as God's people.

Perhaps one of the greatest mistakes of the people of God throughout history has been to attempt to put God into a building. It happened with the tabernacle and the temple in the Old Testament. Today it happens when Christians, by their attitudes, teach children and youth that the church is where we go to be with God. It happens when we call the building in which we worship "God's house."

God cannot be confined to any structure, not even to our church building. One of the results of the "God in a building" heritage is that God appears to be passive, silent, cold, and old, especially to children, youth, and young adults. We are left with a "motionless" God, a God of little or no activity, a God who isn't bothered with human problems.

To be the people of God is to refuse to allow a building to take the place of importance that belongs to the people. Because they cannot be fixed to a place, the people of God are on a pilgrimage and on a mission in the world.

If the building is a hindrance, the church will likely experience a second and greater hindrance to growth—a loss of its mission. The Christian mission cannot be restricted by a building but must grow out of the Christian teachings about creation, sin, and redemption.

Christians affirm that creation is the expression of God's intention for life and that sin is the expression of independence from God's authority. In those two ways all human beings are one. The Bible says it this way: *all* are created in God's image (Genesis 1:27) and *all* have sinned (Romans 3:23).

Another very important Christian affirmation is that though sin breaks fellowship between God and people, God has acted to restore that fellowship. Just as all are one in creation and sin, so God has shown great love for all in sending Jesus Christ to be their Savior (John 3:16). This is the story of redemption. But here the human oneness is broken, for some continue rejecting God's loving forgiveness while others accept it. Those who accept Jesus Christ as their Savior and Lord make up the church. And this is where mission begins.

The church is a special people among the nations of the earth. Having been called out of the world, it is sent back to be among the nations to make disciples. The people of God share a common heritage with all peoples. But their redemption makes them distinct and gives them a mission to the world. The people of God know what it is to be *in* the world but not to be a part *of* the world's life and attitudes that reject God's love and authority. The church, the people of God in the world, is to proclaim God's will and love through demonstration and invitation.

A church that has no sense of mission runs the risk of experiencing a yet greater hindrance to growth. Rejecting the mission means to reject the one who gave the commission (Matthew 28:18-20; John 14:23-24).

Then there is a great temptation for human beings to create God in *their* image. Idols are made by people because they desire gods who do all that they expect, when they expect it done. This kind of god would make them feel comfortable and secure at all times. A god-in-our-image would justify prejudices and never call for accountability.

Such a god would endorse anything a church did, even when it contradicted the will of Jesus Christ for the people of God. A growing church must be guided by the image of God seen in Jesus Christ, not by any god of popular opinion.

A growing church will not allow the building to take the place of the people, nor the people to take the place of God. A growing church believes fully that it is part of the people of God. Because of that conviction, a caring, healthy congregation, whatever its size, will be excited and vibrant, even if in a quiet way. The people of God will always be a church with a mission.

Consider these characteristics of God who calls and of God's people who respond:

- God is active in the world; therefore, the people of God are expected to be active.
- God seeks out people; therefore, God's people need to seek out people.
- God cares for people; therefore, the people of God should be a caring people.
- God saves people; therefore, the people of God should be instruments of salvation.
- God confronts issues in this world; therefore, God's people should confront issues.
- God has hopes, visions, and plans for the church; therefore, the people of God should hope, visualize, and plan for the future of God's church.

Reflect on your church. Are you fully committed to being the people of God, whatever that may mean in terms of ministry and service? Does a ''quiet excitement'' permeate your church and motivate your leaders? Are you occupied with important business because you are God's people?

The Church as the Body of Christ

To speak of the people of God is to speak of the church's identity. To speak of the church as the body of Christ is to describe its task of carrying on the mission of Jesus Christ. To understand the implications of this image for your church, think about what a body is. Take a few minutes to look at yourself in a full-length mirror and say, ''The church of Jesus Christ is like a body because. . . .'' What lessons do you draw from that comparison? Here are some that Paul drew as he developed that term and its meaning for the church.

The first lesson is that just as our human bodies are made up of many parts, so the church is made up of its members. When Paul wrote to the Corinthians, he used the image of the body to teach that unity is not uniformity.

> Christ is like a single body, which has many parts; it is still one body, even though it is made up of different parts. . . . For the body itself is not made up of only one part, but of many parts. . . . As it is, however, God put every different

part in the body just as he wanted it to be. There would not be a body if it were only one part! As it is, there are many parts but one body (1 Corinthians 12:12, 14, 18-20).

Paul goes another step to say that the difference between the parts lies in their function but not in their value. Each member has a special task which the New Testament calls a gift. Paul always wrote about the gifts of the Spirit in the context of the church as the body of Christ (Romans 12:1-8; 1 Corinthians 12:4-11, 27-30; Ephesians 4:7-16). Members of the body of Christ are valued because they are in the body. Their gifts are their different responsibilities.

For Paul, each member is gifted so that the church, through its ministries, will represent Christ on earth. Some gifts help the church grow through the proclamation of the Word in teaching, preaching, and evangelizing. Others demonstrate the great breadth of God's redemptive plan through the church's administration and leadership or through its work of ministering, helping, giving, and showing mercy. Some of the gifts reveal God's unusual power through miracles and healing. All of these gifts, and many more, are given to affect people just as Jesus did in his ministry.

There is a growing interest among many Christians about spiritual gifts in the church. As a member of the Church Growth Committee, you may wish to learn about your own gifts. If so, complete the ''Gifts Analysis Questionnaire'' on pages 125 to 133 of Appendix A.

The second lesson we learn from Paul is that the church as the body of Christ is a sign that points the world to Christ. We can understand this if we refer to John's story of Jesus, the Word of God (John 1:1-14). In Jesus we see what God is like because Jesus was a sign that pointed beyond himself to God (John 14:9).

As the body of Christ, the church is a sign that points the world to Christ as the way to salvation and life. One way the church does this is through its loving, caring, meaningful relationships.

Paul urged the terribly divided church at Corinth to live and work cooperatively (1 Corinthians 12:14-26). He saw little value in their words and outward display of "gifts" as long as members of the congregation showed no care or respect for one another. Helpers were not to be considered of less value than miracle workers, nor were evangelists or teachers to be more respected than administrators. But more important, the joy and pain of each member was to be shared by the entire body. To show respect and care for everyone is to be a body and to follow the example of Jesus (Philippians 2:1-11).

Paul spoke of care and respect but Jesus spoke of love. In the Upper Room, Jesus commanded his disciples to love each other. "Then," he said, "everyone will know that you are my disciples" (John 13:34-35). That kind of love as an unmistakable stamp on a congregation is compelling evidence that the church is the body of Christ. That love is demonstrated in our ways of living and working together more than in our words. When that unusual kind of love fills the church, even those outside sense it and recognize it. It is then that the church's words about the love of God become believable and the church becomes a true sign.

Because the church is the presence of Christ in the world, it is also to be a sign pointing to the reality of a living, glorified Christ. Paul said that by living a holy life in the world, the church was a new kind of body, something uncommon and unfamiliar to the world (Colossians 2:16–3:11). In that way the church is a sign of death to sin, and of resurrection to righteousness. As Jesus was the light, so his followers are to be lights in darkness (Matthew 5:14). As Jesus affected his surroundings, so the church is to be as salt and yeast in the world (Matthew 5:13; 13:33). As Jesus pointed through his life to a God whose will was to be obeyed, so the church by its obedience points to a living, ruling God of justice.

In yet another way the church is a sign. By a life of service it points to Christ the servant. The New Testament word for servant is our word "deacon." Deacons are those elected by a congregation to an office of leadership. In the New Testament, however, the importance of being a deacon was not in the prestige of the office but in the work to be done. Jesus made this clear when some disciples asked for a good position in the kingdom. He told them that service (the work of a deacon) came first. (Read these accounts in Matthew 20:20-28; Mark 10:35-45; Luke 22:24-27.) John makes the same point through the story of Jesus washing the disciples' feet (John 13:3-20). In the world, people may look for status and security but in the kingdom people are called and empowered to serve.

Christian service takes many forms. It may be caring for the physical needs of people (Matthew 8:15; 25:44; 27:55) or responding to their material and financial needs (Luke 8:3; 2 Corinthians 8:4; 9:1). Frequently, in the New Testament, preaching and teaching are called service.

These ways of serving are brought together in a story from the early church. At first the apostles did all the work. As the church grew, so did conflict over administrative matters (Acts 6:1). Then the apostles asked the church to appoint seven to take over the "ministry of the tables" by distributing food and money to the widows (Acts 6:2). They asked for this "help" (a frequent translation of "serve") so that they could continue with prayer and the "ministry of the Word" (Acts 6:4). The word "ministry" in both of these verses is a translation of the Greek word which gives us the word "deacon."

To be a member of the body of Christ is to be a servant who gives completely of one's self. At times the serving, no matter what form it may take, may lead to death, as it did for Jesus and others.

We learn a third lesson from Paul about the body of Christ. To be a living organism, a body needs a head. Christ is the head of the church and he has never delegated that role to another part of the body. He is the director of the church as an institution and is the source of life and hope of the church. As its head he directs and maintains the growth of the church (Ephesians 4:16). But it is the members, acting under the authority of the head, who make that growth visible. Together, Jesus (the head) and the church (the body) function as the presence and power of the living God in the world.

The body of Christ must give evidence that it is just that, the continuation of the presence of Jesus Christ in the world. Are the members of your church aware of and exercising their gifts? Is there a sense of harmony as the parts work together for the building up of the whole body?

Is your church a sign pointing its community to Jesus Christ? Does it sense what it means to be the body—the flesh—of Jesus Christ today? This is what is meant by "incarnation." Can those who are touched by your church detect the power of Christ in your dealings, witness, and presence?

What is your church currently doing that gives evidence of being a serving people in the world? Is there a balance between the time you spend in the church and the time and effort you spend in service in the world? Consider this statement:

> There is, therefore, no question that believers are expected to live in this world as Jesus did. Our lives, values, behavior, attitude, choices, even feelings, are to be in a deep and real way His. We who live in Jesus "must walk as Jesus did" (1 John 2:6).[1]

The Church as the Fellowship of the Spirit

If the *identity* of the church is expressed by the term "the people of God," and the *task* of the church is expressed by "the body of Christ," the *dynamic* of the church is described

in the expression "the fellowship of the Spirit." When Christ ascended into heaven he promised that the Spirit of God would come and be with us. The book of Acts is evidence of the enabling and energizing power of God's Spirit.

The Holy Spirit provides the possibility of a dynamic relationship with God as well as with others in the church. The New Testament word for fellowship has become almost common in English. It is *koinonia* and means partnership or companionship. It is used by Paul to describe our relationship with Christ expressed through the cup and bread (1 Corinthians 10:16) and through suffering (Philippians 3:10). John uses it to describe the partnership that believers have with God as they walk in the light and not in darkness

[1]Laurence O. Richards and Clyde Hoeldtke, *A Theology of Church Leadership* (Grand Rapids: Zondervan Publishing House, 1980), p. 65.

(1 John 1:3-7). *Koinonia* also describes the partnership between believers who share in the knowledge of faith (1 John 1:3), the life of faith (1 John 1:7), and the work of Christ (Philippians 1:5).

While the fellowship we share can be spoken of in very broad terms, it is only through the Spirit that we can enter into it (John 3:6-8). Through the breath of the Spirit we are made alive to God and to others. It is the Spirit that teaches us about Christ and the faith (John 15:26; 1 Corinthians 2:10-12) and helps us in prayer (Romans 8:26-27). The Spirit is the source of power for witness (Acts 1:8) and for ministry through the gifts (1 Corinthians 12:4-11). The Spirit dwelling in us is the mark of our hope (Ephesians 1:13) and the source of our unity (Ephesians 4:3).

Jesus told the disciples before his death that the Spirit would be in the world to convict and to instruct or enlighten. After his resurrection, Christ commissioned the disciples to make disciples of all nations by baptizing them and by instructing them (Matthew 28:20). It seems clear that we form a partnership (a *koinonia*) with the Spirit of God in the expansion of the kingdom. As the Spirit convicts of sin, the church responds with the announcement of forgiveness through faith in Jesus Christ. Those who receive that forgiveness are baptized into fellowship with God and the church. The Spirit opens minds and lives to the fullness of Christ and the church affirms it through the tradition of the apostles.

As the fellowship of the Spirit, the church is drawn into union with God and each other and is also sent on a mission back into the world. How aware is your church of its partnership with both God and one another through the Spirit? How is this shown by the life and ministry of the church? Is there a sensitivity to the leading of the Spirit that prompts gifts to be recognized and a fellowship that encourages them to be exercised?

The Life and Character of the Church

What must a congregation be and do to demonstrate to itself and to the world that it is the people of God, the body of Christ, and the fellowship of the Spirit? While each of those pictures is important, none completely describes what a church ought to be like. There are other ways of describing the character of the church. We will consider four basic ones, even though more may be suggested.

The Church Is Gathered

God set the first "church meeting" at the time of creation. According to Genesis 3:8-9, it seems to have been a custom for God to meet with Adam and Eve at a set time in each day. In this dramatic imagery, Israel's belief was clearly stated: God wants to meet with and talk with the people God has created.

The same picture occurs in Hebrews 10:19-39. The Christian community was undergoing severe persecutions and some Christians surrendered the faith in order to survive. They were encouraged ''not [to] give up the habit of meeting together, as some are doing.'' Instead they were to ''encourage one another all the more . . .'' (verse 25). Gathering shows our love for the presence of God and for each other. Gathering shows that we are ready and willing to engage in conversation with God and with each other.

We gather in response to God's call. As Abraham was called out of his native land to become the parent of a new people of faith (Genesis 12:1-9) so we are called into God's presence (1 Peter 2:9). God's call is the meaning of *ekklesia,* the word used for church most often in the New Testament. The purpose of being ''called out'' was to meet with God for instruction and to take on a new mission.

The idea of meeting together is seen also in the Greek word for synagogue which means ''gathered together.'' Jesus gathered a group of disciples around him to teach and give them a new mission. In a similar way Paul and Barnabas ''met with'' the church in Antioch regularly for a year to teach the people (Acts 11:26).

The early Christians gathered together to learn and worship as did the Jews. The Jews studied the sacred writings in the synagogue and worshiped with sacrifices at the temple. The Christians learned and worshiped in the church meetings. There they were instructed in the apostles' teachings (Acts 2:46-47) and gave their offerings (1 Corinthians 16:2). In their gatherings they celebrated the Lord's Supper and disciplined wayward members (Matthew 18:15-20; 1 Corinthians 5:4). The church is to continue meeting together until that time when people will gather from the four corners of the earth to sit at the kingdom's banquet table (Luke 13:29).

The members of the body of Christ fulfill their purpose best when they have had times of intimate relationship with God and with other members. If growth is to occur, there is a need for members to be linked with one another and to share sustenance and strength. The gathering, whenever it takes place, is vital for both individual and corporate growth.

Are the members of your congregation fully committed to the biblical principle of the gathered body, fellowship, and people? What does your church demonstrate to itself as well as to the world when it is gathered?

The Church Is Sent Out

Someone has said, "The church gathers so that it can be scattered." The church exists to carry out the continuing mission of Jesus Christ. Even as Jesus was sent by God with a mission to perform, so the church has a similar mission (John 17:18). Jesus came to be and to declare the presence and the power of God's kingdom. The disciples, instructed by Jesus, went into the towns of Galilee to do the same thing. After his resurrection, Jesus commissioned them, and us, to continue discipling the nations.

The New Testament shows the early Christians:

— caring (1 Thessalonians 4:9-12; Romans 12:8);
— witnessing (Acts 1:8);
— evangelizing (Acts 5:42; 8:4);
— doing good works (Matthew 5:16; Ephesians 2:10);
— giving hope (I Peter 3:15);
— glorifying God (1 Corinthians 6:20);
— teaching and doing justice (James 4:1-10);
— opposing the forces of evil (Ephesians 6:10-20).

As you consider these aspects of mission, place an "X" beside each mission thrust in which your church is actively involved at present.

The Church Is Faithful

Abraham's faithfulness is still, many thousands of years later, a challenge to Christians to be faithful. His obedience to God's call and mission remains a model for all who follow Christ (Romans 4).

Faithfulness deals with what it is God has called you to be. You *are* the people of God. Even as the steward (slave) of New Testament days was expected to be trustworthy, so today's Christian is to be faithful (1 Corinthians 4:2).

We are to be faithful with our gifts (1 Peter 4:10), with the Gospel (1 Corinthians 9:16-18), and with the truth of God (Colossians 1:25). The stewards are the servants who represent the absent Master (Luke 12:41-48) and work responsibly with the Master's accounts (Matthew 25:14-30). They are the ones who will hear the Master say, "Well done, you good and faithful servant!" (Matthew 25:23).

Jesus pleads for faithfulness in his disciples as true stewards:

Dedicate them to yourself by means of the truth; your word is truth. I sent them into the world, just as you sent me into the world. And for their sake I dedicate myself to you, in order that they, too, may be truly dedicated to you (John 17:17-19).

As the people of God, we are called to give total loyalty to Jesus Christ, and to be devoted to our sisters and brothers in God's family, wherever they are. Later in this chapter you will be asked to define your church's purpose. Then the question to be addressed will be: Are we faithful to God's purpose for our congregation?

The Church Is United

Before his death, Jesus summed up his life in a prayer (John 17). He spoke with God about the model of life he was leaving for his disciples. Jesus had demonstrated faithful, obedient, self-giving service, and a oneness of purpose with God. It was this of which Jesus spoke during the prayer.

"I pray not only for them, but also for those who believe in me because of their message. I pray that they may all be one. Father! May they be in us, just as you are in me and I am in you. May they be one, so that the world will believe that you sent me. I gave them the same glory you gave me, so that they may be one, just as you and I are one. I in them and you in me, so that they may be completely one, in order that the world may know that you sent me and that you love them as you love me" (John 17:20-23).

When Jesus said those words, he was already experiencing the "brokenness" that existed in his small band of disciples; one of them would betray him. Lack of oneness in purpose can be destructive today, even as it was then.

The church at Corinth was wracked with divisions and strife. Paul addressed this church directly regarding its lack of unity and oneness (1 Corinthians 1:10-11; 3:3). He compared those who divided the church by discord to carnivorous animals. To be a carnal Christian was to tear apart the body. He urged them to stop tearing apart the body of Christ.

The unity of the church was a principal theme in Paul's letter to the church at Ephesus. He stressed that the unity of the church depends on God's call and choice, Christ's redemptive work, and the Spirit living in the believers. As there is unity in the Godhead so there should be unity in the church which represents God on earth. This is why Paul detailed all the ways the unity of the church can be experienced. It is as if he were looking at a jewel and naming each facet when he said, "One body, one spirit . . . one hope . . ." (Ephesians 4:4). With humility and with all our energies, we are to work at keeping the unity given by the Spirit (Ephesians 4:1-3).

A growing church is united in every way. Members are loyal to the church's purpose and work diligently to maintain healthy relationships. Disagreements are recognized and are dealt with in love. Persons who are hurt because of these disagreements are not forgotten, but are cared for by the members of the body. The unity of the church also spans distances and differences among people. A growing church will not only send money for the work of churches in another country but will also experience a oneness with those churches despite distance and social, cultural, and language differences.

If Paul were writing to you today, what would he say about the unity of your church?

The Focus of the Church: Memory, Present Reality, and Hope

Mary Semple and Ruth Dobson both arrived at the church early for a meeting of their board of Christian education. They sat and chatted casually while waiting for others to arrive.

Mary, a 35-year-old mother of two children, is a leader in a children's group on Sunday morning. Ruth, in her early sixties, is a children's teacher assistant.

As they waited, Mary remarked, "Did you notice all the children playing in the church parking lot out back? It seems as if every time I come to a meeting, there are more kids playing there. Wouldn't it be great if we could come up with a program that would touch the lives of those children with the Good News in some way? We've just got to talk about that opportunity tonight!"

Ruth responded, "Yes, I saw them. At times it's a problem getting into the parking lot with the children playing there. They don't pay any attention to you if you're coming into the church. Their parents ought to be sending them to our Sunday school; after all, it's not more than a block or two away from any of them. Why, I remember when every child within three or four blocks of this church came to our Sunday school; and we didn't have to do anything special to get them here, either. We had full classes in every department. But I don't suppose we'll ever see days like that again."

Both Mary, with her vision of ministry possibilities, and Ruth, with her warm, glowing memories of the "good old days," are the church. The church of Jesus Christ has a wonderful past it remembers, but the church also has a glorious future it has yet to realize. In between, the church has today, in which it must live and work, rooted in a past while building for the future.

As some people grow older, they lose their dreams and hopes. The same is true of many churches as they grow older. It does not have to be that way for either people or churches. There is a direct relationship between hopes and dreams and the possibilities for growth, however defined.

The aging of a congregation, the pastor, the lay leaders, and even the community itself may often produce an effect known as "orientation to the past." Fresh or new ideas are in short supply, as is the energy with which to implement them. Even a congregation's beliefs about God begin to change. Instead of God being the "strong leader" and "the Spirit who guides" the church into an unknown future, God becomes the "protector of the faithful remnant" or survivors.

Think about life itself. On the one hand, life consists of dreams and visions; on the other hand are memories and history. Sandwiched between is the reality of today.

A "yesterday" church has a strong orientation to its history and its past. Its building is usually very important and much of its limited budget is spent on building maintenance. The emphasis of its programs is on repeating history and the past. In most cases, "yesterday" churches are not eager for new people to join. When new persons do join, it takes them a long time to become leaders. Some "yesterday" churches have endowments which provide income beyond what is received from current contributions. Thus, with yesterday's resources, they struggle for survival. Staying alive and keeping the doors open is of utmost importance.

A "today" church likes what it is doing and wishes to continue its present ministry. This does not mean that it is merely repeating the past nor that it does not change. Rather, it has developed an efficient and perhaps effective method of ministry which it wants to maintain. People in attendance like each other and don't mind newcomers, as long as they are "our kind" of people. Planning consists of program planning, developing a calendar of activities for the year. This is faithfully done on an annual basis. There is no need to look for other issues, problems, or opportunities in the community, since the church is doing what it wants to do and is happy doing it. Tomorrow will be the same as today. (When this happens for a period of time, the "today" church soon becomes a "yesterday" church, doing no more than repeating the past.)

A "tomorrow" church is not satisfied with either its numbers or quality. A "tomorrow" church consistently asks serious questions about its community and what it ought to be doing. It is always conscious of the need to rediscover God's mission. This church believes in the energizing role of the Holy Spirit. The future is there for those who are willing to take it; thus, a longer look into the future is taken regularly. Significant goals are established and kept before the congregation. A realistic assessment of the church's resources is also made. Attempts are made to match resources with ministries. When the resources aren't there and the ministry is thought to be important, then the resources are somehow secured.

There is much enthusiasm about the future. The church's "work" is gladly accepted and viewed as opportunities for the people of God, rather than just "work." Anticipation abounds. The past is fully recognized for what it has meant to the congregation, but no effort is made merely to repeat it.

There are illustrations in the Bible of these three types

of churches. The Pharisees would have been a "yesterday" church. The first generation Christians in some of the churches founded by Paul were "today" churches. They anticipated the immediate return of Christ and did not look to a prolonged future. Most of the biblical writings present a church rooted in a redemptive event from the past, living and working in the present, while looking for the hope of the fulfillment of all of that to which its salvation and mission pointed. It was all summed up in the words from the Lord's Supper, "Do this . . . as a memorial . . . until I come again." Faithful living in the present was an outgrowth of their salvation and preparation for the return of Christ.

Which way does your church look most of the time? Do you spend more time talking about the "good old days," or do you talk more about new opportunities for ministry and witness in your community?

Complete the following exercise to help you recognize the direction of your church's current outlook. The chart below has two triangles, which are joined at their hypotenuse, forming a rectangle. In the triangle on the left side, you will see memories, history, and recollection of the "good old days." As you move to the right (toward the future), there is less and less room for that kind of thinking.

In the triangle on the right, the wider section shows vision, dreams, and enthusiasm about the future. As you move from right to left in that triangle, dreaming is reduced and there is less and less excitement about the future.

On the line which forms the division of the triangles, place an "X" which will indicate where you think your church spends most of its time—looking to the past, present, or future. Are your members more oriented to the past, or the future? If you place your "X" in the middle of the line, most of your time is spent working on today's problems and you are not greatly affected by either orientation.

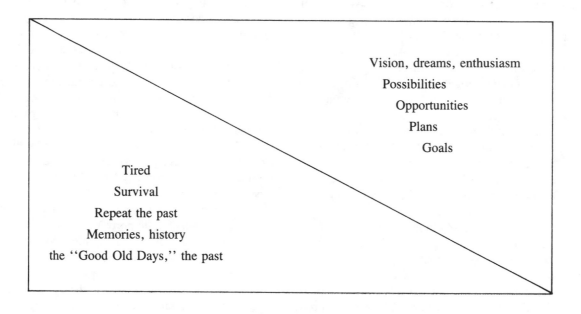

The Purpose and Growth of Your Church

We have described God's intentions for the church. It is now time to translate that into a specific statement about your church's purpose.

Jesus stated in a variety of ways that his purpose in life was to do the will of God who had sent him. Early in Jesus' ministry, he spoke about God's expectations of him (Luke 4:16-19). In verses 18 and 19, note the words "chosen" and "sent." Jesus, reading from Isaiah 61, spoke boldly about the "why" of his ministry. In fact, Jesus' ministry consisted not so much of what Jesus wanted to do, but of what God asked him to do, and expected him to do. Life's purpose for Jesus was to do the will of God.

This is seen most vividly in the Garden of Gethsemane when Jesus' humanity cried out against death on a cross. Jesus had to make a choice. His commitment to his purpose in life, a commitment which could not be dimmed by human suffering, brought Jesus to the cross in a matter of hours.

Almost every church has a statement of purpose. It is usually found at the beginning of a church's constitution or in official church documents.

A statement of purpose explains the long-range reasons why a congregation should continue to exist. Most churches, once they are established and build a building, *assume* they should always exist. That is not always true. Many church members believe their church exists for worship services and programs, but the many programs and services of a local congregation are *not* its reasons for being. Your church's current statement of purpose may mention worship services, Sunday church school, prayer meetings, or witnessing. But not until you have answered the questions "Why are we holding worship services?" or "Why do we offer Sunday church school programs?" will you have answered the "reason for being" question.

A statement of purpose tells the church's "reason for being." It should be the "rallying cry" for a congregation. It should be a constant reminder that the church is the people of God, called into existence by God. Purpose is mission. Purpose is God's calling. Purpose provides identity and direction for what the congregation is to be and do.

God calls each church to *be* something: the presence of God in its community. Each church must determine just how it will be God's presence. Each church has its own role in its community. It is distinct, unique, special, and its origin is in God. Roles can and must change from time to time in order to respond to the changing needs of persons and communities. Many congregations make the mistake of moving ahead on the basic assumption that their church will always be the same, regardless of what happens in their world. Getting at its purpose drives a congregation back to God to discover what God is calling it to be here and now.

A church in a western city discovered its growth was not keeping pace with the fast community growth around it. A deep concern about the situation drove the church to study itself and its community. The study showed, among other things, that the congregation had no identity that pulled it together. The pastor and boards worked on a statement of purpose. The statement that grew out of their work was:

> We are members of the Body of Christ
>   believing and living,
>   going and growing,
>   sharing and caring,
> as an active witness of the Kingdom of God on earth.

The pastor preached sermons on parts of the purpose at regular intervals. Each Sunday morning the congregation recited the statement after the call to worship. On the first Sunday evening of each month it was used as the benediction for the Lord's Supper as the congregation formed a circle around the room.

What happened as the purpose took hold of that congregation? In five years the congregation grew by over six hundred persons. Small group Bible studies and discipleship programs developed. Every day of the week at least one group is now meeting for study and spiritual growth. The congregation is reaching out to the community in many different ways. The congregation has discovered that its reason for existing is the call of God to *be* and *do* something.

Believing that God's call is the reason behind everything you are doing provides much more enthusiasm and excitement than wondering what the reasons are for doing things. Not even a church building can stand in the way. If the church is a living organism (the body of Christ), the building is a secondary part of the picture. It is God who breathes into a group of people the breath of life that makes it a congregation.

Look at your congregation's statement of purpose. What is your reason for being? If your congregation does not have such a statement, it will be important to develop one before proceeding to the next section of this manual. If your church has not reaffirmed, revised, or rewritten its statement of purpose within the last five years, it needs to do so now.

Your Church Growth Committee can work on the statement of purpose if you feel that you have time to do so. Or you can enlist a task force or an existing group within the congregation (deacons, advisory board) to do the study and writing. The group that develops the statement of purpose should be representative of the entire congregation.

Here are some steps your committee may use for writing or revising a statement of purpose:

Step 1— The pastor will preach several sermons dealing with the purpose of the church. (See page 18, step 2.) These sermons will raise the consciousness of the church while the statement is being prepared. The pastor should be a member of the group that is writing the statement of purpose.

Step 2— The Bible study you have already done in this manual has been preparation for building a statement of purpose. Some additional passages that highlight important aspects of the church and its ministry are:

> Isaiah 53—"The Suffering Servant." What is the role of the suffering servant in today's world?
>
> John 3:16-20—"The Object of God's Love." What is God's role in bringing salvation into the world? What is the church's role?
>
> Romans 12:1-21—"The Christian Style of Life." What life-style is expected of the people of God?
>
> Ephesians 1:1-23—"The Lordship of Christ." How does a church respond to the lordship of Christ?

Ephesians 4:1-16—"Christ's Gifts." What are spiritual gifts? From whom do they come?

1 John 2:7-11—"The Test Is Love." Is your congregation reproducing the love of God in its life and ministry?

Step 3— Those who are working on the statement of purpose should review the responses to question 15 on the "Church Member Perception Questionnaire" (page 115) to discover what they think the purpose of the church is. They should have received responses from at least 10 percent of the congregation. When the results are compiled, they will help you to be aware of the congregation's general understanding of the church's purpose.

Step 4— Write a statement of purpose. Remember that the statement of purpose deals with God's call to your congregation concerning your unique role in your community. It should not contain a list of programs, projects, or ministries you are going to offer. These will be developed later. The statement should deal with who you are, rather than what you are going to do.

Step 5— When your group has agreed on the statement that you want to refer to the congregation, forward the statement to the appropriate boards or committees for consideration. Supply any background information needed to explain the process you used to develop the statement.

Step 6— Once the statement of purpose has been approved by the appropriate boards or committees, it should be submitted to your congregation for discussion, modification (if necessary), and action.

Step 7— Publish the statement of purpose. Once it has been adopted, celebrate the statement of purpose in worship and other settings. Keep it before boards and committees as they function. Remember that a growing congregation knows, is proud of, and is loyal to its reason for being. Your pastor should also use the statement of purpose in preaching.

Step 8— Use the statement of purpose in every step along the way as you work at becoming a growing congregation.

Vision Stage

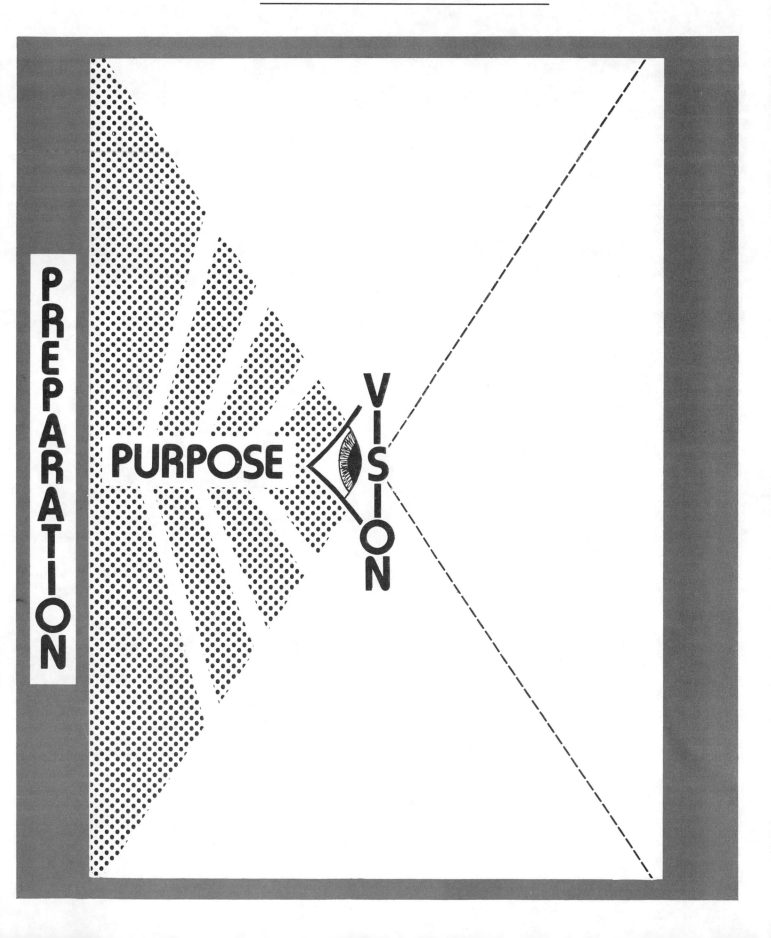

4

The Arenas for Vision

Before you begin chapter 4, take a few minutes to consider the Great Commission. Read Matthew 28:19-20, Mark 16:15, and Luke 24:45-49. Think about what Jesus is suggesting to his followers.

Then read John 17:18 and John 20:21. Perhaps this is the most crucial statement of the Great Commission. Jesus prayed for his disciples in the Upper Room and said: "I send them into the world, just as you sent me into the world."

After his death and resurrection, Jesus reminded his followers: "As the Father sent me, so I send you."

There is a great message here. Jesus did more than draw a casual connection between his mission and ours. He strongly stated that *his* mission is a model for *our* mission as well as the mission of the church. An adequate understanding of the scope of a church's mission must be drawn from an understanding of Jesus' mission.

This chapter deals with arenas of vision, the places where vision needs to be applied. What does the Great Commission mean to your church? to you? What is your vision for ministry in your church and community?

Read Ephesians 3:14-21 in your favorite version. Pray in the following manner:

God, I ask that my mind may be opened to see your light, so that I will know what is the hope to which you have called me, how rich are the wonderful blessings you have promised your people, and how very great is your power at work in all who believe.

One summer afternoon a boy was busy working with his dad's tools. As the afternoon went on, he was seen measuring and cutting pieces of wood, hammering nails, and sometimes taking nails out. From time to time he held pieces of wood in the air for a better look at what he was building. Finally, late in the afternoon, all noise stopped and it appeared as if the project were completed.

Wondering what the boy had been working at all afternoon, a neighbor approached and asked the question, "What have you been building?"

The boy held up an interesting assortment of wood and nails and said proudly, "Here it is. Do you like it?"

The neighbor answered, "Yes," and then asked, "What is it?"

"I don't really know," the boy replied.

"What were you trying to build?" the neighbor asked.

"Oh, I didn't have anything special in mind. I just needed something to do," he responded. "So it doesn't matter how it turned out."

One of the silent messages coming from many congregations in America is the same: "We don't have anything special in mind. We just need something to do." Churches without purpose, goals, and power prove to be as meaningless as the boy's efforts to fill time with aimless building activity. They entertain the persons involved in the effort, but they make no meaningful contribution to the world.

Activity for the sake of activity is *not* one of the marks of a growing church. Congregations with no purpose, goals, or power do not grow either.

Proverbs 29:18 (KJV) reminds us that: "Where there is no vision, the people perish." Also, where there is no vision, churches do not grow, needs are not met, and the work of God's kingdom makes little headway in the world.

Mountain climbing is a rugged sport. It demands a variety of skills, stamina, ability, and motivation. Those who climb mountains tell us that one of the greatest motivators is the vision they have in their mind's eye of what the view will be like when they reach the top. All of the hard work, training, cuts and bruises, as well as risk to life and limb, are worth the effort. The vision keeps them going!

Churches need a vision of what they can be and do. Congregations need vision which will give members something to reach and stretch for, to invest in, to which they can be committed. Your church leaders need to be motivated by some of the possibilities to which they can respond, both in the church and in the community. Your church needs to be "striving and stretching." How else can your congregation tap the resources of the unlimited power of the almighty God?

Sources of Vision

There are a number of sources from which a congregation can catch a vision of what it needs to be and do.

(1) Your statement of purpose has "vision value" if you have determined that God has called you to be a certain type of congregation or to have a special mission in the world. Vision grows out of a church's purpose statement:

> A church's purpose is not the vision, but vision should emerge from a church's purpose. God, who gives vision and shapes mission, whether through the church or the world, desires that *all* creation respond to a loving, forgiving God. If a church believes this, then all "blinders" or resistance to mission must be removed.

> Churches without vision limit God. Most Christians believe God is "all-powerful"; yet God's most limiting factor in the world today is the church itself. Churches often stand "in the way" of God's kingdom. If God is "small," it's because the church has forced "smallness" on God. God is not limited unless we do the limiting.[1]

The very fact that "God has called you forth" can provide motivation if it is kept before your congregation on a regular basis. Members of a congregation must never be allowed to forget that they are the people of God.

(2) Scripture also contains much valuable "vision material." Bible study is of great value to the congregation seeking to discover God's will for the future.

(3) Prayer gives vision to the congregation which constantly asks God who it is to be and what it is to do. Your church growth prayer support group is a living example of using the medium of prayer in the ongoing ministry and work of the church.

(4) Data—charts, graphs, community information, observations, listening, and surveys—provide materials which when analyzed can give new vistas for vision.

Arenas for Vision

In chapter 1, church growth was described as the comprehensive and natural expansion that can and should be expected from the life and mission of the church as the people of God, the body of Christ, and the fellowship of the Spirit. Church growth is something more than numerical growth. The growth of individual Christians and of congregations into a mature faith and in the kingdom's mission are equally important. Growth happens when a dream for something better or different from what exists is realized. Growth begins in the seed of a vision. What is *your* vision for the growth of *your* church? What special dream can your church develop which can be implemented and thus will help it grow?

To build a vision for growth it would help to look at the life and mission of your church from two perspectives. They could be compared to two different ways of looking at a piece of fabric. One way would be to think of the individual threads. The second way would be to notice how the threads are woven into a continuous piece of cloth. Each thread has its own shape, color, and weight but it is not a piece of cloth. The quality of the cloth is determined by the strength each thread gives to the cloth as it is woven with the others and by the beauty it gives as its color and texture are blended with others.

So it is with your church. To build for comprehensive and natural growth you will have to study your congregation's individual ministries (the threads) and then view them as parts of the complete program of the church (the finished piece of fabric). The first step will be to examine each of six major arenas for mission in the life of your church: evangelism, care, worship, education, service to the world, and church administration. Even though there also are other important arenas for ministry and mission, the growth of your church will be helped along if it is designed around these six.

In a growing church none of these arenas of the church's life and mission can stand alone. You cannot afford to choose some and neglect others. As your church grows in all of them, you will become and act as the fellowship, the body, and the people of God. For this reason it is necessary for your Church Growth Committee to look also at the way in which all of these are integrated into the total life and mission of the church. This is essential if your church is to experience comprehensive and natural growth.

Evangelism

The first evangelists numbered eleven men and a handful of women. Would anyone dare to say that a "small" church or group cannot be powerful? Those early Christians were very few, uneducated, and led simple lives, with little organization behind them. They had few great preachers. On top of all these disadvantages, they were hated by both the Jews and the Gentiles.

How could a group like this make such an impact on its society, and eventually on the whole world? The answer is that they were completely "sold" on Jesus Christ, so much so that they obeyed the Holy Spirit fully and told the Good News to everybody they could.

[1] Richard E. Rusbuldt, *Evangelism on Purpose* (Valley Forge: Judson Press, 1980), p. 29.

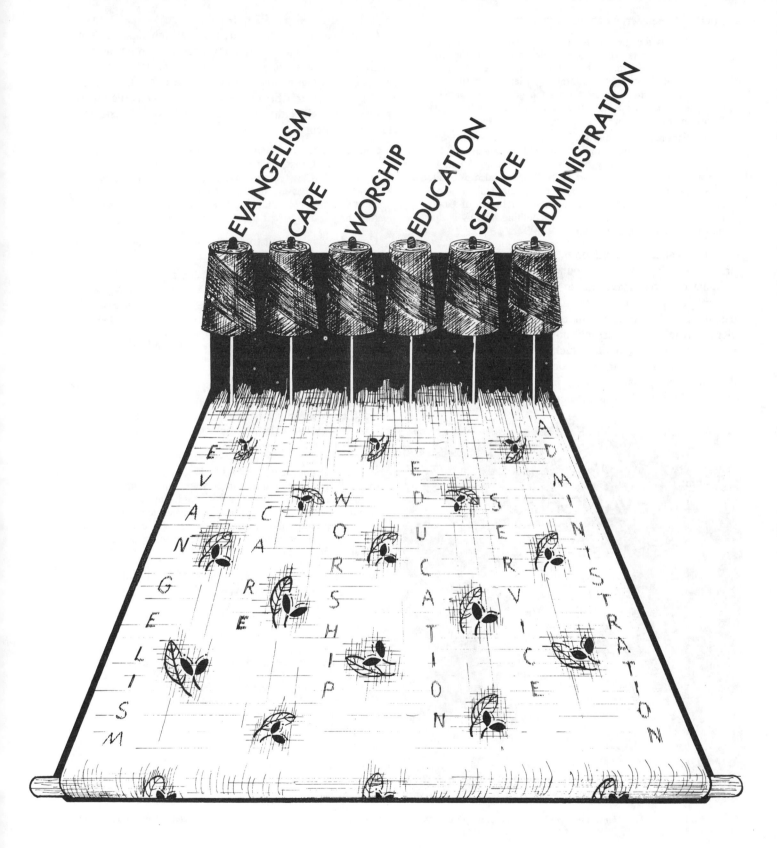

Michael Green writes about evangelism:

Evangelism is not an optional extra for those who like that kind of thing. It is not an acceptable pastime for the man who likes making a fool of himself on a soap box in the open air, or titivating his ego by addressing a large gathering in a public hall. Evangelism is sharing the good news of what God has done for us all. It is the sacred duty of every Christian.

Evangelism is not shallow. It is, of course, often regarded as shallow by those who don't do it, and by some who do. Indeed, a lot that passes by the name of evangelism *is* shallow. But that is not how it is meant to be. It is intended to be the good news of how God takes sinners and builds them into a new society which constitutes the first installment of God's kingly rule in a rebel world. There is nothing shallow in that message and its implications.[2]

Either evangelism is important and is given high priority, or it is not. There is little ground in between.

Some churches leave the so-called "business of evangelism" to the pastor. After all, "that's what we pay a pastor for." But evangelism is not the task of ordained clergy alone. In fact, it may not be their primary task at all. According to Scriptures such as Romans 12, 1 Corinthians 12, and Ephesians 4 (all dealing with spiritual gifts), the gift of evangelism is for the *laos*, the "people of God" (1 Peter 2:9-10). Take a moment to review the definition

of evangelism on page 29. Jesus is such "Good News." *All* of us, not just the preacher, must tell others about him!

The early Christians were known for their enthusiasm for sharing their faith. In your village, town, community, or city, how are your church members known? Are they known as the followers of Christ? It was in Antioch that the townspeople first called the followers of Christ "Christians." Green comments:

It must have been because they kept speaking of Christ, kept working for Christ, kept trying to please Christ, acting as they thought Christ would have acted. . . . They were consumed with a passion for Jesus Christ. He was their Lord, he was their first love; nothing else was so important to them. And the pagans knew it.[3]

Consider this sad but true story of a man who wanted to "check out" today's church:

A Downey [California] resident claims that, in order to satisfy his "curiosity," he attended services at about 500 churches in the Los Angeles metropolitan area in the last five years and found himself ignored at virtually all of them. . . . Donald Thomas, 67, said his personal survey . . . averaged two services a week, . . . He attended not only on Sunday mornings but sometimes on Saturday, Sunday night or Wednesday night.

He contends he was greeted by blank stares, cold shoulders or distant nods at Roman Catholic parishes, Christian Science branches, Mormon wards, Jewish synagogues and Seventh-Day Adventist churches as well as all other varieties of churches.

"With the exception of the greeters (designated handshakers at the church entrances), which I feel are synthetic," Thomas said, "there was only one church where any member said a word of any kind to me." Thomas said that at one lightly attended evening service he and another visitor were asked to stand up during the service and be recognized. Although he lingered in the back of the sanctuary after the service, "everybody walked right by," he said.[4]

Most of the churches we attend would tell you that they are friendly congregations. What would Mr. Thomas have said if he had visited your congregation?

Care

"I myself will be the shepherd of my sheep, and I will find them a place to rest. I, the Sovereign LORD, have spoken. I will look for those that are lost, bring back those that wander off, bandage those that are hurt, and heal those that are sick; . . . because I am a shepherd who does what is right." (Ezekiel 34:15-16).

These words to Ezekiel are indicative of God's attitude toward *your* congregation. Basically, God is saying, "I *care*

---

[2]Michael Green, *First Things Last* (Nashville: Discipleship Resources, 1979), p. 2.

[3]*Ibid.*, p. 78.

[4]John Dart, "He Was a Stranger and Nobody Cared," *The Los Angeles Times,* May 6, 1978. Copyright, 1978, Los Angeles Times. Reprinted by permission.

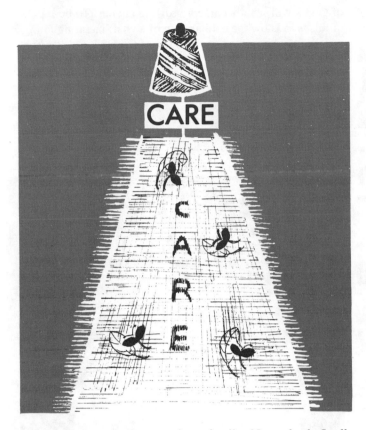

for everyone who is part of my family. Not only do I tell my people I care for them, but I demonstrate it in a variety of ways; I also care for those who are not yet part of my family. I want you to do the same.''

In 1 Corinthians 12:25-26, Paul reminds us:

> And so there is no division in the body, but all its different parts have the same concern for one another. If one part of the body suffers, all the other parts suffer with it; if one part is praised, all the other parts share its happiness.

The importance of caring for each other is seen in the fact that we are told 14 times in the New Testament to "love one another." A search through a concordance under the phrase "one another" shows almost 30 exhortations about the fellowship of a congregation. Here is a partial list of the words and phrases. Draw a circle around each one which describes the basic attitude of the members of your congregation:

have fellowship	be kind to	serve
forbear	wait on	care for
pray for	forgive	confess to
listen to	kiss	bear burdens of
seek after	strengthen	be members of

Lyle Schaller has a "rule of thumb" guide about caring for people. He says that if a person is absent from worship, a class, or group for three consecutive meetings, someone should contact that person in his or her home! Likewise, if someone has been absent for a prolonged period of time, then returns to worship or to a class or group several times, someone should immediately visit that person at home. People give you a message by their presence or absence.

Christian caring goes far beyond making contact with persons who have been absent from meetings. Persons in crisis need the church's caring. Some of the crises to which a caring congregation could respond are hospitalization, fear of hospitalization, illness, accident, marital tension, problem children, alcoholism, drugs, teenage crime, divorce, and unemployment. Are you equipped as a congregation to provide "love to one another," or do you leave these things for the pastor to do?

In a day and age when electronic gadgets provide increasing separation and isolation of human beings, some words from the past may have additional meaning:

> The final grounds of holy Fellowship are in God. Lives immersed and drowned in God are drowned in love, and know one another in Him, and *know one another in love*. God is the medium, the matrix, the focus, the solvent. As Meister Eckhart suggests, he who is wholly surrounded by God, enveloped by God, clothed with God, glowing in selfless love toward Him—*such a man no one can touch except he touch God also*.[5] (Italics added.)

Romans 12:8 indicates that there is a gift of caring. Some of the lay members of your congregation are equipped with that gift. Are you "equipping the saints" for caring?

Worship

In Paul's day the temple was the building where followers would converse with their gods. But Paul didn't want the building to become that important to Jesus' followers. He reminded Christians that people themselves are the dwelling place for God's Spirit (Ephesians 2:19-22). Jesus had said earlier:

> "But the time is coming and is already here, when by the power of God's Spirit people will worship the Father as he really is, offering him the true worship that he wants. God is Spirit, and only by the power of His Spirit can people worship him as he really is" (John 4:23, 24).

Your church ministers to its members and to the community through worship. For most churches the significant worship experience takes place on Sunday morning. However, worship can and should be a part of many other meetings, classes, and events in the life of a church.

A meaningful worship experience has many ingredients, such as praise, confession, forgiveness, thanksgiving, celebration, affirmation, awareness of God's presence, fellow-

[5]Thomas R. Kelly, *A Testament of Devotion* (New York: Harper & Row, Publishers, Inc., 1941), p. 83.

of God's will, can become a growing church. To be a part of this is to know the exhilaration of a vital, maturing faith.

Jesus suggested one of the tasks of the Holy Spirit when he said:

"The Helper, the Holy Spirit, whom the Father will send in my name, will teach you everything and make you remember all that I have told you" (John 14:26).

Congregations need to be alert for every opportunity to

ship, reenactment of the past, hope, learning, a sense of God's faithfulness. Because there are many possible ingredients, not every worship service can offer "everything" to "everyone." Different people find meaning in different parts of worship experiences.

How the ingredients are mixed and presented to those who come is very important. The climate and atmosphere which surrounds the worship experience is vital to a healthy, growing congregation. The attitude of worship leaders is quickly conveyed to worshipers. The range of attitudes extends from being warm, accepting, and affirming to the other extremes of being cold, distant, and unfriendly.

The gathering together of the people of God in worship needs to have top priority in the life of a congregation. In the book of Acts it is clear that Christians needed one another. The gathering together was vital to their growth and development in the Christian faith. Worship services that provide opportunities for those who participate to reach out and touch God, as well as one another, need to be offered today.

Education

A congregation that is teaching and learning the truth of the Bible, the heritage of its people, and the discernment

be taught by the Holy Spirit. This teaching can come in a variety of ways, including worship experience, sermons, small group study experiences, the Sunday church school, and youth groups. Almost everything that happens in the life of a church can provide an educational experience.

The development of capable teachers in all aspects of a church's life is vital for a growing congregation. Paul advised the early church, as well as today's,

Take the teachings that you heard me proclaim in the presence of many witnesses, and entrust them to reliable people, who will be able to teach others also (2 Timothy 2:2).

Note the use of the word "reliable." Today that means committed, trained, and effective teachers.

A growing church also recognizes the value of education and teaching in family units, whatever they may be. Stress is placed on valuing family relationships.

ministry. By having the spirit of Christ, they were to be the sign of the kingdom in the world. They were to represent the righteousness of God and exercise the power of God to set people free from evil's bondage. But as those who had answered the Lord's invitation to follow, they, too, were to call everyone to repent and believe. Their lives of service were closely connected to their work of evangelism. Evangelism often grew out of their service and often prepared the way for the call to repentance. It is word and deed together which demonstrates the love and righteousness of God to the world.

Today Jesus expects the church to be engaged in the same battle with evil in which he was engaged during his lifetime. People are still hurting in our world. Justice has not yet come to many people who are still waiting for deliverance. People are lonely. Others are possessed with the power of greed and evil. There is no promise that the battle will be any easier than it was for Jesus; there *is* a promise that power will be given to those who become involved in this type of warfare. That same power will then help us in our witness to Jesus Christ as the only one through whom true and lasting freedom is possible.

Service to the World

Ephesus was the third most important city in the Roman Empire after Rome and Alexandria. It was a city of temples, the most prominent being that of Artemis, the goddess of fertility. Ephesus was also a center for pagan magic which produced prayers to help people ward off evil spirits. The residents of Ephesus were well aware of the spiritual forces of wickedness and the cosmic forces of darkness that hung heavily over their city. Those who had become Christians, however, had become aware of a greater power through Jesus Christ, who had delivered them from serving these enslaving forces.

In his letter to the Ephesians, Paul dwelt much on the inner life of the congregation. He urged them to build it up so they would become spiritually mature. He urged them to love one another so that there would be support for their mission in the name of Christ. Why? Because there was work to be done and a "warfare" in which to be engaged. We become Christians not to sit passively in sanctuaries, but to become participants with God in the struggle between good and evil. (Read Ephesians 6:10-20.)

The work of the kingdom was evident throughout the entire ministry of Jesus as he countered the forces of evil that bound people physically, emotionally, and spiritually and released them to become new creatures. The disciples were commissioned by Jesus to carry out the same powerful

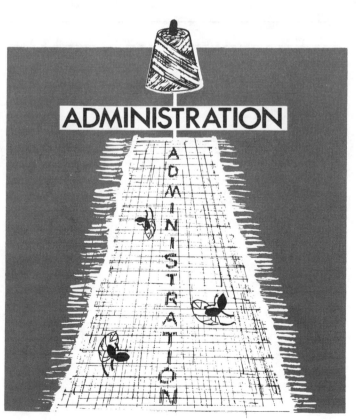

The Ministry of Church Administration

This level of vision puts all the pieces of a puzzle together so the church may see the whole picture. The Church Growth Committee needs to look at the ministry of the entire congregation. Probably no other group in the church is doing this, unless you have a local church planning committee at work.

This whole picture will provide some overall guidance for a vision for the entire church. Perhaps some of this vision has already emerged in the work on a statement of purpose.

Think for a moment in terms of a picture of your church. What do you want your church to be and to do? How could your church grow comprehensively and naturally? How will all your church's resources be mobilized to accomplish that vision?

Before you move to the next chapter, describe a dream, for each area below. Draw on the sources for vision (church purpose, Scripture, prayer, and data from the "Church Member Perception Questionnaire" in Appendix A, page 115).

Evangelism–

Care—

Worship—

Education—

Service—

Administration—

5

An Eye to the Future

Before you begin this chapter, read Acts 16:1-10. Read verses 6 through 10 a second time.

Sometimes vision comes *to* a person, as in Paul's case. It was almost impossible for Paul to avoid the vision because it was so clear and startling. When someone pleads, "Come and help us," we will respond in most cases if it is within the realm of possibility.

But sometimes we have to *discover* the vision. It may already be there, but hidden from sight or at least difficult to see. Vision and opportunity are before every church in every community in America. There are ministries that need to be offered, hurts that need to be healed, people who need to be heard, sacrifices that need to be made, witness that needs to be provided, people who need to be won to Jesus Christ.

What is your vision of your church and community?

Pray, asking the Holy Spirit to work in your Church Growth Committee to unfold the vision of ministry for your church. Pray for God's wisdom in opening your eyes to opportunities; ask God to help you look in the right places and directions.

As you begin work on this chapter, all of the data about your church and community from Appendix B should be in your hands. This data can be helpful if it is used wisely but it can misdirect you if it is treated superficially. The three types of data you have are complementary. Each helps to clarify and validate the perceptions of the others.

Here is an illustration of the relationship of the different kinds of data from football.

The referee was ready to give the two-minute warning for the first half of a game between Dallas and Tampa Bay. Part of the statistics for the game to that point were:

	Dallas	Tampa Bay
Total yards gained on offense	197	-17
First downs made	7	0

The score was 10 to 3. Who had 10? From these statistics, you would conclude quickly that Dallas had 10. But if you had been an observer at the game you would answer differently. Tampa Bay had recovered two fumbled kickoffs to score 10 points without gaining one yard of ground offensively.

In the same way, your committee must look closely at *all* the data you have been given. Your job is to be certain that you understand what the data says about your church and its potential for growth. A good analysis of the data will give you that understanding.

What to Look for in Analysis

To be able to work your way through the mass of data, it is necessary to focus on just certain kinds of information. As you study the data, look for these three things:

1. *What can be affirmed.* Chapter 1 proposed that satisfaction with a church's life and ministry helps it to grow. As a church moves in its life cycle from growth to decline, positive feelings tend to be unexpressed. Nevertheless, feelings of satisfaction about the church do exist. Look for those as you study the data, and think of how they can be celebrated by the church so its self-worth will grow.

2. *New directions for growth.* Whenever a church grows, it is meeting the needs of more people. Decline begins when a program continues even though the need changes. That is why your committee must be attentive to the needs people say are not being met by the present ministry of the church. Some will be needs of church members and others will be needs of community residents. A new direction may mean that some programs should be modified, some abandoned, and some added. Growth occurs as churches go in new directions to meet the needs of people.

3. *Needs for pastoral care.* In studying the data you may notice negative feelings about the church that do not coincide with what is happening in the church's life. These may be cries for help and love. If you notice such statements, refer them to your pastor for follow-up.

How to Analyze the Data

In your next meeting you will be given a "Data Analysis Summary" sheet from Appendix C (page 181) for each arena of ministry. Fill in the name of one of the arenas on each sheet.

Review the observation data from Appendix B (pages 137-140). You may also want to review the responses to the "Church Member Perception Questionnaire," on page 115, Appendix A. Note the items that are consistently rated high in each arena of ministry. Record them on the Data Analysis Summary sheet for that ministry in the space marked "To be affirmed." In the right-hand column, mark "O" to indicate the source as observation.

Then note the needs that are to be met and record them on the summary sheet in the space marked "New Directions." Do the same for "Needs for Pastoral Care."

In working with this data be careful not to be misled by the answers to some questions. Even though people were asked to indicate how the ministries are being carried on, it is not unlikely that some wishes will slip in. These can be detected by a careful comparison of responses. For example, one person may say that evangelism is the responsibility of all members (Observation for the Ministry of Evangelism, number 4 Appendix B, page 137). However, when you compare the same person's responses to statements 2, 7, 10, 12, and 14, it may be noticed that members are not doing evangelism. This could indicate that an important expectation is not being met.

Now is the time to analyze the observation data from the community. Study the "Windshield Survey Information Sheet" (Appendix B, page 142) returned by the survey teams. Record your conclusions on the "Data Analysis Summary" sheet in the following manner:

To Be Affirmed—Things that are "givens" about the community with which the church ministers. For example, how conveniently located is the church to the community residents? What are the housing patterns? Are there community service projects or institutions? How do people relate to each other?

New Directions—These would be opportunities for new ministries and may be related to things listed under "To Be Affirmed." What should the church do differently if it is in a bad location that cannot be changed? Can the church participate in some community service projects? Are there groups in the community that seem untouched by a church? And so on.

After completing a review of the observation data, begin the same process with the statistical data from Appendix B. The statistics will be the clearest way of validating whether the church is reproducing itself or not and at what rate. In Appendix C (pages 177 to 180) there is a series of questions to help you analyze each set of statistics as it relates to each ministry. You will want to refer to the written history of the church (see Appendix B, page 143) to answer some of the questions. List your conclusions on the "Data Analysis Summary" in the appropriate categories. Indicate the sources by putting an "S" in the right-hand column. You may want to refer again to the "narrative statistic" of church history, especially in terms of what can be affirmed. Some findings will duplicate what you noted from the analysis of the observation data.

The final part of the analysis will be to review the listening data. This study will be similar to what you did for the observation data. For each of the findings you record on the summary sheet, put an "L" in the right-hand column. Again, there may be some findings duplicated by an "O" or an "S" or both.

Synthesis

Having examined your church's life and ministry, your Church Growth Committee has now reached an intersection with roads going in different directions. The decisions you make from this point on are critical. They will determine the direction your church will take for a number of years. Which way should you go? Here are some guidelines to help you make that choice and to help you create a vision for the growth of your church.

1. Your Church's Life Cycle

One ingredient in the process of creating a vision is to describe what your church is like today. Churches go through a cycle of growth, stability, and decline just as individuals, businesses, and nations do. To identify your church's phase in its life cycle, review your church's history and the "Data Analysis Summary" sheets in terms of the following characteristics:

a. What is your church's sense of self-worth? Are members enthusiastic about belonging to the church? Do they speak often about the good experiences or are they more often negative and critical? Are they comfortable inviting visitors to church?

b. What is the status of the church's programming? Does it have a healthy balance of activity and ministry from its past, in its present, and for its future? Over the past year were most board discussions about keeping your church going or about more effective ways of meeting needs of people in your church and community? Did decisions tend to negate or create new ideas?

c. What has been your church's ability to reproduce itself? Has attendance and membership increased or decreased each year over the last 10 years? At what

rate did it change? What was the cause for the increase or decrease?

Now circle where your church seems to be on the life cycle chart on the following page. (It is possible to have characteristics of different phases at the same time.) Think about why you are there and how long you have had those characteristics.

CHURCH LIFE CYCLE
Characteristics

Phases		Self-worth	Programming	Reproduction
	1. Growth	Feels good about what the church is and where it is going.	Builds on past achievements. Sets and works on new directions.	Increase is greater than decrease.
	2. Stability	Feels good about what the church is and what is happening now.	Maintains and repeats the strengths of the past only.	Increase equals the decrease.
	3. Decline	Doesn't feel good about itself.	Remembers the past. Hopes for a repeat of the past.	Decrease is greater than increase.

2. Horizons for Growth

Most stable or declining congregations have a potential for growth. In their past there were times of growth and renewal. That could happen again in new and greater ways. Your church's history has likely shown that it grew in the past because it was then alive to the needs of its community. Growth can happen as your church looks beyond itself to catch the vision of what God wants it to be and do. The Church Growth Committee can help create that vision by surveying the broad horizons of the church's present and future ministries. Use a copy of page 183 (Appendix C) for each arena of ministry. Review the "Data Analysis Summary" sheets. Give special attention to those points that come from more than one data source. Record the information from the summary sheet of each ministry onto a "horizons" worksheet for that ministry. The answers to the following questions will help you place the information in the appropriate place(s).

a. What *strengths* does your church have in this arena of ministry? What do many say can be affirmed? What has been effective?

b. What *opportunities or challenges* call your church to new ventures? What new directions have you discovered?

c. What is the *potential for growth* in your church's sense of self-worth, in ministry, and in its ability to add new members (reproduce)? Is there a potential for growth from the community that your church did not recognize before?

d. What will your church *need* to take advantage of the opportunities, respond effectively to the challenges, and realize its potential for growth? Is it money? space? people? training? resources? organization?

e. What *problems* must be dealt with in order to grow?

f. What *issues* have yet to be clarified?

3. Focus on Special Concerns

A church that wants to start growing cannot do everything that appears on its "horizons." Therefore, your Church Growth Committee must focus on certain aspects of each ministry. In preparation for your next meeting complete a copy of page 184 (Appendix C) for each ministry. Think back over all that you have learned about your church and community. Recall your newly developed statement of purpose. Review your church's life cycle and the opportunities for ministry on its horizons.

In reviewing these sources, look for the needs, problems, issues, and opportunities which you sense are keys to growth in your church. Among these may be concerns such as increasing professional and volunteer staff, using facilities creatively, and initiating ministries to the unchurched. List especially the concerns that come from a broad base of the congregation.

At the next meeting, each committee member will share his or her concerns with the committee. If all have done their homework well, you will have generated more ideas than your church can pursue in a reasonable period of time. There will be validity in almost everything suggested on the different "focus" worksheets. But because your church's time and resources are limited, you must become yet more selective. Part of your task at the next meeting will be to form a vision for your church's future ministry from these worksheets.

4. A Vision for Growth

In the Bible, vision for the people of God concedes that what is currently happening is not God's final plan. No matter how good or effective the status quo may be, the Bible never suggests that it is the end of what God wants to do through the people of God. Biblical vision always struggles with life as it *could* be when God's will and power are released through human activity. This was the hope of Joel (2:28-32), the reality of Pentecost (Acts 2), and the last words of the New Testament (Revelation). Vision is catching sight of the things that you believe God wants you to see and to do in the future.

You began working on your vision by developing a purpose and analyzing your ministries. Then you described your church's place in its life cycle, scanned the horizons of its ministries, and finally focused on concerns about growth. Your next task will be to consolidate all of your work to this point into a vision of the future ministry of your church. Read what follows in preparation for your next meeting. Study the Scripture passages mentioned below. Review your own "focus" lists so you will be ready to weigh all the options.

From the focus worksheets of the committee members, compile one list for each arena of ministry on a clean copy of the focus worksheet. Weigh all the possibilities and implications of each concern as you consider what you believe to be God's intention for your church.

Reduce the list for each ministry to the top three-to-five concerns. Perhaps some could be combined. Others may be unrealistic at the present time but could be part of a later vision. The final list should include the most pressing concerns for your church if you are to experience that com-

prehensive and natural growth about which you studied earlier.

You now have 6 lists which together contain from 18 to 30 concerns. The total number is much too large for your church (or any church) to handle effectively. Discuss each idea, asking the following questions:

- What are 'the fields ready for harvest' around us that God wants us to see and work in? (Read John 4:27-38.)
- What fields should we see that need planting or cultivating? (Read I Corinthians 3:1-9; Matthew 13:1-23.)
- What are the loudest cries from the community, our congregation, and the world to which we should respond?
- How would God want us to change from what we are now?

As you discuss the lists, build a consensus in the committee by narrowing the focus to one or two ideas for each arena of ministry. These will make up the vision for your church's future ministry. Remember that you are not trying to design programs. You are now at the stage between Purpose and Program. What you do here will help to assure that your programs will fulfill your church's purpose.

As you form that consensus, list your concerns on the worksheet titled "The Vision" on page 185 (Appendix C). Keep this sheet for the work of the next chapter. Take time to pray about what you have just decided. Ask God for wisdom, courage, and strength to make that vision happen.

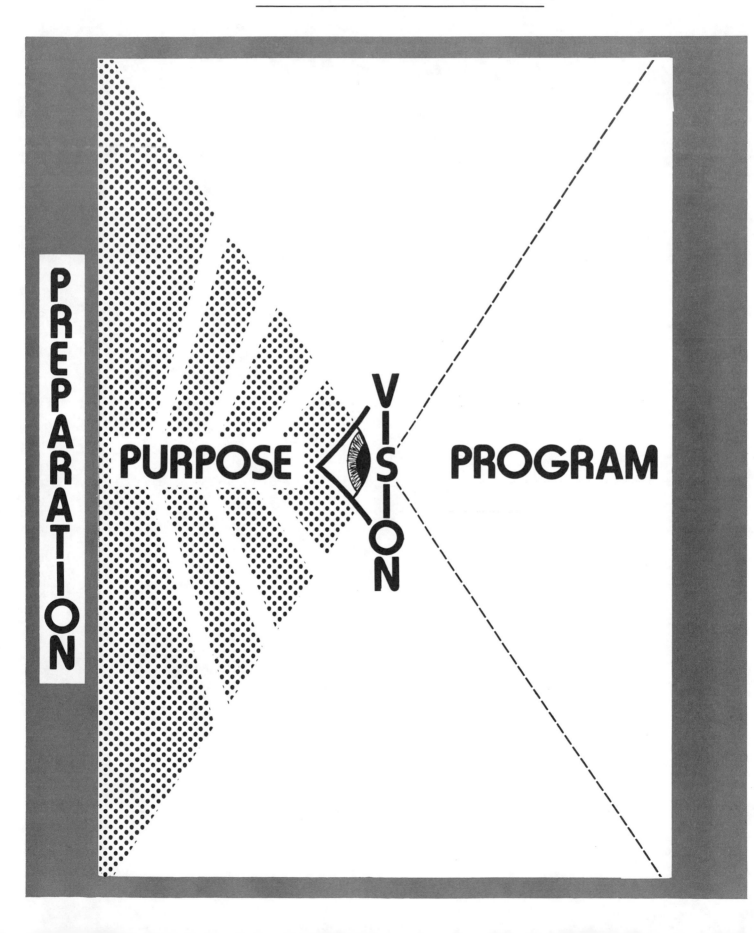

6

Goals for the Growing Church

Poor Jonah! He had a goal: to get out of the belly of a big fish. Of course he wouldn't have needed that goal if he had done what God had wanted him to do in the first place.

God wanted Jonah to go to Nineveh, the capital of the great empire of Assyria, Israel's deadly enemy. And when he didn't go, Jonah was thrown into the sea and swallowed up by a great fish. Read Jonah's prayer from inside the fish in chapter 2 of the Old Testament book of Jonah.

God has a plan for your church, too. It is the task of your Church Growth Committee (and others who assist you) to determine what it is. It probably won't be as glamorous or as threatening as going to Nineveh, but it might be even more important. Set good goals; set goals based on God's plan for your church.

Pray Jonah's prayer, pausing over verse 7. Ask God's guidance for you and your Church Growth Committee as you work through chapter 6.

As you prepare to develop goals, take a look at what your committee has done so far. You have:

- studied Scripture together;
- discussed a definition for a growing church;
- enlisted church growth prayer support persons;
- worked on (or secured others to work on) a statement of purpose for your church;
- collected data (with the help of others) for analysis;
- studied the data, searching for a variety of concerns; and
- reduced those concerns to six or seven major ones which have become your vision.

That vision contains the potential for motivating your church to make some plans and pursue the future you have dreamed about. The next step in this process is developing goals.

What Is a Growth Goal?

There are many definitions for the term "goal." Here are some ingredients of a growth goal as it is used in this handbook. A growth goal

- expresses a long-range hope because it
  —can be accomplished in two or more years.
  —is a picture of the final result and not the intermediate steps.
- motivates the members to act because it
  —reflects the vision and helps fulfill the purpose.
  —is a challenge that stretches but is realistic.

—will make a difference in the church's life and ministry.
  —can be resourced and achieved.
  —can be celebrated both in the process of being done and at the end.
  —can be evaluated.
- is easily communicated and remembered by members because it
  —is short and concise.
  —contains only one subject.
  —has no reference to how it will be accomplished.
  —is personal and not abstract.
- is developed cooperatively and owned by most church members.

Why Do We Need Growth Goals?

Most people have had the experience of watching a child or teenager trying to blow up a balloon. Even those watching sometimes find themselves huffing and puffing in order to offer encouragement for the child to continue the task.

The goal? A blown-up balloon! Everyone watching knows what the child is trying to accomplish and, almost unconsciously, wants to get involved because it is exciting to contemplate the end result.

That is one of the key functions of a goal statement. It should provide an easily grasped picture of what is hoped for. It should be so interesting, pertinent, attractive, and challenging that people want to join in working toward its accomplishment.

Many church goals today have little value because no one knows what they are really saying. There is no immediate "capturing" of supporters for the goal by the goal statement. And some goals are meaningless because, even if they are accomplished, they will make little difference. Consider the following cartoon.[1]

[1]Reprinted with special permission of King Features © 1983 King Features Syndicate, Inc.

A church may say, "We will be an evangelistic congregation." So what? To write a goal like that is like throwing a snowball at the earth.

Goals should motivate people. Motivation is a good word but when it is used, it is often confused with inspiration.

A simple illustration may help untangle these two words. Imagine yourself at home. You are restless and want to take a brief vacation. The car, with a full tank of gas, is in the garage. You and the car are ready, but you are doing nothing. You don't know where to go and what to do. Without a clear sense of direction you are not yet free to act. Applying these two words to this illustration, you are *inspired*, but until you are *motivated* the car's motor won't be running and you won't be on vacation.

In the previous chapter you took the first steps toward building a direction for growth when you reduced a great assortment of ideas to a select list of concerns. These became your vision. Now your committee will lead your church and its leaders in charting the course for your journey to growth. What happens in the next few weeks may determine if your church will ever take that trip.

Being captured by a sense of call and mission can be inspiring. But little will happen until you and the church are prompted to act in ways that will cause growth. That prompting or motivation comes about through the combined work of the Holy Spirit and the human response of planning and commitment. The human side of motivation can be traced in the following steps:

1. Have a challenge to reach.
2. Accept ownership or partnership in that challenge.
3. Have specific responsibilities to fulfill.
4. Be adequately resourced and trained.
5. Receive recognition for work done.
6. Know that the work will be achieved and evaluated.

Motivation is created by goal statements that give direction to your congregation's vision. Goals imply that something is going to happen as a result of the dream you have expressed in the goal statement. It is also assumed that goals, which are set and implemented through the combined efforts of many people, foster shared responsibility in the church. If pastor, Church Growth Committee, key leaders, and congregation all are involved in formulating and affirming the goals, you may assume that they will be motivated to work toward reaching them.

Ephesians 4:13-16 provides a good illustration of goal development:

> And so we shall all come together to that oneness in our faith and in our knowledge of the Son of God; we shall become mature people, reaching to the very height of Christ's full stature. Then we shall no longer be children, carried by the waves and blown about by every shifting wind of the teaching of deceitful men, who lead others into error by the tricks they invent. Instead, by speaking the truth in a spirit of love, we must grow up in every way to Christ, who is the head. Under his control all the different parts of his body fit together, and the whole body is held together by every joint with which it is provided. So when each separate part works as it should, the whole body grows and builds itself up through love.

In this Scripture passage several hoped-for accomplishments are stated on the goal level:

> we shall be mature people . . . reaching to the very height of Christ's full stature.

Each Christian could take that passage as a goal for his or her individual faith journey. It would not be easy to attain that goal since, for Christ, full stature included a cross. But it is a goal which Paul offered to every person who became a follower of Jesus Christ.

In verse 16, there is another goal:

> So when each separate part works as it should, the whole body grows and builds itself up through love.

When individuals mature in the faith, then the body of Christ—the church—is also going to be more mature and function more effectively. The goal is the mature church of Jesus Christ, which reflects him in every aspect of its corporate and individual life. That is the picture, the hoped-for accomplishment!

Who Writes Growth Goals?

An important task for the Church Growth Committee is to prepare goal statements for presentation to the congregation. However, the committee does not work alone in this process. The pastor, the moderator of your church, and key leaders of boards and committees should work with your Church Growth Committee on this important step. This is one way to obtain broader ownership of the goals. These key leaders will be the ones to do the program work that will move the congregation toward growth. They will lead best in accomplishing those goals they create or help to create.

In a multi-board church, all those who serve as chairpersons of committees, boards, and task forces should be involved in the process of writing goals. In a single board church, it is wise to involve most of the members of the advisory board unless the size of the group is more than fifteen persons. Be sure to involve persons who are the key leaders in the six arenas of ministry: evangelism, care, worship, education, service to the world, and church administration.

Consider the following possibilities, though you may think of others. The task of the Church Growth Committee is to enlist the participation of the responsible people and may include giving them assistance in developing goals, objectives, and program plans.

Evangelism	—Committee on Evangelism Evangelism Task Force Diaconate
Care	—Nurture Committee Lay Pastoral Care Committee Diaconate
Worship	—Worship Committee Music Committee Diaconate
Education	—Board of Christian Education Christian Education Task Force Sunday School Committee
Service to the World	—Social Concerns Committee Task Force on Outreach Missions Committee
Church Administration	—Church Growth Committee Diaconate

How to Write Growth Goals

There are ten steps to writing a growth goal:

1. Review your vision.
2. If new persons are participating in goal writing, brief them on how you arrived at this point and share pertinent data so that they understand your conclusions about vision.
3. Decide with which part of the vision you will begin to work.
4. Discuss what is already happening in that part of your church's ministry.
5. Identify what is *not* happening and what needs to happen.
6. Try to clarify the picture of what needs to happen

in order to translate that picture into a growth goal.
7. Make an attempt to develop the goal so that it describes what you want to have happen in the life of your congregation.
8. Test your statement using the guidelines on page 73. Is it a goal?
9. Complete the development of your growth goal statement.
10. Ask the question: Will what we have described make a significant difference in the life of our congregation if it is accomplished? If your answer is "no," go back to Step 5 and try again.

An Example of a Growth Goal

To help you understand what is required in moving from a part of the vision to developing its growth goal, here is an illustration taken from the planning work of a real congregation. Having collected data through observation, statistics, and listening, the church listed these conclusions:

- No new people are coming to our church.
- There is apathy towards evangelism.
- There is not much caring.
- Attendance has declined over a seven-year period.
- Pastor and people disagree too much.
- The pastor doesn't visit.
- We believe our church should be growing; we want our church to grow.
- Some tension exists.
- We have several good Sunday school classes.
- Our congregation is perceived as "cold."
- There is an "I don't care" attitude.
- We can't agree on what needs to be done.
- Some people want to do something.
- There is fighting among members.
- Deacons don't visit.
- Some people can't relax when they go to church.

Parts of the vision which grew out of those conclusions were:

- We need to be reaching and keeping new people for Christ and our church.
- We will learn to get along together and learn how to handle conflict.

The first part of this vision relates to evangelism. However, it is a concern which spreads through the total life of the congregation. It is complex, and there is no simple answer. Yet, the members of this church had to ask what they wanted to see accomplished in response to this part of their vision. The growth goal they developed was: "That we consistently reach new people."

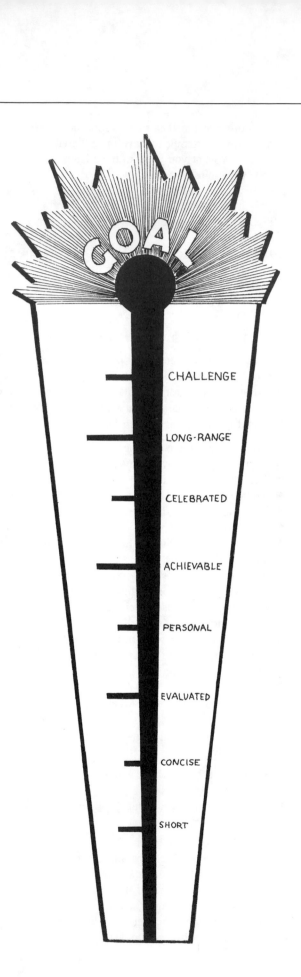

CHALLENGE

LONG-RANGE

CELEBRATED

ACHIEVABLE

PERSONAL

EVALUATED

CONCISE

SHORT

When they tested this goal by the criteria listed on page 73, they discovered the following about it:

- It is short, concise, and has only one subject.
- It is realistic and would make a difference if implemented.
- It is easily communicated, grasped, and understood.
- It is a challenge and would motivate them.
- It is long-range but suggests steps that could bring it about.
- It can be owned by the pastor and the congregation.
- The church was able to see what it would be like if the goal were accomplished.

A goal such as this implies that every individual and organization in the church could be involved. A look around the congregation would soon tell if progress was being made toward accomplishing the goal.

Now turn to the task of developing growth goals for your congregation. You should develop at least one growth goal for each arena of ministry. These goals will aim at meeting the vision you described on page 185.

Use the growth goals worksheet on page 187 (Appendix C) for writing the goal or goals that will help fulfill each part of your vision. (Duplicate as many copies of the worksheets as your Church Growth Committee and other boards and committees need.)

Each chairperson of a board or committee who has worked with the Church Growth Committee in the goal development process should share the goals as well as the background and process of developing the goals with their groups. They should also enlist their ideas and suggestions for refinement of goals. Suggestions for modification or revision should be communicated immediately to the chairperson of the Church Growth Committee for consideration. After that the top five or six goals are ready to be taken to the congregation for approval.

Who Uses Growth Goals?

It is hoped that those who develop and vote on goals will be the people who use them. Goals can be those of the whole congregation (churchwide goals), as well as those of groups with accountability for the six arenas of ministry. Orlando E. Costas states:

> People need to do their own goal-setting if the goals are to be accomplished by them. They need to be involved in the decision-making process if they are to carry out the decisions.[2]

Here are some of the ways different people may use the goal statements:

[2]Orlando E. Costas, *The Integrity of Mission* (New York: Harper and Row Publishers, Inc., 1979), p. 30.

The pastor may use them
- to provide direction for the overall ministry;
- as the subject of sermons or small group study;
- to aid in the role of communicator and motivator.

The Church Growth Committee may use them
- to build involvement of others in writing goal statements to be used by subgroups in the life of the church;
- to reflect the dreams and vision for the church.

Boards and committees could use them
- as a guide and framework for all their work;
- to aid in recruitment of workers.

The congregation in general could use the goal statements in many ways. Some suggestions follow.

1. The goal statements can be the subject of Sunday school lessons. A creative teacher can be enlisted to develop a lesson plan for each of the goals.
2. An interesting leader can use the goals in dialogue with youth groups.
3. Banners with short, concise statements on them can be made and hung in the sanctuary, vestibule, or elsewhere around the church.
4. The statements can be printed in the bulletin on a regular basis.
5. They can be the subject of articles in the church newsletter.
6. Short skits and dramatic pieces can be presented in worship experiences to highlight goal efforts as well as accomplishments.
7. Solo and choir music can address goal statements in a variety of ways.

7

Objectives for the Growing Church

When you travel by auto from one place to another, you have a general idea about the miles involved. By watching your odometer, you can measure your progress rather easily. When you arrive at your destination, you will know whether you have had a fast trip or if you were delayed at certain points. Much of our everyday life is measurable because of certain obvious criteria for measuring—clocks, odometers, bank statements, thermometers, barometers, and cardiographs.

It is not so easy to "measure" the different elements in the life of your church. Just how much does God expect from your congregation? What is "enough" ministry? What is "too much?" How does a congregation know whether it is "coasting" rather than stretching itself to do God's bidding?

Read John 14:9-14. The above questions are intensified by Jesus' words in verse 12 which read: "Whoever believes in me will do what I do—yes, he will do even greater things, because I am going to the Father." What are these "even greater things" Jesus mentions? How are they reflected in the ministry of your congregation? Are they part of your new growth goals?

Objectives are targets to help you reach one of your goals. They allow you to measure the progress you have made toward your goal. As you complete the objectives, you can measure the progress you have made. If you develop demanding objectives, obviously you will be saying to yourselves that it is no longer "business as usual." How far can you stretch yourself as a church? Will you risk writing down the "greater things" God expects from your church?

Pray for God's guidance upon all those groups who will be developing growth objectives for the future of your church.

As you move forward in your planning for growth, a review will be helpful. To keep your ideas clearly defined and to assist you in developing objectives, remember that:

- In chapter 1 you studied a description of the growing church: *Church growth is the comprehensive and natural expansion that can and should be expected from the life and mission of the church as the people of God, the body of Christ, and the fellowship of the Spirit.*
- Your congregation adopted a statement of purpose which answers the question, "Why does our congregation continue to exist?"
- Your Church Growth Committee developed a vision to answer the question, "What are our most serious concerns for the next five or more years?"
- You developed growth goals to answer the question, "What do we hope to accomplish through our church's ministry?"

and *now*

your task is to write some growth objectives which will help you accomplish your growth goals.

Why Develop Growth Objectives?

The game of golf provides a good illustration of measurable objectives which are related to a goal. The goal in golf is to complete the eighteen holes at the "par" (score standard) established for that particular golf course. If you can do better than that, you're an exceptional golfer.

A golf course normally consists of eighteen holes. Each of these holes has been given its own par, equal to the number of times you should hit the ball to get it into the cup on the green. When all of these individual pars (targets) are added together, they make up the total score for reaching the goal, which is the par for the course. By accomplishing each one of the eighteen holes at the established par, you can reach your goal for the course (if you're good, lucky, or both!).

It is good for a golfer to concentrate on each separate hole, as each is a "measure" recorded on the score card. *Each* hole is an important objective for the golfer.

In the same way, each objective toward each of your church's goals should be viewed as important. An objective is a measurable target by which you will accomplish some part of your goal.

A frustrated lay leader said:

> For years I've given my time in leadership in the church and the frustration has always been, "Are we making any progress?" Our evaluation was always subjective and based only on the programs we were doing. Now that we have measurable objectives, we can know if we're making progress. If we are, we can celebrate and feel good; if we're not, we can do something about it and try something new.

Good intentions focused on church growth don't necessarily produce meaningful results. Having objectives toward church growth will at least let everyone know what you are trying to get done. Good intentions more often produce the desired results when they are stated as measurable objectives.

There are some very good reasons for setting up measurable targets (objectives) to accomplish your goals.

- They divide a long-range goal into short-range steps.
- What at first appears to be a tedious, mechanical process can become a vitalizing experience.
- Challenging assignments provide motivation, especially when they are achievable in short periods of time.
- It is healthy when a group stretches itself beyond what is average or normal.
- The objectives belong to everyone, not only to the pastors or the lay leaders.
- Accountability is lodged with persons or groups.
- Evaluation is simplified.
- You will know, when you evaluate, whether or not you have helped to achieve your goal.
- There is much satisfaction for volunteers when specific targets are set and reached. This is a system of rewards.
- When an objective is reached, it is cause for celebration. In many churches, only dollar or money targets are established and nothing else is ever celebrated.
- Earlier you were advised to ask yourselves the question "What does God want to accomplish through us?" When you measure what is happening and there is accomplishment, you can see and celebrate what you have prayed about and realize that God *is* working through you.

There are also a number of reasons why many churches aren't interested in being specific about what they are trying to accomplish:

- It takes time to develop detailed, measurable objectives.
- Objectives move you from generalities to specifics.
- Accountability for objectives is lodged with persons and groups, which is threatening.

- Some people don't want their performance "measured."
- Some say that setting numerical targets is not biblical.
- Some claim that God will give the "increase," so it is wrong for us to set targets.

When Should Growth Objectives Be Developed?

Now that the growth goals have been approved by the congregation and assigned to the respective committees and boards, it is time to develop the objectives. It is better for each committee or board to hold a separate, specially called meeting for this purpose than to try to do the task while in the process of conducting regular business.

Another option is to bring together all groups that will develop growth objectives and have them all write their objectives at the same time. Your committee can serve as resource to each of the groups.

Since it is possible to develop more than one objective for each growth goal, sufficient time must be provided so that the full scope of each goal can be exhausted by the group that is working on objectives.

Who Develops Growth Objectives?

Your Church Growth Committee should not develop objectives for other boards and committees. In order to have ownership of its growth objectives, each committee or board needs to participate in developing those objectives.

You have most likely developed at least one growth goal for each of the arenas of ministry. Each of those goals should now be given to a group that will do the basic work of developing growth objectives. Because of size, some churches have only one board that does all the work. Other churches are blessed or burdened with many boards and committees. Regardless of its size, each church must have those persons who as part of their mission accept the responsibilities of leadership. These will be the persons to do the basic developing of the objectives as well as to lead in their accomplishment and evaluation. If there are administrative growth goals, it may be appropriate for your committee, with the pastor, to develop those respective objectives.

Other boards and committees, such as the trustees, may be asked to participate in developing objectives for each of the arenas of ministry. As an illustration, if one of your growth goals has something to do with a certain age grouping, be sure that these people are represented in the formulation of growth objectives.

If the persons who chair the boards and committees feel confident of their role in leading their group through the process of developing growth objectives, then there is no need for a member of the Church Growth Committee to work directly with them. However, if the chairperson is somewhat uneasy or unsure of the process of developing growth objectives, then a member of the Church Growth Committee should be present as a resource person to the group. Often just the presence of a resource person instills enough confidence in the group members to enable them to function very effectively while performing what, for many, will be a new task.

A significant part of your organization for developing objectives is to alert your prayer support persons to pray for this particular step. Continue to offer concentrated prayer support for every step of your church growth effort.

How to Develop Growth Objectives

A growth objective is a target to be reached, a step to be taken which will help you accomplish your growth goal. To accomplish most of the goals you have written, you will need several objectives. Each objective should be stated so that its progress and achievement can be measured. Questions such as these should be answered in a growth objective:

- What task will be accomplished?
- When? (beginning when? accomplished when?)
- Where? (if applicable)

A growth objective can use any time frame, from a few months to several years. An objective which is to be accomplished in less than two years is called a short-term objective; one to be accomplished in more than two years is a long-term objective.

Certain steps need to be followed in order to produce a good objective:

1. Be sure that those who will be responsible for carrying out the growth objectives are involved in developing the objective.
2. Study the goal statement. Answer these questions:

   - What is currently happening that addresses this goal?
   - What could we do that we are not now doing which might help us attain this goal?
   - Identify some ''targets'' or ''steps'' that emerge from the discussion. List them so that all can see.
   - Which targets or steps are best? Why?

3. Decide on the most important steps you need to take.
4. Write the growth objectives.

   - Begin by using the word ''to,'' followed by an action verb. For example: ''to enlist,'' ''to identify,'' ''to discover.''
   - Avoid words such as know, understand, hope, or grow, which are too vague and impossible to measure.

- Point out with whom the action is to be done.
- Reflect the growth goal to which it is addressed.
- Produce one key result (not several).
- Tell when the action will begin and when it will be finished.
- State how many or how much of what is expected.

5. Check your objective against the illustrations that follow in this chapter.

Some Illustrations of Growth Objectives

In this section, using the illustration of a growth goal from the previous chapter, we will develop some possible growth objectives.

Growth Goal: That we consistently reach new people.

In the discussion that is held regarding this goal, some of the factors that might be listed include:

- No one has specific responsibilities for evangelism.
- It's been assumed that this is the task of the pastor and the diaconate.
- We don't have enough leaders to do all that needs to be done now.
- We are a friendly congregation, at least to those who are on the ''inside.''
- We don't know our community very well.
- No one wants to ''do'' evangelism.
- There are many people in our community who are unchurched.
- We have many inactive members.
- We seem to have a lot of disagreement over how some

things should be done; it's usually over trivial matters.

- We don't know how to "really welcome" and "assimilate" new people. We say "hello" and that's about it.
- Our pastor has had no special training in evangelism and can't provide us with much direction.

In light of this kind of dialogue and listing of pertinent factors relating to the growth goal, here are *some possible growth objectives*:

- *to create* a group within six months whose primary responsibility is the ministry of evangelism.
- to *secure training* within twelve months for our pastor and at least (no. of) persons who will be responsible for contacting new people.
- to *visit* in the homes of at least five unchurched persons each month during the next two years, beginning (date).
- to *bring* a comprehensive report to our congregation at the time of our next annual business meeting (give date) which will tell us something about how we handle our differences.
- to *poll* all visitors/newcomers within the first week after their visit to our worship services to discover their reactions, beginning next month (give date).
- to *increase* worship attendance by 10 percent (number of persons) within (number of) years, ending (year). Using this format, objectives stating numerical increases can be written for each Sunday church school class, youth ministry, each age group, each small study group, each choir, and every type of worship service, business meeting, and fellowship activity. It is always important to give the number of people you have targeted when you state a percentage increase.

Many more growth objectives could address this growth goal. As you look at these illustrations of objectives, which appear to be more basic than others? Some objectives will be much more important than others.

Each group that develops objectives for your church will need to decide which are most important. Ask each group to arrange its list of objectives in order of priority before submitting it to your committee. Suggest the following guidelines for their use (and for your committee's use later with all the objectives you receive).

Beside each growth objective, write one of the following:

MUST	—This growth objective must be done, even if no others are accomplished.
OUGHT TO	—Given the time and energy, this objective really should be undertaken.
WANT	—It would be nice to achieve this objective; it's something you want to do, but it just may not get done.

Another way to look at these words is:

MUST	—is *high* priority.
OUGHT TO	—is *medium* priority.
WANT	—is *low* priority.

Record Growth Objectives

Use the worksheet on page 189 (Appendix C) to record objectives for each of your goals. Make as many copies of the page as you need to develop objectives for each goal.

What Do You Do with Growth Objectives?

After your growth objectives have been completed, your committee may wish to study them and make further suggestions or recommendations to the group that developed them.

After that, your committee will:

1. Bring all of your growth objectives before the church members in a business session and secure their approval. This option provides an opportunity for all members to share in deciding the thrust of the congregation's ministries for the next few years. Then assign the objectives to the respective groups for the "how to" step.

   A variation would be to share the growth objectives during a worship service, using worship, music, and drama to share creatively with all of your people what you hope to be doing in the next few years. Since many more persons attend worship services than business meetings, there is usually a strategic value in this option.

2. Assign the growth objectives to the groups that developed them for the next step, which is planning how to carry them out.

Your Church Growth Committee should keep a full set of all growth objectives for reference. Each group should also have copies.

8

Programs for the Growing Church

In John 10:25, Jesus said, "The deeds I do by my Father's authority speak on my behalf . . ." Jesus made what we do (our works) very important. Everything we do is a message which should reflect the love of God.

Growth program plans are your church's "works." They represent your church's understanding of God's will for it at this time.

These programs (works) speak to your community, to your church members, to the poor, and to the powerful. What message will be given by your programs to those whose lives you will touch?

Read John 10:22-30 and reflect on Jesus' relationship with God and the influence it had on his life and ministry. For Jesus, all he did had to reflect the intense intimacy with God. It should be the same for each Christian and for each church. Consider how your church's purpose should affect the programs offered to the members and to the community.

Pray that God will guide those who develop program plans and that these plans will reflect God's will for your church.

You have now moved through a process which looks like this:

You began with your *church's purpose*
   and moved to identify your *concerns for vision,*
      out of which emerged a number of *growth goals*
         for which you have *growth objectives;*
           and now

How do you ACCOMPLISH the *growth objectives?* The answers to that question will be your *growth program plans.*

What Is a Growth Program Plan?

A growth program plan is simply the best strategy for reaching a growth objective. A good program plan will

- describe what is to be done;
- name who is responsible;
- determine a schedule;
- list resources or training;
- identify costs;
- allow for evaluation.

You can choose between many program options to achieve your objectives. Be sure you select the best one. As you create the programs for future ministries, carefully examine every present program. Some may be retained, others changed, and a few abandoned because they are ineffective.

Who Creates Growth Program Plans?

In most cases the groups that develop growth objectives should also create the related program plans. In this way they will assume responsibility for the proposed programs.

A member of the Church Growth Committee may need to be assigned as a resource person to groups that may not feel comfortable with the task of creating a growth program plan. Otherwise, groups should be able to create their own plans using this manual.

How Do You Develop Program Plans?

Ideas are very important in the creation of effective program plans. Consider every possible way to achieve each objective. It is not unusual for people in nongrowing churches to seem to have no new ideas. The "Ideas and Resources" section has been distributed to the persons who will write program plans to help stimulate some new ideas.

In your next meeting you will begin building program plans by listing every possible strategy for achieving an objective regardless of leadership, costs, time or resources. Some may be existing programs and others will be new ideas. Be open and creative. Suggest even what at first might appear to be a "way out" idea. Do not stop to analyze any of the ideas or to discuss details. Let the ideas flow. Be different! Be daring! Record your list for future use.

Now that you have many ideas, select the best suggestions for your church's ministry by asking:

- Which will best help to achieve our objective?
- Which could our members do best?
- Can some be combined or modified?

Next, reorganize that list in order of priority. Limit the number of ideas you will attempt so that your resources will not be spread too thin. Now you are ready to create a good growth program plan with the components that were listed at the beginning of this chapter. Before you start that work, study the following illustration.

Illustrating a Growth Program Plan

Using the illustration of one growth objective from page 81, here are several growth program ideas that may be developed into program plans by that church's evangelism committee.

Growth Objective: Within six months, *prepare* a plan for reaching out to new people.

Ideas for Growth Programs:
1. Identify where unchurched persons live and work and how they can be reached.
2. Enlist every Sunday church school class to bring at least two new persons into the class during the next year.
3. Enlist every member of the congregation to invite new persons each week to the worship services during the next year.
4. Provide training in witness for the entire congregation through three one-day sessions during the next two months.
5. Develop a system for recognizing those members who bring new people into the church.
6. Keep records of attendance at worship and enrollment in Sunday church school for the next year and report the progress monthly in the church bulletin and newsletter.

A Growth Program Plan

A plan for the first program may look something like this—Joan and Jim will do a phone survey of the community within one-half mile radius of the church by June 1 to determine who are unchurched and what some of their needs are.

To do that they will:

- obtain a directory which lists phone numbers by addresses from the Chamber of Commerce;
- develop questions to ask the community residents;
- recruit and train six volunteers to call;
- prepare a report from the responses for the committee's June meeting, noting the efficacy of this approach.

At that meeting the committee will determine if another survey should be done including the community up to a mile from the church.

Recording Your Growth Program Plans

Now you are ready to create your "growth program plans." You will find a worksheet on page 191 (Appendix C). Many may be needed, so reproduce them for the use of groups that will write the plans. Create the plans you selected from your priority list by putting appropriate words or phrases in each column. Note all the resources needed to accomplish them. The Church Growth Committee should keep copies of all the growth program plans the church is working on in order to complete its task.

Looking Ahead

To begin thinking about the rest of your task, reflect on the steps for motivation given on page 74. You have already accomplished the first three steps listed below.

1. Your goal statements have given you challenges to reach.
2. The various boards and committees have been involved in the development of growth goals and the congregation has contributed to and affirmed that work. Therefore, there is a broad base of ownership of the challenges.
3. The objectives and growth program plans you developed designated specific responsibilities. The three steps yet to be done (listed here as 4, 5, and 6) will be discussed in chapter 9.
4. Provide adequate resources and training.
5. Receive recognition for work done.
6. Achieve and evaluate the objectives.

You will recognize that steps 4, 5, and 6 cannot be done without having good program plans. You can now begin to see growth occur. This can be as exciting for you as it is for new parents to watch their baby grow and develop.

IDEAS AND RESOURCES

Here are some ideas and resources that may stimulate your thinking as you develop program plans for evangelism, care, worship, education, service to the world, and church administration.

Evangelism

Nothing seems to break the bonds that hold a declining church to its past like evangelism. The church that is winning new people to faith in Jesus Christ has an excited, renewed atmosphere. New people with new faith bring new ideas and new possibilities into churches. A dynamic witness to the love, power, and justice of God that challenges people to commit their lives to Jesus Christ is a key to growth in any church.

As you look through the program ideas which follow, remember that biblically based evangelism (see pages 58 to 60) begins with individuals who:

- have a vital, joyous faith;
- are possessed by a call to share that faith;
- are convinced that all need to know Christ as Savior and Lord.

Evangelism continues with the integration of new believers into a community of faith and moves on to their participation in the total work of the kingdom. Evangelism that grows out of the Great Commission (Matthew 28:18-20) is related to all other ministries carried out by the church. Those who accept Christ as Savior are to be baptized into a caring, worshiping congregation. They are to be instructed in their new faith and enabled to express their faith through service. A good evangelism program will affect and be affected by everything the church does.

Organization for Evangelism

If your church does not have a specific group responsible for outreach, it is important that some group be given that responsibility. Even the smallest church needs to have a committee responsible for planning evangelism and seeing that it is done. It is not enough to say that evangelism is everyone's responsibility. Anything that is everyone's responsibility too easily and too often becomes no one's responsibility. Evangelism is the work of the entire congregation but it requires permanent leadership in the form of a standing committee.

One author describes such a committee as the steering wheel that controls the four wheels of a car. He compares the wheels to the entire congregation involved in an orderly and linked process of contact, cultivation, commitment, and conservation. The committee, as the steering wheel, nurtures a spiritual climate for evangelism in the church; de-

signs, stimulates, and coordinates evangelistic activities; and enables the contacting and nurturing of prospective and new members.[1]

If your church is to have a vital program of evangelism, two things are essential: a commitment of the church to evangelism, and the consecration of leaders who will coordinate and direct the evangelism program.

Those leaders, who make up the evangelism committee, may be thought of as associates of the pastor. For that reason it is appropriate for the pastor to seek out those church members who have:

- a personal commitment to Christ as Savior and Lord;
- a strong conviction that people are made new through faith in the redemptive work of Jesus Christ;
- a desire and ability to share their faith;
- a vision of a renewed church through new converts (These persons will have a burden for people who are outside the church and not living in the joy of forgiveness and faith.);
- confidence in the local church and its role in the salvation and spiritual growth of people;
- an ability in and/or a commitment to the need for planning, training, and coordination of activities;
- an ability to keep confidences.

If these people, gifted in leadership and highly interested in evangelism, are already involved in another area of ministry, they should be relieved of those responsibilities so that they can give their total attention to evangelism. Just as Jesus called his disciples from other tasks and occupations, so must the church. And just as Jesus prayed before choosing the disciples, so the church today should pray for the leading of the Spirit in choosing leadership. Use Luke 6:12-13 as a model for prayer when building an evangelism committee. Pray, "Lord, who should lead us in evangelism? Whom have you set apart for this work?"

The pastor needs to work patiently and prayerfully to disciple the leaders of the committee. He or she may take the committee through a book such as *Basic Leader Skills,* by Richard Rusbuldt (Valley Forge: Judson Press, 1981). This will build the team relationship of pastor and committee and lead the church to growth.

The committee must continue to work closely with the pastor, enabling the congregation to become an evangelizing church. To do this the committee will need to:

- create a climate for evangelism in the congregation;
- enlist, train, and support workers in evangelism;
- identify and organize evangelistic activities;
- build and carry out a program of follow-up.

[1] George Sweazey, *Effective Evangelism: The Greatest Work in the World* (New York: Harper & Row, Publishers, Inc., 1976).

Each of these tasks will be covered in detail in the pages that follow.

Creating the Climate for Evangelism Through Pastoral Leadership

One of Paul's last words to Timothy was an exhortation to be an evangelist (2 Timothy 4:5). But pastors may not be evangelistic by nature. Taking care of the needs of members can become such a preoccupation that evangelism is lost.

And yet it must not be so. As the model and equipper for the church, the pastor has a responsibility to make evangelism a priority. One way to do this is through sermons.

Unfortunately there is little written on preaching evangelistic sermons. Some basic helps exist in chapter 10 of *Effective Evangelism,* by George Sweazey (New York: Harper & Row, Publishers, Inc., 1976). An excellent explanation of the role of the listener in the preaching communication process can be found in *Listening on Sunday for Sharing on Monday,* by William D. Thompson (Valley Forge: Judson Press, 1983).

The other part of the pastor's leadership is to recognize and enable members who are gifted teachers. The "Gifts Analysis Questionnaire" on pages 125-133 can help interested laypersons determine what gift or gifts they have.

Creating the Climate for Evangelism Through Congregational Study

You may want to provide Sunday church school classes on evangelism for adults. Here are three books, each with a study guide for thirteen sessions, which can be used as Sunday church school curriculum:

John: The Gospel of Life, by George Vanderlip, answers "What is the Gospel?" by relating John's use of creation, revelation, and redemption to the ministry of Jesus and our ministry today.

Going Public with One's Faith, by R. James Ogden. A study of eight people from the Bible who help readers understand the meaning of witness.

The Gospel for the Person Who Has Everything, by William Willimon. Examines ways of sharing the gospel with the good, modern American who senses no need for God.

All of these books are published by Judson Press, Valley Forge, Pennsylvania. Leader's guides are printed and distributed by American Baptist Literature Service, Judson Book Store, Valley Forge, PA 19482-0851.

You may want to have some small group discussion and study at a time other than the Sunday church school hour. These books could be used as well as the following:

Christian Mission in the Modern World, by John R. W. Stott (Downers Grove, IL: IVP). Defines mission, evangelism, dialogue, salvation, and conversion to show that the mission of the church includes evangelism, discipleship and social concern with action.

First Things Last: Whatever Happened to Evangelism?, by Michael Green (Nashville: Discipleship Resources). A study of evangelism in the early church and how it can be done today.

Opening the Door of Faith, by John R. Hendrick (Atlanta: John Knox Press). Begins with the stories of how seven people came to their faith commitment. Examines the readiness of people to respond and the way in which both congregation and individual members play certain parts.

Two Half Gospels or a Whole?, by William R. Herzog, II (Valley Forge: American Baptist Literature Service). A short pamphlet which will stimulate discussion and study as it ties the word and action of evangelism together.

Creating the Climate for Evangelism Through Congregational Sharing

Give frequent opportunities for people to share stories of faith at work.

An excellent starting point is to have a lay renewal weekend. This program is designed to enable people to rediscover their commitment, to grow in their faith, and to support each other in applying their faith.

Provide time in worship services for testimonies that reflect current growth in relating faith to life. Members can give a "witness" for a minute or two about something in which they have been or will be involved as representatives of Jesus Christ and the church. One or two members could give a brief statement before each Communion service about the meaning of the Lord's Supper for them. Someone who has experienced an unusual answer to prayer could introduce the time of prayer.

Ask new members to be prepared to give a statement when they are received into membership. This statement could include why they chose the church as their family in Christ, what they are ready to bring to it, and what they expect to receive from it. Those who are being baptized could speak about their commitment to Jesus Christ as Savior and Lord.

Few people can speak easily on the spur of the moment. Ask people in advance to prepare a testimony and provide any help requested.

Enlisting Workers for Evangelistic Outreach

The evangelism committee leads the outreach of the church by providing organizational and support structures. Its primary role is not to do evangelism, even though the committee members may be effective in evangelism. Effective organization that promotes growth recognizes the differences between leading, doing, and enabling each person to do the task for which he or she is most suited by ability and gift.

Effective workers are those who demonstrate their gift for evangelism by witnessing and leading others to Christ. These people can be discovered if the church uses the "Gifts Analysis Questionnaire" (pages 125 to 133) or conducts a seminar on spiritual gifts.

Evangelists represent both Jesus Christ and the church. Therefore, they should be brought together, as Jesus brought the disciples together to train them to send them out in pairs.

Training for Evangelism

There are two approaches to lead people to commit their lives to Jesus Christ. These two approaches may be compared to two ways of making sure a suit fits you. Suppose you see a suit that catches your eye in a store. You try it on and discover it is the only suit of that style in stock and it is not your size. The suit could be altered to fit you or you could work at gaining or losing weight until you fit the suit.

One way to evangelize is to assume that the gospel is an unchangeable series of statements that everyone must accept to be saved. This method works with only a limited number of people. The other method assumes that the gospel can be adapted to fit people in the same way that a suit can be tailored without changing its style or cut. How people receive and understand the gospel depends much on the lives they live. Following the examples of Jesus and Paul, the concepts of the gospel are communicated best in the vernacular of the person who is being addressed. This method reaches more people than the other.

Some textbooks which can be used in training for evangelism are:

Good News Is for Sharing: A Guide to Making Friends for God, by Leighton Ford (Elgin, IL: David C. Cook Publishing Company, 1977). The author emphasizes "building bridges" to people and between people and God. He therefore presents many methods of sharing the Good News and gives practical pointers for telling your own story of faith. There is a study guide as well as an abridged form of the book and a videotape. All may be obtained from the publisher.

Communicating Good News, by David Augsburger (Scottdale, PA: Herald Press, 1972). The author is a theologian and psychologist, but above all a committed evangelist. In this book he focuses evangelism on the receiver rather than the sender in the process of communicating the Good News. The style of this book is very contemporary and can be read easily.

Support Evangelism

Those who relate to people outside the church need a

support group in which they can deal with the joy and pain of evangelizing. There will be "afterglows" when sharing has led to commitment. There will be pain when witnessing is answered by rejection. A support group of evangelists also provides a prayer bond. This is one part of the work that a committee and pastor cannot neglect. To forget this is to allow burn-out.

Those doing weekly visitation or community canvassing also need a support system. The evangelism committee, with the pastor, organizes and directs this group.

Some churches set aside one evening a week for visiting. The evening begins and ends with prayer at the church. There may even be a short time for sharing what happened on the visits. Other groups arrange to pick up assignment cards from the pastor or the church secretary and visit at their convenience. These workers need a special time for meeting, but probably not more than once a month.

The pastor is the best person to lead this meeting. Though it begins with prayer and praise, many requests will be generated by debriefing the experiences. The sharing time is not a time for gossip. Confidences must be kept and personal details must not even be hinted. However, problems may be shared discreetly so that the way in which they were handled can be examined. This will sharpen everyone's skills and prolong enthusiasm.

Evangelistic Activities

The coming of Jesus Christ and his teachings into the world underline important lessons for evangelism. One is that few seek out the gospel. It must be taken to those who seldom recognize that they need it. Another lesson is that evangelism must combine both compassion and message. Compassion without a message gives no ultimate hope. A message without compassion is a heartless voice.

The most effective and essential activity for evangelism is prayer. Prayer generates power that no program can. Evangelism that does not begin and exist through prayer will soon become manipulation and coercion. It is easy to think of open doors in relation to human situations, but don't forget the doors God can open. These doors are found by prayer.

As a Christian witness, ask God to open your eyes to the opportunities around you and to help you meet those opportunities with creative imagination. Add work to your prayer by searching out people with needs.

When we talk about types of evangelistic activity, we are simply referring to meeting people where they are so that they are confronted by the love and power of Christ. Types of activities are as different as the opportunities that grow out of the settings in which people live. To determine the activities which fit your situation you will need to draw on your community analysis done in chapters 4 and 5.

Identifying Opportunities

Some opportunities are identifiable by age group. Children need places and times to build friendships and to learn values. Youth may need a place for recreation and unwinding. Young singles need an alternative to secular clubs. Young parents seek help in the task of parenting. Middle-adults need to fill time once given to children. Senior adults long to know that life doesn't end when society says it is time to retire.

Personal experiences common to everyone open doors for the gospel. Sickness, accidents, business failure, divorce, births, marriages, promotions, and anniversaries present needs to be met. Some opportunities arise from tragedy, others from joy. The words of counsel and invitation to someone at these moments can open the door to eternal life. The gospel that saves from sin is able to respond to problems of lesser dimensions as well.

Greeting new people in the community is a great opportunity for outreach. The church should welcome the new neighbors with food and friendship when the moving van arrives.

Some opportunities demand that we understand what created a problem and recognize the pain of living with its consequences. The gospel can lift the guilt and burden from a pregnant teenager or a juvenile offender, from a prisoner or an addict. The gospel also lifts up those whom society puts down because of their race or class. It reaches out in love to migrant workers and the poor, to the handicapped and shut-in as much as to the affluent and healthy.

When we respond to human needs with grace and sensitivity, doors open. Acts of social concern say that God cares about people in their human and social dilemmas. As the church, we are able to meet the deeper needs of people for life in Christ. Because our good works are not the whole gospel, service opens the door for evangelism.

Opportunities for evangelism also come about as Christians break down barriers. Some barriers are the result of inappropriate actions of Christians and of churches in the community. Some barriers exist because people don't know what the church or the Christian life is all about. Loving, caring words and deeds can break down barriers of ignorance and negative experience.

The seasons of the year renew opportunities. Society has turned holy days into holidays. The Supreme Court has ruled that it is not against the First Amendment to sing Christmas carols in public schools because they are a part of our culture and not something uniquely religious. At Christmas and Easter the church can say something uniquely religious—something of God's redemptive love and power. It could help turn holidays back into holy days.

The media provide us with many open doors. Space may be bought in newspapers and on billboards or time on radio and TV. All of these provide evangelistic opportunities when used imaginatively and in the language of unchurched people.

The National Evangelistic Association (2323 Broadway, Lubbock, TX 79401) sells 60-second church commercials called "Bright Spots." On request, the association will send you samples for examination and a price list.

Activities in the Community

Here is a list of ways to find persons with special needs or interests through which you can engage in the ministry of evangelism.

Bible clubs in homes for children on weekdays.

Children's choirs and plays.

Youth recreation programs.

Community sports programs.

Forums on issues affecting youth.

Christian films.

Christian contemporary music programs.

Young adult programs with social and recreational focus.

Discussion groups on singles' issues.

Parent effectiveness training.

Weekday Bible studies in homes of members.

Day care or nursery school.

Single parents' evening which will provide child care one evening a week or every other week so the parents will have some free time.

Professional or business groups for men and/or women.

Training in home and car repairs.

Hobby classes.

Drama or fine arts group which could prepare productions for church services.

A touring club for "empty-nesters" to give middle-adults a chance to vacation in groups with friends.

Tutoring program for children, youth, and non-English-speaking residents.

Volunteer work in institutions.

Big Brother or Big Sister programs for needy children or children of single parents.

Doing repairs for people who can't do them or pay for them.

Providing transportation.

Serving Meals On Wheels.

A senior adult social program.

Visitation in homes and institutions.

Telephone counseling.

Forums on topics of community interest.

Work on community improvement.

Apartment house study groups.

Visitation in prisons (if there is one nearby).

Opening homes of members to youth offenders who are being rehabilitated.

A literature rack with tracts and Bibles in laundromats or shopping centers.

A booth at a county fair with literature about your church's programs.

Such a list would be endless if it included suggestions to deal with all the specific situations in your own community. However, the church is more than a social service agency and doesn't use care as a way to "trap" people. While responding to people's needs, evangelism moves beyond that.

A day care center evangelizes when some members get acquainted with families and share the gospel with them. When the community uses the church's facilities, members should take part in the activities and take opportunities to speak of Christ's love.

Crusades

One way a church can communicate the gospel to large numbers of people at a time is through a preaching mission, a revival, or a crusade. Whatever it may be called or however it may be organized, the key to the effectiveness of an event lies in the amount and type of preparation. This preparation, along with much that has been said earlier about service and meeting needs, is called "pre-evangelism." What happens in a crusade of one evening, a long weekend, or a week depends on what has been happening in the community through the members of the church for weeks before.

If you are interested in this type of evangelism, refer to *Planning a Festival of Evangelism,* by Owen Owens (Valley Forge: American Baptist Literature Service).

Because it is difficult to attract people for a week-long crusade today, other plans have been tried. Some churches have encouraged members to build friendships with non-Christians over an extended period. Groups have been organized for fun and discussion to which members could invite their friends. Here they had opportunities to meet other Christians and to begin sharing or exploring the meaning of the Christian faith. These people were prayed for intensively and then invited to a special service held on a weekend evening. This service aims at being a catalyst for the commitment to Christ.

Other churches have built their revivals around three or four special meetings during a long weekend. A special speaker is invited and sometimes special music is featured. Special meetings are held for youths on a Friday evening and a breakfast for adults on Saturday morning. Gatherings may be held on Saturday afternoon in houses of members for people interested in discussing the meaning of the Christian faith. Large meetings for inviting people to make commitments are held on Saturday and Sunday. This type of preaching mission requires the same "pre-evangelism" mentioned above.

The organization of such meetings requires at least the following work and planning:

1. A year before this special meeting, decide the purpose of the meeting, find a theme, set a date, build a budget, and decide on the number and the type of leaders to be involved.
2. Begin to pray for the effort as contacts with the evangelist and other leaders are being made. Make commitments with these leaders as soon as possible.
3. Organize the congregation into the following groups:

   ● prayer committee to organize chain prayer, cottage prayer meetings, prayer notices in church bulletins and newsletters, and to participate in regular prayer meetings;
   ● publicity committee to announce the campaign in local media and through leaflets and posters;
   ● music committee to arrange for local or outside instrumentalists, vocalists, or choirs;
   ● usher committee;
   ● hospitality committee to care for the needs of the leaders;
   ● counselors and follow-ups;
   ● visitation committee;
   ● special events committee.

4. Set goals for attendance and build the anticipation of the church. Plan special sermons for several weeks before the meeting.
5. Evaluate the preparations and results, noting the strengths and weaknesses with special observations that would help the leaders of the next meeting.

The outline of the planning will also apply to a week-long evangelistic crusade. If the speaker comes for a week, you may arrange for special activities during these days. A guest evangelist might speak on a local radio station, address students in high school, visit an institution where the church holds regular services, and visit in homes. If such a schedule is desired, it should be clearly stated when the evangelist is invited. Not all evangelists want to be that involved during the week.

Individual Contacts

The most basic and effective pre-evangelism is outlined in the first three steps of "Operation Andrew." This program gets its name from Andrew, who, having met Jesus, brought his own brother Simon to Jesus (John 1:40-42). This program trains Christians to bring unchurched and uncommitted friends either to a faith commitment or to a meeting where the invitation will be given. Its five steps are:

1. Pray for one to ten people whom you know and who to the best of your knowledge are not yet Christians.
2. Cultivate their friendship.
3. Invite them and bring them to a meeting.
4. Encourage them in Christian commitment.
5. Support them as they join the church and become growing, witnessing Christians.

Statistics from mass evangelism campaigns point out that those who have had a nurturing relationship for an extended period before attending a meeting make the most of their commitment and stick to it over the long term. These people have established trust and friendship with Christians in the church before making their commitment at mass evangelism campaigns.

As long as there are unchurched people in a community, making contact should not be difficult. The biggest problem is that the longer someone is an active church member, the more that person breaks contacts with people outside the church. God does not intend that Christians become isolated from the world. God wants everyone to be saved and has commissioned those who are saved to be the bridge builders.

W. Oscar Thompson, a former professor of evangelism at Southwestern Baptist Theological Seminary, popularized a life-style evangelism called *Concentric Circle of Concern* (Nashville: Broadman Press, 1981). He says that the most important word in evangelism is relationship. Evangelism begins in the relationship between an individual and Christ as Lord. From there evangelism should not focus on the unknown person but rather on meeting the needs of those in the immediate family. Then it moves successfully outward to relatives, close friends, neighbors, business associates, and acquaintances, before reaching the unknown persons God sends into our lives at different moments.

Thompson advises Christians to put names of people in each category and pray for them regularly, asking God to make them ready to respond to Christ.

Your church could have a Commitment Sunday when all members are given the opportunity to list those people for whom they are committed to pray. Those who make that commitment become prayer partners by supporting each other in the witnessing task.

Other contacts are those who visit the church or those who are counseled by the pastor during crises. New people moving into the community are likely prospects, as well as inactive members of the church, those reached through special services held in the church building, and those who are a part of some special outreach such as a sports program, Scouts, a church circle, a day care program, or study groups. Another overlooked group of people includes the unreached ones in the families of some church members.

Most contacts will be neighbors and friends of the members. Evangelism in the neighborhood is done most naturally by residents. This is especially true in densely populated areas such as apartment houses, mobile home courts, and city areas with row or multiple housing units. Members in these areas could open their homes for Bible study groups, community forums or organizations, and house parties.

A house party provides a social setting for a few invited church members to meet some friends and neighbors of the host. After light refreshments the people begin directed conversation by using questions that will help them become better acquainted. The hosts end the evening with a brief witness about the meaning of the church in their lives and what it means to believe in Jesus Christ. Time is left for questions or discussion and an invitation is given informally for the guests to feel free to ask any personal questions or to visit the church for a Sunday school class and worship service.

Another way to initiate contacts in the neighborhood is for the church to do either a door-to-door or a phone survey. A phone survey gives opportunity for ministry to members who are not able to get out easily, such as shut-ins or parents with young children at home. It can be done at convenient times and in any kind of weather. On the other hand, the door-to-door survey establishes face-to-face contact which makes communication easier.

These surveys are not merely for collecting data. Through them the church is presented as a listening, serving, understanding representative of Jesus Christ. The information gathered describes needs the church may be called on to meet. While the first purpose is to discover, the ultimate purpose is to share Jesus Christ and his call to believe and follow. Here are some helps for doing a survey.

1. Get a street directory of the neighborhood near the church building. A Chamber of Commerce could give you information about it or may even lend you a copy. These directories may be from six to eighteen months old by the time they are circulated and revised. Utility company address lists, if available, lack phone numbers.

2. For a door-to-door survey, prepare an attractive brochure about the church. Include a brief history of the congregation, a short note from the pastor, announcements about activities, and one- or two-sentence testimonials from some neighbors who are members.

3. Determine the area you want to cover and divide it into so many residences per person or team that will call by phone or in person. Door-to-door calling does not require

having names and phone numbers. However, it helps if information cards are prepared ahead of time. If a community has roadside mailboxes, names may be checked before going to a house or apartment.

4. Develop a model for calling. It must be remembered that you are making contacts that may lead to future visits and conversion. Therefore, the model must make an introduction between two people who do not know each other and must aid in opening up a conversation. "A Model for Tele-Survey" is given in Appendix C, page 193.

5. Prepare a card to record and file the information that will be asked for. Also, *prepare a system for follow-up.* It is better not to contact neighbors than it is to contact them, raise their hopes, and then lose them because of no follow-up. Devise a system in which persons bring the information back to the church so that future contacts can be made with these people.

6. Train the callers. Let them practice making several calls in role-playing situations. Then let them call on each other by phone or at home to get a feel for something more real. They may even try calling on several active church members in a "pastoral" way. These books, published by Judson Press, would help in this training. They are:

How to Make a Friendly Call, by Willard D. Callender.

Comprehensive Pastoral Care: Enabling the Laity to Share in Pastoral Ministry, by Samuel Southard.

Pastoral Care for Personal Growth, by Thomas H. Conley.

Also available from American Baptist Literature Service is *Growing as a Caring Community,* by William C. Cline.

Evangelism Demands Follow-Up

Building bridges to people and between people and God is often called pre-evangelism. Evangelism is the act of inviting someone to become reconciled to God through faith in Jesus Christ. The follow-up is called post-evangelism or sometimes "after-care." At this part of the process new believers are instructed, nurtured, and guided in fulfilling some of the gospel's expectations such as joining a church, establishing the habits of Christian discipleship, and becoming involved in the work of the kingdom.

The starting point of follow-up would most likely be a pastor's class. The content of such a class will vary from church to church. However, the following outline is basic to most of these class sessions:

1. My new relationship with God.
   What it means to be saved.
   How I can grow in my new life.
2. My new relationship to the church.
   History of the denomination.
   History, purpose, and program of the local church.

Expectations of the church and the new member.
3. My new relationship to the world.

As an ambassador for Jesus Christ among those with whom I am in contact every day.

As an aid for the church's mission to the world by praying, giving, and doing.

The process of reception into the church should be a spiritual high point in the life of the new members. There should be opportunity for meeting the church leaders and for sharing the story of faith and their commitment to Christ and the church. Leaders as well as the new members should be able to share their stories briefly. The focus in this sharing should be first on what Christ means and then on what belonging to the church means.

The service of reception should be an act of faith and fellowship rather than merely an organizational vote. The new member should have the opportunity to give a brief testimony. The "Hand of Fellowship" could be given by a sponsor. This would be a person or family assigned to the new member; this person or persons would have the following responsibilities for a year:

1. Introduce the new member to the congregation at the time of his or her reception. Stand with him or her in the reception line to introduce the members to them.
2. Invite him or her to a Sunday school class or be sure that the person joins a class.
3. Be sure that he or she understands the church's program and polity.
4. Be sure he or she is on the mailing list and has completed a congregational information form.
5. Introduce him or her to other members at a social setting in the sponsor's home during a dinner or a time of refreshment.
6. Become a friend. Notice when he or she misses a worship service or other activity and call to inquire why.
7. Report any needs he or she may have to the pastor.

The congregational leaders should begin working on integrating new members into the life and ministry of the church from the time of their reception. The three Rs of integration are:

- Relationship—new members need to belong to some group.
- Responsibility—every member should have some specific part in the mission of the church.
- Renewal—one part of the church's task is to strengthen and revitalize the faith of its members.

If new members do not experience these three things within one year, they will become high risks for dropping out. This fact has been highlighted by Lyle Schaller in his book

Assimilating New Members (Nashville: Abingdon Press).

In that book, Schaller also points out the many devices by which congregations squeeze out new members. One of the most subtle forms of exclusion is for a congregation that has a strong sense of history to lack contemporary goals. This is why the planning process is so important to the ministry of evangelism in the church. Having current goals that will involve new members in tasks, groups, and roles is vital to the preservation of those who are won by the outreach of the congregation.

Care

Because the Christian church is a community of support, care, and nurture, God has given some of its members the gifts of caring, helping, encouraging, and showing kindness. The church is to reach out to the world while being hospitable and showing love to one another within the fellowship.

A congregation begins to be a caring people when members sense they have something to share and exercise the will to share. True care grows out of a faith relationship with Jesus Christ that is shared with others and forms a fellowship. The point of focus for true care and fellowship is Jesus Christ (1 John 1:3). The biblical basis for care and fellowship was given on pages 48 and 60-61. Here are some program suggestions to help grow a caring congregation.

Lay Renewal

This program has given many churches a new sense of fellowship, a new understanding of the ministry of the laity, and a new commitment to outreach. It is usually a weekend event prepared with a church by a trained coordinator. The coordinator and a team of visiting laypersons share what Christ is doing in their lives. This sharing often takes place in small group meetings which build a trust relationship between those attending. The team, in these groups, helps the church members discover and express what Christ is doing for them and in them.

There is, however, a danger in the small group experience. A group can turn inward, closing itself off from any outside the group. This is usually unconscious and comes about as the group focuses on the needs of its members and the relationship being built between them.

Such a group can be revitalized by opening itself and intentionally and regularly including new people in its activities and life. This changes the nature of the group and must be the desire of its members. Groups can share with the entire congregation through regular reports in the church bulletins or newsletter. This demonstrates that the smaller groups belong to a larger congregation. It also attracts new people into the groups.

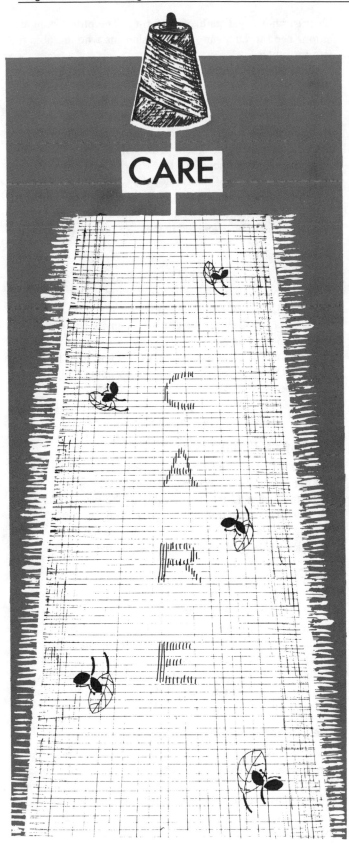

Information about lay renewal programs may be obtained from:

1. Macedonia Ministries, Board of National Ministries, American Baptist Churches, Valley Forge, PA 19482-0851.

2. Evangelism Section, Board of Discipleship, P.O. Box 840, Nashville, TN 37202.

3. Faith at Work, 11065 Little Patuxent Parkway, Columbus, MD 21044.

Diaconate's Shepherding Program

While small groups meet the needs of some members, this program will be able to care for others, especially the inactive or marginal members. Deacons (both male and female) are "pastoral assistants" responsible for the care of church members. But their most urgent task is to touch the disconnected or loosely connected members. Here is a plan for the shepherding ministry of the diaconate.

1. Make a list of all members who are not actively involved in some group such as a study group, a choir, a church school class, or a women's or men's fellowship.

2. Each deacon selects up to eight family units (a family unit includes *all* persons living at the same address). These are people the deacon may know or would like to know.

3. Pray regularly for each person in that group.

4. Visit each family unit at least twice a year. Visit to become acquainted, to become friends, to discover needs, and to encourage participation in the life of the church. But never visit to get a financial commitment to the church.

5. If they are absent from worship, call them, if appropriate, to express interest and concern, being sensitive to any need.

6. Minister to them at special times by personal visits, cards, or phone calls. Inform the pastor of any need for his or her presence and care.

7. Each deacon may invite these people to his or her home for a meal or an evening once a year. Add a few other church members to broaden the fellowship. When introducing people, or at other times, say something appropriate about the life and ministry of the church.

8. Set aside a day or weekend each year for training in visitation and listening skills. Experienced workers can help new ones while sharpening their own skills.

Helper's Band

Care means that churches must respond with aid in times of some crises. Make a list of the members able to supply aid such as transportation, food, house-sitting, pet care, child care, housework, companionship, or shopping. Designate a person to contact the helpers and to organize the schedule of help. With such a plan, response to crises can be given in a very short time. A prayer chain (see page 96) can become part of this program.

Sponsors

Here is a program of care for new members. Sponsors are members selected for their skill at hospitality and their commitment to the church. They will help new members get to know the church and enable the church to know the new members by:

1. Greeting the new members at church each week for several weeks and introducing them to other members.

2. Visiting in their homes and encouraging them in their new commitment, praying with them, and urging them to pray regularly for the church and pastor.

3. Being conscious of any sign that they are getting off to a bad start. If something has gone wrong, try to make it right. Inform the pastor or deacons if necessary.

4. Posting their pictures on the bulletin board with a brief biographical sketch.

5. Encouraging them to attend a social occasion for honoring new members. Offer transportation if possible.

Training is necessary for people who undertake the ministry of care. Here are three resources, selected from many, because they present three different levels of training.

1. William Cline has developed a six-hour training program in listening and visiting skills called *Growing as a Caring Community: Training and Resources for a Program of Membership Renewal, Retention, and Reclamation* (American Baptist Literature Service, Valley Forge, PA 19482-0851).

2. Richard Rusbuldt has designed a 15-hour training program called Lay Pastoral Care (LPC). It includes fifteen hours of training and guidelines for setting up and carrying out a ministry of care through the laity. Information about this well-proven program is available through the LPC Office, American Baptist Churches of Pennsylvania and Delaware, Valley Forge, PA 19482-0851.

3. Paul Welter makes the professional skills of a counselor available for everyone in his book *You Can Help a Friend!* (Wheaton, IL: Tyndale House Publishers, Inc., 1978). This book gives clear and easy steps for learning how to help persons in ways best suited to those persons.

Care and the Shut-in

Jesus said that one of the questions that will distinguish between those who enter eternal life or eternal punishment will be "What have you done for those whose movements are restricted by sickness or imprisonment?" (see Matthew 25:31-46). That such persons need the care of those who are able to get around would seldom be questioned. Yet this care is not readily put into practice. Nor is it always thought of in terms of programs.

Many shut-ins are very caring people, able to understand the frustrations and pain of suffering. Therefore, congregations need to be aware of those shut-ins who are able to care for others.

The ministry of care is "burden bearing" through support and encouragement. When people notice care shown to the member of a church or are told about it by the member, they will ask, "Why do they do that?" The Lord gives us the answer: We love Christ by loving others; we minister to Christ by caring for others. This will be the measure of our obedience (Matthew 25:31-46).

God never intended the care of the Christian community to stop at the doors of a building. It is to flow over into the world. In this manual that care is called "Service to the World" and will be discussed in that section (see page 100).

Worship

Worship, according to the words used in the New Testament, is work, service, joy, thanksgiving, and life. It is our response of awe to God's judging and saving power (Hebrews 12:28-29). It is a gift of ourselves and our good deeds to God (Romans 12:1; Hebrews 13:16). In worship, Christians acknowledge the majesty of Christ, joyfully thank God for Christ's victory over death and sin, and confess their hope in Christ's return and the kingdom's ultimate triumph. Below are three of the ways in which the character of true Christian worship can be shown.

The Day of Worship

While the first Christians met every day (Acts 2:46), it was not long until the primary gathering was on the Lord's Day (Revelation 1:10), the first day of the week. This was the day of resurrection (Luke 24:1) and, as the day of meeting, declared that Christians were convinced that God had final authority over death as well as over life.

The Content of Worship

Worship is a dialogue with God. The congregation addresses God in prayer, hymns, and offerings through which it praises God for mighty deeds of giving, renewing, sustaining, and directing life. Prayers and hymns fill many pages of the New Testament.

God speaks to the community through the words of Scripture that call us to act. God is also present in the signs of bread, wine, and water.

The Gathering for Worship

While God is present in the physical signs mentioned above, God is also present in the lives of the worshipers. Christians worship *together* because they have a common faith in Christ. Corporate worship is the gathering of God's people, the reassembling of the body, and the molding of the fellowship.

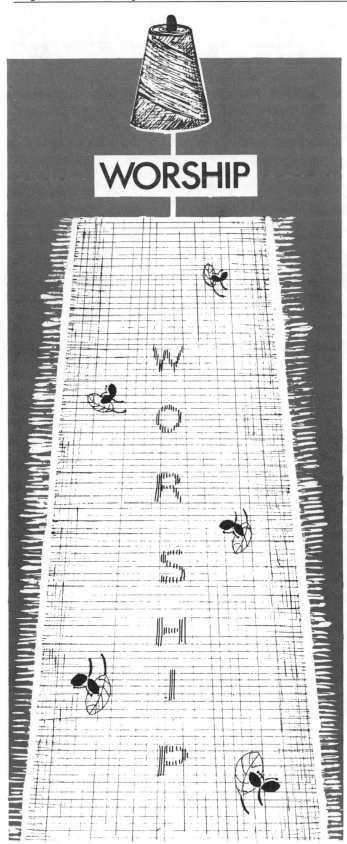

Additional material on the biblical background of worship was given on pages 61-62. Here are some program suggestions to help grow a worshiping congregation.

The Worship Committee

The responsibility for worship belongs to the pastor and to either the diaconate or a worship committee. Most often the committee limits its activity to preparing for communion and baptisms and arranging for flowers and ushers. However, the committee, with the pastor, can do much to build a growing worship experience for the church. A vibrant worship brings in people. These kinds of services are most often thematic as the proclaimed Word is reinforced by related prayers, music, and other liturgical content. Resources are available to help the pastor and committee. Here are a few:

1. *We Gather Together: Worship Resources for the Church of the Brethren* (Elgin, IL: The Brethren Press) is a guide for the worship committee. There are sections on the meaning of worship, the work of the worship committee, and the content of worship for adults and children. The notebook is full of examples.

2. Every worship committee should have a library of aids and books. Two of many that could help renew the worship experience are:

Writing Your Own Worship Service, by G. Temp Sparkman,

Open to Glory, by Carol Doran and Thomas H. Troeger.

Both of these books are published by Judson Press, Valley Forge, PA, 19482-0851.

The worship committee can sponsor a churchwide study about worship. This study could take place during the Sunday church school hour or on Sunday evenings for a month. In addition to the books mentioned above and the extensive list of books given in *We Gather Together,* another resource is *Listening on Sunday for Sharing on Monday* by William Thompson (Judson Press, 1983). This book was written at the request of the American Baptist Churches Evangelism Team to show how a congregation can become a partner in the preaching ministry through living out the sermon's message.

Worship Renewal Through Membership Renewal

Vital worship begins in a vital commitment to Jesus Christ. Revivals or lay renewal weekends (pages 89, 92) can help to renew or maintain a high level of commitment among the members of the church. Another way to experience renewal is to have a day in which members can make a recommitment of loyalty to Christ and to the church. Some suggestions for preparing that service are:

1. Put it on the church calendar a year in advance and

speak about it from time to time in the pulpit and in the newsletter.

2. Several weeks before the day, send each member a letter explaining the service and procedures for declaring individual recommitment. Include any or all of the following: the church's covenant and statement of purpose, a loyalty recommitment statement and a time and talent commitment form. The recommitment statement could say:

MY COMMITMENT TO FAITHFUL MEMBERSHIP
IN THE _____ CHURCH
FOR 19____

I have read the church covenant and statement of purpose carefully and accept them as a guide for my relationship with Christ expressed through my membership in this church. Therefore, I sign my name signifying that I am renewing my commitment to be a faithful member of this church.

_____   _____
(name)   (date)

3. The diaconate could collect the cards during a visit in the homes or the members could bring them to the church.

4. Designate a specific Sunday for a service of renewal. Focus the elements of the service on the meaning and responsibility of membership in the church. Have a way to make the act of recommitment (or commitment) visible, and conclude with the Lord's Supper.

Prayer and Worship

The heart of worship is prayer. Prayer is a discipline of the Christian life which requires constant attention. The worship committee can schedule training programs and the pastor can preach an annual series of sermons on prayer. There are many books that aid growth in this discipline. William Krutza was asked to write *Prayer: The Vital Link* (Judson Press, 1983) as a companion resource to this book on church growth. His book contains a seven-hour study program for the renewal of personal and corporate prayer. One of its goals is to build prayer groups in a church. Here are some suggestions for the use of these groups:

a. Prayer Cells

Prayer cells are formed to pray for specific needs or projects. They come together as needs arise and disband when the prayer need is gone. They meet in homes most often and the leader and host divide responsibility for calling people about the meeting and for handling the different tasks at the meeting. The meeting may begin with a song and the reading of Scripture related to prayer.

b. Prayer Chain

Here is another way to link those expressing special interest in praying for those expressing special needs. Members of the chain are recruited by public announcement or by personal invitation from the pastor or even from the diaconate. The members select a leader to activate the chain as needs arise. The size of the group should be limited to twelve people. If there are more, a second or third chain with its own leaders should be started. A chain may decide to meet quarterly for fellowship and study. Making arrangements for this meeting is the responsibility of the leader and may provide opportunity to introduce new members into the chain.

As prayer needs are made known to someone in the church, the pastor or the diaconate contacts the leader of the prayer chain. The leader then contacts the members of the chain, requesting prayer for the specific need. Some needs may call for acts of caring as well as prayer. This ministry of prayer may therefore be combined with the ministry of care discussed on pages 93 and 94. The prayer chain may pray for someone undergoing surgery, while another group provides food for the family and flowers and visits for the hospitalized person.

Prayer requests should be kept on the list for as long as necessary. This may require some follow-up by the leader. Share answers to prayer with the prayer chain. You may even want to use some as testimonies in a worship service.

c. Prayer Support of the Church Members

Some churches have grown a praying congregation by giving all members a prayer card with the names of fourteen members on it. They are asked to pray for one member each day, praying through the list twice each month. The lists are changed two or four times a year and new cards distributed during visits of diaconate members to the homes of church members.

These prayer cards can be made easily out of 5" x 7" cards. List the names on the left side; to the right put three or six double columns—one pair of columns for each month the list is to be used. Each day as the member prays for a name on the list a check mark can be entered beside the name of that person.

Regular opportunities should be given in worship services to share the blessings of being a part of a congregation which prays for its members.

NAME	Jan.		Feb.		March	
	1	2	1	2	1	2

96

d. A Day of Prayer

Before a special event in the life of the church, call the congregation to a day of prayer. This event could be a nominating committee beginning its work of selecting new leaders or the launching of a major effort in education or evangelism.

Prepare a large clock, then ask members to sign up for one or more 15-minute periods. People can come to the church to pray or pray at home. More than one person can sign up for a period of time and families could sign up for larger blocks of time to pray as a unit. Make a selection of Scripture passages related to the event available so that people can read them during the prayer time. Follow this up with a sharing time during your next worship service.

Music Programs

Worship is incomplete without music. Through music we express feelings and thoughts at the same time. It is also an excellent medium for telling the Good News. A church should seek to have as broad a range of music in its worship services as possible so that the most people can be reached. Involve as many people and age groups as possible through a music program which includes soloists, ensembles, and choirs which give concerts for the community as well as participate in the worship services. Instrumental music is also important. A good organist or pianist leads a congregation into joyous singing. To a visitor, musicians are as visible as the pastor. Good musicians attract people and communicate God's story of redemption with the power of mood, rhythm, melody, and harmony.

While musicians are important in worship, the congregation's music is more important. Growing congregations tend to be singing congregations. Singing congregations tend to be joyful congregations.

There are excellent suggestions about music in worship in *We Gather Together* and *Open to Glory* which were mentioned earlier as resources for the worship committee. Another book for the committee, the pastor, and those responsible for the music program is *Ministry and Music,* by Robert Mitchell (Philadelphia: Westminster Press).

Giving and Worship

In worship we declare that Jesus is Lord and we are his subjects. Part of worship is to recognize that our possessions are not exclusively our own. Jesus demanded a place of priority in our lives, even over our money (Mark 10:21). An offering is not just the way a church collects money. It is a sign of our dedication to God. Therefore worship leaders should prepare the Call to Giving and the Offertory Prayer thoughtfully and well.

Of all the motives for Christian giving, the first must be joyful obedience in response to God's love, rather than a reluctant or forced submission. Christian giving begins with God giving to us and continues as we give to God and, in God's name, to others. A growing church will grow in giving. A very effective stewardship program building over five weeks on the theme of commitment to Christ and to Christ's ministry is *Call to Commitment*. This program was developed by Rev. Floyd Harbold and is distributed through American Baptist Literature Service, Valley Forge, PA 19482-0851. In 1983 Judson Press (Valley Forge, PA) published a study book by A. Q. Van Benschoten, Jr., titled *What the Bible Says About Stewardship*. This book would be an ideal study to complement the programmatic resources in *Call to Commitment* in launching a new church year of ministry.

Worship and the Shut-In

It is easy to limit worship to an activity done within the walls of a church building. This limits worship to people who are able to travel and cuts off those who are immobilized. People in institutions should be included in worship. A group from a church could prepare a worship service for a shut-in. However, the group should allow opportunity for shut-ins to lead them in worship or in parts of the worship service also.

Family Worship

Worship is more than an activity of the gathered people on the first day of the week. It is a constant outpouring of praise from God's children. It is, therefore, natural for the worship committee to encourage worship as a part of a day's activities in all family units of the church.

Provide members with a daily devotional guide to be used in the home. Since these guides are generally produced quarterly, they could be taken to members' homes by the diaconate members.

Give members opportunities to tell what family worship means in their lives and homes. Some members may be recruited to demonstrate an actual family worship period during a worship service built around the family theme. Promote family worship regularly in the church newsletter and from time to time in the pulpit.

Special devotional materials may be prepared by the congregation for the periods of Lent and Advent. Development of the projects may take two years. During the first year ask members to write devotionals for each day. Publish these before the season of the second year and distribute them to the congregation. Once again, enlist some members to write new devotionals for use the following year.

Education

There is repeated emphasis in Scripture on the need to learn God's will. Those who believe in God are expected

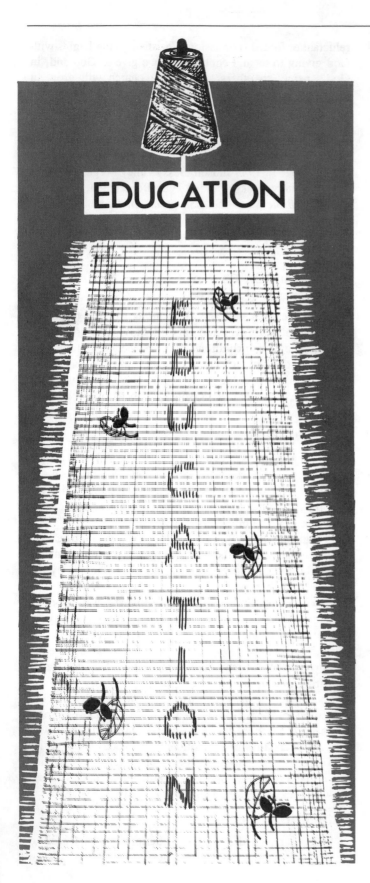

to commit time to learning God's will. The Christian education program is a key part of the discipleship task of the church. But Christian education programs also have a cutting edge for evangelism in that they provide instruction for those who are searching for God. (Additional comments on the biblical basis for education are found on page 62.) Therefore, education in the church serves two purposes: to help believers mature in the faith and to help unbelievers become familiar with the faith and its demands. Here are some suggestions about how to do that.

A Rally Day

Public and private schools recruit and register students. Why doesn't the church do it for educational programs? Some churches with commitments to the importance of education grow through an annual recruitment day. This special day is for presenting the church's educational opportunities to both church members and nonmembers not yet involved in the program. Here are some suggestions for this rally day.

1. Set the date a year ahead and prepare for it. Have each class and activity build lists of prospective members. Prepare a brochure to advertise the program.

2. About three months before the rally day, prepare a prospect list of children, youth, and adults to be invited.

3. Enlist and train those who are active in and enthusiastic about the church's educational program as visitors. Invite older children and youths to visit their peers.

4. One month before the rally day, begin visiting the homes of the prospects. Explain the program and invite them to the rally day.

5. One week before the special day send a letter to all who were visited, reminding them of the date and time and encouraging them to attend.

6. Present an attractive and positive description of the church's education programs. Use pictures and words; statements from children, youth, and adults who participate; and program descriptions from leaders and teachers. Give time for registration. The meeting should provide a time for those active in the education programs to mix with those who were invited. Refreshments would help the conversations to be more relaxed.

7. Encourage the program leaders and teachers to follow up.

Divided We Grow

Growth in Sunday church school comes most often through multiplying classes. The size of a class depends on the method of instruction used. Lecture methods may be used in large classes more easily than discussion or sharing. Small group methods are effective only with small groups. Large group methods always work best on large groups. Some considerations for the growth of the church school are:

1. *The number of classes available.* You may want to expand the options in the Sunday church school program. Some people may not attend because they are not attracted by what existing classes are doing. Create classes that meet special interests and needs.

2. *The size of a classroom.* If a class gets too large for its room, do not force it to move. Classes pick up "real estate" and don't like to be evicted. This is especially true of youths. Try starting another class.

3. *The actions and attitudes of the current members of the class.* Encourage all classes to become active in inviting new members to attend and join. Classes should work on building attitudes and actions that welcome people rather than prevent them from attending.

4. *The support of training.* Train, pray for, support, and praise teachers.

5. *The visitation program.* Remember that visitation is a part of the education program. Visitation is essential whenever people who meet together occasionally are scattered the rest of the time. Visitation builds friendship and friends become loyal to their group.

Decision Day

While the role of Christian education is to instruct people about the faith, part of that instruction is to invite people to commit their lives to Jesus Christ as Savior and Lord. All who are able to understand the call to make an open commitment to Christ should be encouraged to do so. A decision day can be a chance for persons to make that commitment to Christ.

Teachers should be trained how to present the claims of Christ and how to lead people of various ages to a faith commitment. Prior to decision day, they should share their faith with their classes. When children are involved, the teacher should contact the parents to explain the purpose and plan for the day. Encourage parents to speak with their children about their relationship with Christ or to talk with the pastor about it.

On that particular day the classes which have been invited to the program should be brought together for a worship service. After the call for commitment is made by the pastor, people may respond either by signing a card or by moving from their seats to a place at the front of the meeting room. If they come forward, teachers should be present to stand with the pupils and to talk with them about their faith commitment. This part of "Decision Day" should be individualized. Those who made decisions should be invited to join the pastor's (or new members') class.

After-School Program

If your church neighborhood has little or no supervised activity for children or youth, there is an excellent opportunity for opening up new homes to the gospel by starting some good after-school programs. Younger children's programs could include recreation, crafts, music, and stories. Older children could have some competitive sports, discussion of interesting and current topics, films, music, help with school work, and instruction in the Bible.

Training Teachers in Home Visitation

Church school teachers need to have some knowledge of the home situations of their pupils. They should be given training in visitation skills and encouraged to do this at the beginning of the church school year. These visits will open up relationships with the parents and give opportunity to enlist their cooperation in the education of their children in the faith. If the families are not church families, a visit will open up possibilities for future contacts to witness.

Teachers can also "train" their pupils to do some visiting by taking them to see a sick pupil or having them recruit a friend to attend their Sunday church school class.

Teaching Discipleship

As part of the midweek services or on Sunday evenings, the Christian education committee/board could sponsor a series of discipleship seminars for adults and youth. As part of their growth as disciples, invite the participants to covenant to do the following:

1. Spend thirty minutes each day in Bible study, reflection, and prayer. Keep a journal of the Bible study reflections, noting especially what thing(s) you feel led to do for others that day.
2. Maintain a prayer list of at least three non-Christians as well as the pastor, church leaders, some church members, family, friends, and acquaintances.
3. Witness to others of your faith experience in Christ.
4. Do two hours of work per week in the church.
5. Meet weekly with the discipleship group for one hour of study, sharing, and prayer.
6. Tithe for the thirty-day period and speak in the discipleship group of its meaning in your life.

This experience could last for thirty to sixty days.

Bible Conference

If your church has had evangelistic meetings or revivals and is seeking to have a different experience, the Christian education committee/board could sponsor a three- to five-day Bible conference with an outside speaker. The activities for organizing this special ministry are the same as those for organizing a rally or campaign (see page 90).

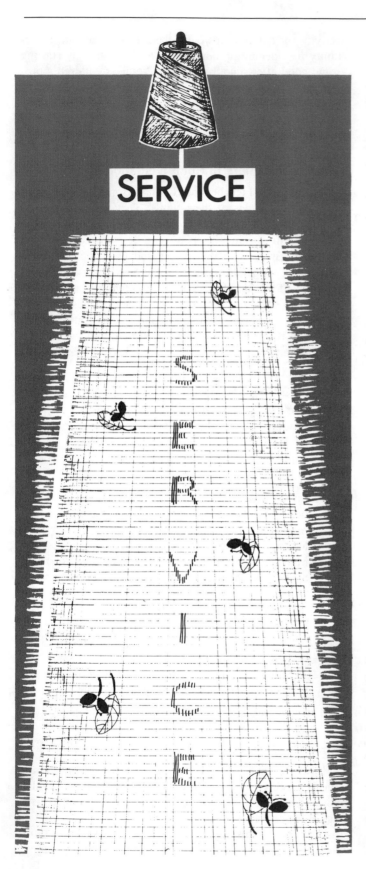

Service to the World

The church gathers to praise God, care for one another, and learn. But the church is also a sign in the world of the presence and power of God's kingdom. This was discussed briefly on pages 45-48, and 63. Much more could be said about it, drawing on many great passages from the prophets and Jesus. However, one short passage in Philippians 2 sums up the church's role and priorities.

Paul starts the second chapter in Philippians by speaking about the transformation that occurs as different people join in a common bond under the lordship of Jesus Christ. This divine bonding brings about the unity of the body. And this body is recognized through the change from self-interest to concern for others (verses 3-4). All of this has been modeled by Jesus Christ (verses 1-5).

Paul then lifts a hymn of praise about Christ out of the liturgy of the early church. Jesus expressed concern for humanity by giving up his status of glory and taking on an identity with the human race. He did this according to the will of God whose power brought him back from the dead and glorified him above all (verses 6-11).

Finally Paul turns back to the church urging it to be a new people in its care for one another, in its worship, and also in the world. All the works of the church are in reality God working for God's glory. The church is to work in unity and holiness so that it will be an option which the world will want to choose (verses 12-16).

Paul states that although the church is in the world it is to be different from the world. From the prophets he borrows the image of light (Isaiah 42:6; 49:6). Simeon compared Jesus to light at the time of His birth (Luke 2:32). Later Jesus called his followers the lights of the world who through their good works would glorify God (Matthew 5:14-16). As light, the church is to dispel the darkness that is in the world.

Paul assumes that the purpose of God in saving us is to complete God's work. This is done as we are transformed and then transform the world. We are saved through faith to do the work that God intended to be done from the time of creation (Ephesians 2:8-10). The church is to be a model community in the world.

The Committee for Service in the World

Regardless of the church's size, someone or some group must be committed to guiding the church in meeting the needs of the community and the world. In most churches the diaconate or a mission committee is responsible for this. Yet service in the local community often tends to be haphazard because other important work has to be done. The diaconate is concerned about the spiritual life of the church. The mission committee is busy raising money so that missionaries can do work somewhere else.

As important as these tasks are, they are best done along with community service. We are created so that as we look to Jesus, we also look outward and become involved in the lives of others. We do not fulfill God's will only by providing money for others to do the work. God has a task for each of us to do in the places where we live and work. Therefore, service in the world must be seen as the church doing mission in its own community, as well as supporting what others do elsewhere. The committee can be organized in the same way as an evangelism committee. Its task will be to help the church serve God in the world both at home and elsewhere, through action and through giving.

Learning About Service

The church has always had difficulty relating its life of faith to its life in the community. It is easy to allow our commitments to the social order to direct our lives. Then when our faith asks us to cut across what is, or to "upset the apple cart," we become uneasy. It is difficult to live out the conviction that God is working in the world and commands us to get involved. If we do get involved, it seems difficult to become confident of God's presence and help in ministry, especially when the work gets hard.

We all need constant reminders of both God's command and God's great provisions for all who dare to obey those commands. The reminders can come in at least three ways.

The first way is the reminders that come through life. Being in the fellowship of the church is a living reminder of God's presence. Being part of the world's brokenness is an unmistakable reminder of what God wants us to do.

Reminders also come through God's Word proclaimed. In sermons the pastor can emphasize the resources God gives for our involvement in the world.

And, finally, reminders come through studies. Here are two books, either or both of which would be excellent for a monthly study of three to six months.

1. *A Passion for Jesus; A Passion for Justice,* by Esther Bruland and Stephen Mott (Valley Forge: Judson Press). This book provides an excellent study on the biblical base for our service in the world.
2. *The Mustard Seed Conspiracy,* by Tom Sine (Waco, Texas: Word Books). This book will give practical application for your service in the local community and the world.

Any church can focus on at least one community need *and* on at least one community issue. A *need* is something people understand clearly and can resolve or meet by taking some action. An *issue* is something that needs to be studied and clarified so that appropriate action can be taken.

Getting Involved in the Community

Draw on the work of the Church Growth Committee from chapter 5 to determine the needs and issues facing the community. While studying the community, seek out those people who can best describe these needs so as to motivate the congregation. Select specific needs that can be accomplished in a short period of time. Refer to the list of "pre-evangelism" activities suggested on page 89. If you don't find the right suggestion in that list, find others suitable for your community.

Prepare a weekend program to introduce the congregation to community needs. Such a program could give variety to an annual service emphasis. Launch the weekend of activity with a Friday evening seminar. The aim of this meeting would be to motivate the congregation for responsible Christian action in the community. The pastor could present a brief meditation. Then community representatives could describe the needs.

Reserve Saturday morning and afternoon for work in these areas of need. Allow the members to choose the area that interests them most. Provide a wide variety of activities including cleaning, building, reading stories for a blind person, tutoring, and so forth. Saturday evening could be a time for "storytelling" as workers return to share what the work meant to them.

Have a potluck dinner on Sunday afternoon or evening to discuss possible future actions with the membership. It will have been necessary for the committee to have done the planning suggested in this manual. This would be a good time to present the growth goals and growth objectives in such a way that the congregation would be excited to own and share in them.

Growing in Awareness

The service committee can sponsor a few evening sessions during the time of a local political campaign. Invite candidates to speak to the members. Allow time for questions. It may be possible and helpful to have two opposing candidates present their views at one time. The meeting could be open to the community and refreshments served so that members would have a chance to become acquainted with their neighbors.

The same things can be done if the community is involved in the struggle over an issue such as a bond for building a community facility or a strike of the police or schoolteachers. Every community is faced with an issue during the course of the year. The church needs to be informed so that the members can ask the question, "As a Christian called to be a light in the world, what *should* I do and what *can* I do?"

Similar meetings could be held to discuss national and

world issues. The environment, the economy, peace, hunger, unemployment, and the homeless are but a few of the issues that can be dealt with. Denominational leaders and local school or political offices can supply resources and speakers for many of the issues.

People-Related Activities

The community can encourage the church to participate in community programs that relate to the needs of children, youths, senior citizens, or shut-ins. Every community has someone who needs an extended family. Such needs can be met through Big Brothers/Big Sisters programs or by adopting "grandparents." Your county public health office probably has a list of people with special needs.

Train church members in working with people of special need. The books mentioned on pages 91 and 94 can be of help in this area. Coordinate the training with that planned by the diaconate, the evangelism committee, or the education program. Trained people find it easier to visit, telephone, write cards, or help others with transportation or shopping needs.

Mission Promotion

The church is not involved in mission only in its own community, it is also enabling others to do mission elsewhere. Following is a list of activities for promoting your church's interest in mission around the world:

1. Maintain a mission bulletin board in a very conspicuous place in the church. Use maps of the world with pictures on them to highlight mission activities in the United States and other countries.
2. Build a year's calendar of mission themes to be highlighted. These could be related to special offerings or to specific months in the following manner:

   September and October—international missions.
   November and December—retired ministers and missionaries.
   January through March—the church mission carried on nationally.
   April through June—relief efforts at home and abroad.
   July and August—local mission projects.

3. Emphasize the monthly theme in the church newsletter, the weekly worship bulletin, the bulletin board, and Sunday church school.
4. Organize a White Cross day twice a year. Make this a churchwide project by enlisting the help of youths and men as well as women. Hold it on a Saturday from mid-morning to mid-afternoon. Provide a light luncheon. Dedicate the projects and recognize the workers during a Sunday morning service either before or after the workday.
5. Pray each week for one or two missionaries whose work is related to the theme or field being highlighted that month. Their names and work should be listed in the bulletin. Have church members write the missionaries a note saying that they were prayed for and send them a copy of the bulletin.
6. Post pictures and letters from missionaries so the congregation can see them. Read paragraphs from these letters each week before the time of prayer or the offering. Print some paragraphs in the church newsletter.
7. Recruit church members to become "pen pals" to missionaries by sending them cards for birthdays, anniversaries, holidays, and at least one personal note per year.
8. Conduct a missions conference for several days once every other year. This could be alternated with a Bible conference or evangelistic campaign.
9. Promote mission studies for all ages in the Sunday church school. During each study arrange to have a furloughed missionary from that field in the church for a day or have a phone conversation with one still on the field.
10. Sponsor a tour of a mission field and prepare to do a work project under the supervision of that field. Such projects are needed on home fields as well as on fields overseas.
11. Encourage increased giving to missions by providing more information about what mission is doing.

Evaluation Stage

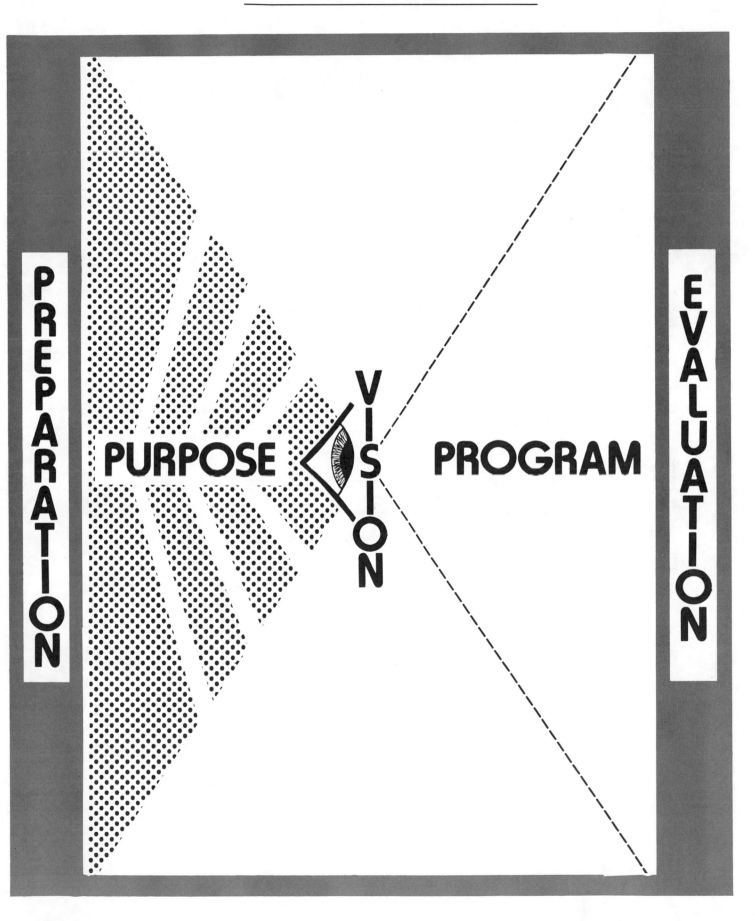

9

Ongoing Growth

Your committee has held many meetings to carry out the church growth planning process. The task has not been easy. You learned the hard truth of what was said on page 27, "Church growth is complex." Because there were no easy solutions, there may have been times when you thought about stopping. You may have wondered if anything would ever come from all your work. But you stuck to it and some things are about ready to happen for your church.

You now know that growth of this kind takes time. It usually doesn't happen overnight. As your committee, the pastor, and congregation wait for the seeds you have planted to take root and grow, all the fruits of the Spirit are needed. Ask God for strength to continue the process, patience to notice even the small signs of growth, and confidence in the Holy Spirit to wait with anticipation.

As you wait, you need to continue working for the realization of your church's growth. There may be obstacles, few or many, small or large. Faithfulness is required if you are to stay with the task and experience growth in your church. If you believe that God wants your church to grow and the church wants to grow, then you can take on the tasks to be done during the next year with a strong and joyous faith. From now on, the work pace will not be as intense nor the meetings as frequent. Others can join you in doing the work to make your church grow in whatever way it can for God's glory.

What follows in this chapter describes the four tasks that make up the ongoing work of your committee. It would be helpful if the full committee could remain intact for the next year. However, some of your members may be led to resume other commitments. If they should resign, assign replacements as soon as possible and introduce them to the past and future work of the committee.

Telling the Story

Your committee has only recently initiated the process for building growth program plans. It is now important that some of them be shared with the congregation. The congregation will not necessarily be interested in all the details. However, it is helpful and wise to bring to the church's attention the important things that are going to be happening. This will create awareness of the church's ministry, generate support for it, and help recruit new workers and leaders.

Information about the program plans can be presented through newsletters, at business meetings, or on bulletin boards. Highlight the growth goals and the growth objectives the congregation has adopted. Then share briefly some plans for reaching those objectives. If you use a bulletin board or a newsletter, you may want to present only one arena of ministry at a time.

Just as church members need to know what is going to happen, so they want to know what has happened. Celebrate the completion of a program plan or even significant steps in its completion. Don't whisper the news, "shout it" so all will hear! This rewards those who worked hard and excites many others. But repeat the story several times. Tell it in newsletters and bulletins, in meetings, and from the pulpit. Rejoice about it in prayer and testimonies. Share it many times and in many ways.

One congregation that had determined to make every effort to grow, appointed several persons to be "communicators." Some with camera skills were to take pictures and slides at a wide variety of occasions and settings. They were alerted to special events by the growth committee. They were told specifically to get pictures with people in them; everything one does in planning is (or should be) directed toward people. When people see faces attached to goals, objectives, and plans, interest is heightened.

The pictures taken by the communicators were then shared in many ways. Some were placed on special bulletin board displays. Some were presented to classes at regular meetings. Others were shared in slide presentations at business meetings and fellowship gatherings. The pictures carried a message: They told the story of what the church was doing in its efforts to grow.

Pictures and slides are just one way to communicate with a congregation. Tape recorders or videotape are other possibilities. Remember that different classes and groups might also be willing to become involved in the process of "telling the story."

In a sense you are being asked to "promote" your church growth efforts. "Telling" is "selling"; without it, you will limit the possibilities of support and enthusiasm.

To summarize, remember that if your church's statement of purpose is not kept before the congregation on a regular basis and in a variety of ways, it will soon be forgotten. We have short memories; we need to be reminded often. Goals and objectives need to be mentioned from time to time. Your congregation will be as supportive and enthusiastic about the growth process as you help it to be. Also, please note that "telling the story" is something you need to organize and get started; you don't need to do all the actual "telling and selling" yourselves.

In all your promotion of the story, do not forget to focus on the workers who have made it possible. Never assume that growth happens by itself any more than promotion does. Recognize those who work. From time to time have them mentioned for prayer or praise. People who work need food. Part of their need is satisfied by being recognized. Recognition keeps our human motors running more than almost anything else does.

Monitoring Program Plans

The process outlined in this handbook is based on a major assumption: Those persons and groups who develop program plans are the same persons who will carry them out. In other words, the "developers" become the "doers." It is assumed that because they have been involved in the creation of the growth program plans, they will have a high degree of ownership in the accomplishment of those plans.

"We made a lot of plans, but little ever happened." Those are well-worn words. Some churches have "papered the walls" with all kinds of plans on newsprint, but they never went any farther than the newsprint. You need to check out your assumptions about those who have developed the program plans.

This can be done by establishing checkpoints. A checkpoint is a date upon which you mutually agree that a review should be made concerning progress of the program plan. For instance, if the group that wrote some program plans for the Sunday church school said they would start two new classes during the next year, you could negotiate with them to check out progress halfway through the year. At that point, if no new classes have been started, and no one is even talking about it, it is obvious that the program plan is in trouble. It is at this point that your Church Growth Committee needs to engage in conversation with the group that is responsible for the objective under which that program plan was placed. You need to discover what is wrong, and what needs to be done.

Sometimes quarterly checkpoints are better than waiting six months or longer. If you check earlier and decide there are problems, you will have more time to make corrections, solve problems, or even rewrite the program plan if it is necessary.

The Church Growth Committee should receive copies of all program plans as they are written. You need them in order to know what they are and what kind of timetables they call for. You will need to decide how you will assign the monitoring of the program plans among your members. Monitoring does not require attendance at more meetings. A telephone call to the chairperson of the group, committee, or board responsible for a program plan will, in most cases, quickly tell you whether or not they are on target. This type of checking will also remind groups responsible for program plans that you are taking the pursuit of church growth and their part in it seriously. It will also demonstrate your sincere interest in and concern for what they agreed to try to do.

Evaluation

The process of evaluation has been around for a long time. In Genesis, near the conclusion of the story of creation, we read that God looked over everything made and concluded it was good. Evaluation is asking, "How well did you do what you set out to do?"

Jesus spoke about evaluation in the parables of the talents and the fig tree which bore no fruit. Paul suggested that running a race was not enough; you are to run *hard* in order to win. Since the church is doing the work of God, the church leaders should try to do the best job possible. "Business as usual" is not enough for the work of the kingdom. Church growth doesn't "just happen." It takes not only hard work, but also the right work. And to determine how well you are doing, there needs to be some evaluation.

Evaluation is the last and perhaps the most valuable step in growth planning. It is not something done as an afterthought or as an exercise to be done because someone "expects" you to do it. The step of evaluation is the last growth planning step you will take. It is valuable for two reasons. First, evaluation will tell you how well you have done what you set out to do. Second, it will provide some guidance and hints about the future.

There are two levels of evaluation. One is program evaluation and deals basically with the results of the growth program plans. The other deals with the effectiveness of the growth objectives and growth goals.

On page 83 you learned that a growth program plan includes the following:

- tells who is to be affected or helped by the plan;
- briefly describes what is to be done;
- pinpoints responsibility for carrying out the plan; and
- states when the plan is to be completed.

Groups that have developed growth program plans and

are responsible for carrying them out should be referred to these statements at the appropriate time. Questions relating to the "who, what, and when" may be asked. Additional questions such as these can be posed: What happened? Was it what you wanted to have happen? How worthwhile was it for the persons involved? How did this program plan help your church to grow? What did you do in the plan that was "really good"? What could have been done differently? Should the plan be repeated, modified, or thrown out?

These kinds of questions should be asked by every group that has written a growth program plan. This level of evaluation is not the task of the growth committee but of each of the responsible groups that has written and carried out growth program plans.

The answers to these questions can open a new future for many of your program efforts. Some of the programs may not be needed, while others give strong evidence of their value for the future. Some may have great value for a growing church while others may not be necessary, even though they are well received. A careful evaluation needs to be made of everything you are doing in order to determine how best to utilize your resources in the future.

The other level of evaluation, evaluating the objectives and goals, is the task of your Church Growth Committee. When you total the results of the program plan efforts, you will have an accurate idea as to whether you have accomplished your objectives. You need to collect reports from the various growth program plan groups so that you can evaluate the objectives. This is usually done on an annual basis; however, other time frames may be used if you so desire.

On page 81 you noted that a growth objective answers these questions:

- What task will be accomplished?
- When? (beginning when? accomplished when?)
- Where? (if applicable)

Properly developed growth objectives already describe your targets. Did you reach them? Did you surpass or fall short of the target? If the objective has not yet been reached, is it realistic in light of what you have learned so far? How much more time should be given to reach it? What change should be made in the plan? What movement toward growth was provided by this objective? Why should the objective be continued, dropped, or adjusted?

These are but some of the questions to be asked of each growth objective. When you evaluate objectives, be sure all the persons who helped develop them are present. This includes in particular the persons who chair the boards and committees of your church.

After all the growth objectives have been evaluated, your committee should look at your church's growth goals. Since goals are usually longer-range statements, you may not notice their completion for a number of years. However, it is important to study the goal statements and determine if the objectives at which you are working are actually doing the job you want done. If not, note changes you want to make when new objectives are developed. There may also be a time when goals need to be revised and new goals developed. In most cases this is the ongoing task of the Church Growth Committee.

Successes should be reported to the congregation as suggested at the beginning of this chapter. The congregation should be kept informed about the progress which is (or perhaps which is not) being made regarding efforts to grow. This should be done positively and, if possible, in an enthusiastic manner. The next section will provide some ideas for doing that.

Celebration

A growing church knows how to celebrate. It is important for the membership to be informed about accomplishments, whether small or large. It is just as important to celebrate "baby steps" as it is large-size steps. Celebration is good for the overall health of a congregation.

You can celebrate successes and accomplishments at every step of your growth planning process. When you have successfully adopted a church statement of purpose, it should be celebrated with an event to which all church members are invited. The statement of purpose gathers every member of your congregation into its fold; all should celebrate.

When a growth goal is completed, it is a cause for celebration. Progress toward the achievement of growth objectives can also be celebrated. The use of music, drama, worship experiences, testimonies, fellowship events, outdoor programs, and many other methods are suitable means for celebration activities.

Over the years most churches have paid tribute to successful fund raisers, building fund targets, and financial campaigns. There is much satisfaction to be gained by recognizing these accomplishments. However, there is no need to limit celebration to the raising of money. Celebration and thanksgiving to God should follow every victory or accomplishment a church experiences. In fact, celebration should even be part of our difficulties and failures because our standing with God doesn't depend on our victories. The church should be a celebrating people.

Consider how much celebration takes place in the Bible. Israel was told that they would find strength in celebrating the deeds of God from the past and the promises of God for the future. Unfortunately, Israel's life seems to be summarized by three activities: sinning, slighting God, and suffering. When Israel failed to remember, Israel fell. God pursued her with the messages of the prophets who all seemed to say, "Remember," "Repent," and "Rejoice." The faith chronicled in the New Testament carries the prophetic message to us today. Listen to Jesus in the upper room, Paul in prison, or the early church under persecution. There is a constant theme of remembrance and joy. Amid the darkness of the end time, listen to the jubilant celebration of the redeemed as revealed in Revelation.

We have much to celebrate: a supper of thanksgiving, a baptism of hope, the caring communion of believers, the working love of the faithful. The growing church is indeed a celebrating church.

10

"Thy Kingdom Come"

The path ahead may seem overwhelming at times. The leaders of the growing church must often remind the people of God that growth is part of God's mission. God's promises must continually be lifted up: "So also will be the word that I speak—it will not fail to do what I plan for it; it will do everything I send it to do" (Isaiah 55:11); "I will build my church; and not even death will ever be able to overcome it" (Matthew 16:18); "And so I am sure that God, who began this good work in you will carry it on until it is finished on the Day of Christ Jesus" (Philippians 1:6); "Greater works than these will he do because I go to the Father" (John 14:12, RSV). The *plus factors* of God's presence and power have to be considered . . . and trusted.

No other institution in our society possesses this guarantee. The Holy Spirit's ministry in us cannot be plugged into the all too familiar computer. God's power is part of the "evidence of things not seen," part of what people who are aware of the supernatural recognize daily. This was the secret of Moses' unusual leadership against incredible odds and in the face of a people who lost the dream so quickly and so easily (Hebrews 11:23-31). The growing church leader's single valuable contribution to the enterprise is to keep that vision in spite of all odds from without and within.

The growing church rooted in the presence, power, and promises of God will not be like cut flowers that wither easily and quickly. The growing church will, in spite of obstacles, gather to declare God's presence and power. Celebrating victories, even small ones, gives the church a sense that God is with it. Testimonies in worship services are reminders of God's constant grace. Baptism, which declares that people have begun a new life in Christ, clearly reinforces the realization that the gospel is still mighty to save. The Lord's Supper, perhaps the single most moving reminder of Presence, is a powerful means of grace to the church struggling to keep its focus in a sometimes dreary existence.

The environment of the 1980s, within which God calls the church to bear its witness, is a steady reminder of how much the church needs to be a partner in God's mission. As a bridgehead of the kingdom, it is part of the "already"
but "not yet." The challenge to join God in the kingdom enterprise of peacemaking is sharply etched against the backdrop of the horror of nuclear war which now threatens the existence of the human species. God's concern that "justice roll down like a mighty river" has never been in such clear perspective as we see the incredible gulf fixed between the "haves" and the "have-nots." Daily headlines of pollution and water shortages and statistics regarding the extinction of species and the irretrievable loss of fixed resources tell us that God needs us to join the battle for the earth, to be part of the creation-mandate to "have dominion . . . and to till the garden," rather than to exploit and use it up.

The world is peopled with some three billion humans who are unreached by the saving gospel of Jesus Christ. In the United States alone 41 percent of the adult population or 61 million adults have no steady religious affiliation. In light of these statistics, the implication is clear for the church that believes in the Great Commission "to go and tell" and the great commandment "to love."

God's *purpose,* the primary instrument of which is the church, calls for a recruitment program we have never seen before. God wants more people to become part of the great mission of personal salvation and societal renewal. God is up to something very big! The church which believes that will become part of it!

The growing church is a renewing church. It probably will grow numerically. Net growth in a mobile society is not always easy. No one can look down upon the church that reports little or no net growth in any year. Nor can anyone argue that merely showing a net growth is *the* sign of faithfulness.

To aim at mere numerical growth may be to miss the mark. Perhaps, at bottom, growth is a by-product of faithfulness to the mission of salvation and societal change. "It is required of stewards that they be faithful." The successful Christian is a faithful servant. God gives the increase!

Go now. Join the band God has raised up for these special times. Go and hold forth the vision of God's mighty growing kingdom!

Appendixes

Aids for Planning

Appendix A

Attitudes and Gifts for Growth

CHURCH MEMBER PERCEPTION QUESTIONNAIRE

The following statements focus on important aspects of the life and ministry of your church. Select the word which, from your perception of and experience with your church, best completes each statement.

1. Member satisfaction with the worship, fellowship, and work of my congregation is:
   high _____ average _____ low _____

2. My personal satisfaction with the worship, fellowship, and work of my congregation is:
   high _____ average _____ low _____

3. Those who participate in worship look forward to that experience with anticipation and enthusiasm:
   very much _____ some _____ very little _____

4. I usually look forward to the worship experience each week with anticipation and enthusiasm:
   very much _____ some _____ very little _____

5. Our church is organized for evangelism:
   very well _____ somewhat _____ poorly _____ not at all _____

6. Our church is committed to a ministry of evangelism:
   very little _____ somewhat _____ highly committed _____

7. The priority our congregation's leaders give to the ministry of evangelism is:
   high _____ average _____ low _____

8. Our church is involved in the life of our community:
   very much _____ somewhat _____ not at all_____

9. Our church's image in the community is:
   positive _____ neutral _____ negative _____

10. Our church's ministry of outreach to our community is:
    intentional _____ accidental _____ nonexistent _____

11. Our church's membership is:
    growing _____ declining _____ I don't know _____

12. Our Sunday church school is:
    growing _____ declining _____ remaining the same _____

13. Our board or committee of Christian education has specific growth plans for our Sunday church school:
    yes _____ no _____ don't know _____

14. Is "something missing" in your church or church school which could contribute to growth?
    yes _____ no _____ don't know _____

    If your answer is "yes," and you can identify what is missing, record it here:

    _____

    _____

    _____

    _____

15. What do you think God wants to be through our church now and in the future?

    _____

    _____

    _____

    _____

QUESTIONS REGARDING THE ROLE OF THE HOLY SPIRIT IN YOUR CHURCH

1. Do you know what the role of the Holy Spirit is in the life and ministry of your church?
2. On the basis of what you know, what do you believe the role of the Holy Spirit *ought* to be in the life of your church?
3. Knowing your church's membership as you do, which of the following activities would generate the most interest to learn about the work of the Holy Spirit? (In the column marked "for me," put a number beside each activity. At the next meeting total the numbers given by all the committee members and enter that in the committee's column. To fill out the congregation's column, distribute the list at a congregational meeting or worship service. Add the numbers for each activity and put the total in the congregation's column. The higher the number for an activity, the broader the interest in it may be.)

In order to learn more about the work of the Holy Spirit, I would have:

1—little interest in
2—some interest in
3—great interest in

For the congregation	For the committee	For me	
_____	_____	_____	a. hearing a series of sermons on the Holy Spirit.
_____	_____	_____	b. participating in a series of worship services designed to give me a new awareness of and knowledge about the Holy Spirit.
_____	_____	_____	c. being part of a small group study on the Holy Spirit.
_____	_____	_____	d. preparing a two-year program for a deeper experience and awareness of the work of the Holy Spirit.
_____	_____	_____	e. studying about the Holy Spirit in church school.
_____	_____	_____	f. having an all-day retreat for the church boards (or deacons) to study about the role of the Holy Spirit in our church.
_____	_____	_____	g. reading some books from the church library during my personal devotions about the Holy Spirit.
_____	_____	_____	h. developing a list of our church's theological assumptions about the ministry of the Holy Spirit.
_____	_____	_____	i. praying for the guidance of the Holy Spirit in the work of the church and in my life.
_____	_____	_____	j. (other) _____

You may add any other activities to the list that would be appropriate for your church. Resources for additional study are listed on pages 41-42. Keep the results of this in mind for the planning part in chapter 5 and following.

QUESTIONS ABOUT YOUR CONGREGATION

Consider the following questions about your congregation in light of the challenge of producing a growing church. Place a check mark in the appropriate column.

	Not at all	So-so	Very much
1. Our congregation is enthusiastic about its calling and ministry in the name of Jesus Christ.	———	———	———
2. Our congregation is committed to the "priesthood of all believers" and to the ministry of the laity.	———	———	———
3. Our congregation is open to new ideas, worship suggestions, and programs.	———	———	———
4. Our congregation is open to new people worshiping and joining our fellowship.	———	———	———
5. Our congregation is openly warm and friendly.	———	———	———
6. Our congregation is concerned about the personal needs of those within our fellowship.	———	———	———
7. Our congregation is concerned about persons in need in our community.	———	———	———
8. Our congregation is thoroughly committed to becoming a growing church.	———	———	———

QUALITIES THAT CONTRIBUTE TO GROWTH

Rate yourself on a scale of 1 to 10, with 10 as the highest possible score, indicating maximum efficiency. Place an 'X' on each line at the point which best describes you.

a) My attitude towards a growing church and the task I have to do shows:

1	2	3	4	5	6	7	8	9	10
no enthusiasm			little		some			great enthusiasm	

b) My personal faith is vital, contagious, and visible:

1	2	3	4	5	6	7	8	9	10
definitely not				somewhat				very much so	

c) I handle diversity within our congregation:

1	2	3	4	5	6	7	8	9	10
very poorly		not very well			somewhat			very well	

d) My picture of the needs of my church and community is:

1	2	3	4	5	6	7	8	9	10
not realistic		partially realistic			fairly realistic			very realistic	

e) As a communicator with the groups I lead, I am:

1	2	3	4	5	6	7	8	9	10
poor			fair			good			excellent

f) As a communicator with the congregation, I am:

1	2	3	4	5	6	7	8	9	10
poor			fair			good			excellent

g) As a communicator with those outside our church in our community, I am:

1	2	3	4	5	6	7	8	9	10
poor			fair			good			excellent

h) I am open to meaningful, constructive change:

1	2	3	4	5	6	7	8	9	10
not at all				somewhat				very open	

i) I relate to others:

1	2	3	4	5	6	7	8	9	10
poorly			fairly well			well			very well

SUMMARY SHEET FOR QUALITIES THAT CONTRIBUTE TO GROWTH

Average the responses for the Church Growth Committee (CGC) and the church's leaders (CL) and record them below for each question. Under *Comments* summarize the discussion about differences and similarities in scoring. Your aim is to help the church grow. Discover what can best bring that about. Remember Ephesians 4:18-19. Be constructive! Be honest! Be supportive!

Question	*Averages*		*Comments*
	CGC	CL	
a. Attitudes	____	____	_____
b. Contagious faith	____	____	_____
c. Handling diversity	____	____	_____
d. Knowing needs	____	____	_____
e. Communicator with groups	____	____	_____
f. Communicator with congregation	____	____	_____
g. Communicator with outsiders	____	____	_____
h. Open to change	____	____	_____
i. Relating to others	____	____	_____

GIFTS ANALYSIS QUESTIONNAIRE

The Holy Spirit has given all Christians spiritual gifts. The discovery and use of gifts by church members is important to the life of the Body of Christ.

The Spirit's presence is shown in some way in each person for the good of all (1 Corinthians 12:7).

We have many parts in the one body, and all·these parts have different functions. . . . we are all joined to each other as different parts of one body. So we are to use our different gifts in accordance with the grace that God has given us. . . . (Romans 12:4-6).

Each one, as a good manager of God's different gifts, must use for the good of others the special gift . . . received from God (1 Peter 4:10).

Christ wants to build up his church and kingdom. He does this through gifted members. Therefore, each member must discover his or her spiritual gifts. Each member must *use* his or her spiritual gifts. Each member must develop his or her gifts.

The questionnaire which follows will help you discover your gifts. The results of this questionnaire will be *only tentative,* however. You may not actually have the spiritual gifts you identify by taking this questionnaire. Two more things should happen before you will be sure:

1. Others should observe your gifts and tell you what you do well.
2. You should actually use your gifts in ministries and experience a degree of success.

How to Complete the Gifts Analysis Questionnaire

Each statement in this questionnaire has five response spaces following it. They are: very little, little, some, much, very much. These represent percentages on a scale of 0-100% as follows:

Very little	=	0 - 20%
Little	=	20 - 40%
Some	=	40 - 60%
Much	=	60 - 80%
Very much	=	80 - 100%

Read each statement. Decide to what extent the statement has been true of you during the past five or ten years. Check the appropriate column. Your first impressions are usually correct.

Pages 125 to 133 are taken with permission from *Discover Your Gifts,* a workbook published by the Christian Reformed Home Missions, Grand Rapids, Michigan.

THE FOLLOWING IS TRUE OF ME...

	(1) Very Little	(2) Little	(3) Some	(4) Much	(5) Very Much
1. I am able to organize ideas, tasks, people, and time, for Christian service.	☐	☐	☐	☐	☐
2. I have used a particular creative ability (writing, painting, drama, etc.) to benefit the body of Christ.	☐	☐	☐	☐	☐
3. I am able to distinguish between spiritual truth and error.	☐	☐	☐	☐	☐
4. I have been used to encourage people to live Christian lives.	☐	☐	☐	☐	☐
5. I like to talk about Jesus to those who don't know him.	☐	☐	☐	☐	☐
6. I have had the experience of knowing God's will with certainty in a specific situation even when concrete evidence was missing.	☐	☐	☐	☐	☐
7. I assume responsibility for meeting financial needs in church and community.	☐	☐	☐	☐	☐
8. I enjoy providing a haven for guests and do not feel put upon by unexpected visitors.	☐	☐	☐	☐	☐
9. I take prayer requests of others seriously and continue to pray for them.	☐	☐	☐	☐	☐
10. I motivate groups toward specific biblical objectives.	☐	☐	☐	☐	☐
11. I have a knack for turning compassion into cheerful deeds of kindness.	☐	☐	☐	☐	☐
12. I have pleaded the cause of God to the people of the church and/or world.	☐	☐	☐	☐	☐
13. I enjoy doing tasks that help others minister effectively.	☐	☐	☐	☐	☐
14. I have been responsible for the spiritual lives of Christians with good results.	☐	☐	☐	☐	☐
15. Others understand as I explain the Bible or the Christian life to them.	☐	☐	☐	☐	☐

THE FOLLOWING IS TRUE OF ME....

	(1) Very Little	(2) Little	(3) Some	(4) Much	(5) Very Much
16. I like to help plan things in which people are involved.	☐	☐	☐	☐	☐
17. I would enjoy expressing myself creatively for God through artistic expression (music, drama, poetry, etc.)	☐	☐	☐	☐	☐
18. I see a serious danger when false teachings and false practices creep into the church.	☐	☐	☐	☐	☐
19. I am sensitive to suffering, troubled and discouraged people, and want to help them see God's answers to life's problems.	☐	☐	☐	☐	☐
20. I would like to be able to share the Gospel freely and effectively with unbelieving persons.	☐	☐	☐	☐	☐
21. I find myself accepting God's promises at face value and applying them to given situations without doubt.	☐	☐	☐	☐	☐
22. I feel moved to give when confronted with financial needs in God's Kingdom.	☐	☐	☐	☐	☐
23. I am sensitive to the acts of kindness which make such a difference for guests or strangers.	☐	☐	☐	☐	☐
24. I am sensitive to the prayer needs of others and concerned to give the needed prayer support.	☐	☐	☐	☐	☐
25. I have a desire to help, lead, guide, and direct people in some aspect of the Lord's work.	☐	☐	☐	☐	☐
26. I would like to minister to those who have physical or mental problems.	☐	☐	☐	☐	☐
27. I have spiritual insights from the Scriptures relating to people and issues which make me want to speak out.	☐	☐	☐	☐	☐
28. I sense when others need a helping hand and am ready to give it.	☐	☐	☐	☐	☐
29. I am concerned to see the spiritual needs of believers met and am willing to be personally involved in nurturing and discipling ministries.	☐	☐	☐	☐	☐
30. I earnestly desire to explain Bible principles to others.	☐	☐	☐	☐	☐

THE FOLLOWING IS TRUE OF ME....

	(1) Very Little	(2) Little	(3) Some	(4) Much	(5) Very Much
31. I am able to make effective plans to accomplish goals.	☐	☐	☐	☐	☐
32. I have significant artistic ability (music, drama, writing, painting, sculpting, etc.) which I have put to good use in God's Kingdom.	☐	☐	☐	☐	☐
33. I have detected phony or manipulative persons and teachings when others have not.	☐	☐	☐	☐	☐
34. People in the Christian community have been stirred up to love and good works by my counsel and encouragement.	☐	☐	☐	☐	☐
35. I have been instrumental in leading others to believe in Christ as their Savior.	☐	☐	☐	☐	☐
36. In specific cases God has given me assurance that He would do what seemed unlikely.	☐	☐	☐	☐	☐
37. I give cheerfully and liberally in support of the Lord's work.	☐	☐	☐	☐	☐
38. I have a knack for making strangers feel at ease in my home and at church.	☐	☐	☐	☐	☐
39. I pray for others, recognizing that their effectiveness depends upon it.	☐	☐	☐	☐	☐
40. I enjoy leading and directing others toward goals and caring for them for the sake of Christ.	☐	☐	☐	☐	☐
41. I enjoy working with people who suffer physical, mental or emotional problems.	☐	☐	☐	☐	☐
42. I have proclaimed timely and urgent messages from God's Word to the people of today.	☐	☐	☐	☐	☐
43. I like to work at little things that help build the Body of Christ.	☐	☐	☐	☐	☐
44. I assume responsibility when I see a Christian being led astray.	☐	☐	☐	☐	☐
45. I am able to communicate truth clearly and concisely.	☐	☐	☐	☐	☐

THE FOLLOWING IS TRUE OF ME....

	(1) Very Little	(2) Little	(3) Some	(4) Much	(5) Very Much
46. I would enjoy giving direction to an important church ministry.	☐	☐	☐	☐	☐
47. I have the potential to be very creative in an area that could be used in building up the Church.	☐	☐	☐	☐	☐
48. I tend to look beneath the surface and perceive people's motives.	☐	☐	☐	☐	☐
49. I believe that people will grow to spiritual maturity through counsel and instruction from the Word.	☐	☐	☐	☐	☐
50. I have a burden for friends and acquaintances who do not believe in Christ.	☐	☐	☐	☐	☐
51. I have a sense for moments when "the prayer of faith" is needed.	☐	☐	☐	☐	☐
52. I am willing to maintain a lower standard of living in order to benefit God's work with my financial support.	☐	☐	☐	☐	☐
53. I tend to be more aware of the needs of guests than of my own.	☐	☐	☐	☐	☐
54. I have an inner conviction that God works in response to prayer and want to be used to help others through prayer.	☐	☐	☐	☐	☐
55. If I had the opportunity I would enjoy leading, directing, and motivating others in some aspect of the Lord's work.	☐	☐	☐	☐	☐
56. The sight of misery makes me want to find a way to express God's love to hurting persons.	☐	☐	☐	☐	☐
57. Given the opportunity, I would like to be an expository preacher of God's Word.	☐	☐	☐	☐	☐
58. It is my nature to like to do work that helps others do theirs.	☐	☐	☐	☐	☐
59. I sense in myself a shepherd's instinct when I know of Christians who need spiritual counsel.	☐	☐	☐	☐	☐
60. I am concerned to help others learn what the Bible teaches.	☐	☐	☐	☐	☐

THE FOLLOWING IS TRUE OF ME. . . .

	(1) Very Little	(2) Little	(3) Some	(4) Much	(5) Very Much
61. I have a sense for delegating important tasks to the right people at the right time.	☐	☐	☐	☐	☐
62. I am aware that people have been blessed through my creative or artistic ability.	☐	☐	☐	☐	☐
63. I have developed an ability to discriminate between good and evil in today's world.	☐	☐	☐	☐	☐
64. I am glad when people who need comfort, consolation, encouragement and counsel seek my help.	☐	☐	☐	☐	☐
65. I am able to share the Gospel in a way that makes it clear and meaningful to non-believers.	☐	☐	☐	☐	☐
66. I am able to go on believing God will act in a situation in spite of evidence to the contrary.	☐	☐	☐	☐	☐
67. I help people and the Lord's work through generous and timely contributions.	☐	☐	☐	☐	☐
68. My home is available to those in need of hospitality.	☐	☐	☐	☐	☐
69. I am conscious of ministering to others as I pray for them.	☐	☐	☐	☐	☐
70. I have accepted leadership responsibilities and have succeeded in helping a group work toward a goal.	☐	☐	☐	☐	☐
71. Sick, helpless and shut-in persons are helped when I minister to them.	☐	☐	☐	☐	☐
72. God uses me to build up, encourage and comfort other Christians by speaking to them of spiritual things.	☐	☐	☐	☐	☐
73. I find practical ways of helping others and gain satisfaction from doing this.	☐	☐	☐	☐	☐
74. The Lord has used me to watch over, guide and nurture other believers toward spiritual maturity.	☐	☐	☐	☐	☐
75. I hold the interest of those I instruct.	☐	☐	☐	☐	☐

THE FOLLOWING IS TRUE OF ME....

	(1) Very Little	(2) Little	(3) Some	(4) Much	(5) Very Much
76. I have a sense for how and when projects or ministries need to be better organized.	☐	☐	☐	☐	☐
77. I sense a latent creative ability (in drawing, writing, music, etc.) which I would like to use for the kingdom of God.	☐	☐	☐	☐	☐
78. I am usually aware of people who wear masks or are pretending.	☐	☐	☐	☐	☐
79. I would be willing to spend some time each week in a counseling ministry.	☐	☐	☐	☐	☐
80. I am able to sense when a person doesn't know Jesus Christ and I hurt for him or her.	☐	☐	☐	☐	☐
81. I sense what Jesus meant when he said, "If you have faith as a grain of mustard seed, you will say to this mountain, 'move hence to yonder place' and it will move, and nothing will be impossible to you."	☐	☐	☐	☐	☐
82. I have a conviction that all I have belongs to God and I want to be a good steward of it.	☐	☐	☐	☐	☐
83. I have a genuine appreciation for each guest to whom I minister.	☐	☐	☐	☐	☐
84. I would be pleased if asked to be a prayer partner to someone involved in a ministry.	☐	☐	☐	☐	☐
85. I am usually quick to sense when a group I am a part of is "spinning its wheels", and I want to do something about it.	☐	☐	☐	☐	☐
86. I sense it when people are hurting in some way.	☐	☐	☐	☐	☐
87. I think more Christians should speak out on the moral issues of the day, such as abortion, easy sex, racism, etc.	☐	☐	☐	☐	☐
88. I wish I had more opportunity to assist others in their ministries.	☐	☐	☐	☐	☐
89. I would love to be in a position to equip saints for the work of ministry.	☐	☐	☐	☐	☐
90. I get excited by acquiring knowledge out of God's Word.	☐	☐	☐	☐	☐

Key Chart

HOW TO USE THE KEY CHART

STEP 1—Place the numerical value (1–5) for each statement of the Questionnaire (1–90) next to the corresponding number in the Key Chart.

STEP 2—In Chart A, add each row of three numbers, and write the total in the adjoining box in the "Totals A" column. In Chart B, do the same in "Totals B" column.

STEP 3—Circle the highest scores in the "Totals A" column. Circle three or four, but not more than five. Write the names of those gifts in Box A, "Working Gifts," with the highest-scored gift first, the next highest second, etc. (In case of ties, it doesn't matter which one is listed first.)

STEP 4—Now circle the scores in the "Totals B" column which scored high but were not circled in Step 3. Write these gifts in Box B, "Waiting Gifts," beginning with the highest.

STEP 5—Place in Box C any gifts not listed in Boxes A and B. These are likely not your spiritual gifts, but you have, of course, a responsibility (role) in each of them.

STEP 6—Note the gifts in which your Totals B score is significantly (2 or more) higher than your Totals A score. This may indicate a gift which should be developed and used.

BOX A	BOX B
Working Gifts	**Waiting Gifts**
Highest Scored Gift _____	Highest Not In Box A _____
2nd _____	2nd _____
3rd _____	3rd _____
4th _____	4th _____
5th _____	5th _____

BOX C

Not a gift but a role

_____, _____

_____, _____

_____, _____

_____, _____

CHART A				Totals A		Totals B	CHART B		
1	31	61	Administration				16	46	76
2	32	62	Creative Ability				17	47	77
3	33	63	Discernment				18	48	78
4	34	64	Encouragement				19	49	79
5	35	65	Evangelism				20	50	80
6	36	66	Faith				21	51	81
7	37	67	Giving				22	52	82
8	38	68	Hospitality				23	53	83
9	39	69	Intercession				24	54	84
10	40	70	Leadership				25	55	85
11	41	71	Mercy				26	56	86
12	42	72	Prophecy				27	57	87
13	43	73	Service				28	58	88
14	44	74	Shepherding				29	59	89
15	45	75	Teaching				30	60	90

When You've Finished Your Key Chart

Some people are surprised by the gifts which their questionnaire reveals; others are not. Whichever category you fall into, two things must be said:

- Congratulations! To be aware of gifts which the Holy Spirit gives is an exciting experience and one which is significant.
- Remember that to be sure concerning which gifts you have, you must hear what other members of the body are saying and must also test the gifts in ministering situations.

Something should also be said about those gifts that are listed in Box C, which for you are not gifts but roles. Don't think less of yourself or of these gifts because they appear in Box C. No one has all the gifts. And even those who don't have a particular gift—giving, for example—continue to have two functions with regard to it:

a. One is to encourage and pray for those who have these gifts. The fact that *you* don't have the gift another has demonstrates the meaning of being the Body of Christ (Romans 12:4-6).
b. The other responsibility is to be diligent in each of these areas as a member of the church. For example, if the gift of giving is last on your list, you recognize that while God may not call upon you to give 60% of your income you still have a responsibility to give.

Appendix B

Gathering Church and Community Data

OBSERVATIONS OF THE CHURCH

The data gathering process begins when your committee members disclose their perceptions of what is happening and their feelings about the church's ministry. The answer to each statement (on pages 137-140) must reflect precisely how each committee member sees or perceives what is happening in the church's program.

Most statements have three possible answers. Circle the word in the parentheses which best describes your observation at this moment. Should you want to choose another word to complete the sentence, write it above the words in parentheses.

Ministry of Evangelism

1. Our church has (very much, some, little) concern about personal evangelism.

2. I have (very much, some, little) concern about personal evangelism.

3. We (plan and pray for, hope for, take for granted) the ministry of evangelism.

4. The ministry of evangelism is the job of (the pastor, church leaders, all members).

5. We (regularly, occasionally, never) offer training to our members in methods of personal evangelism.

6. We (often, sometimes, rarely) baptize people.

7. Visitors in our worship service are (warmly welcomed and invited to return, welcomed, greeted, ignored).

8. We (always, sometimes, never) consider our Sunday church school as a tool of evangelism.

9. We (do, do not) maintain a file of newcomers and prospective persons to be contacted by our church.

10. (Many, some, none) of our members invite new persons to visit or attend our church.

11. We baptize mostly (children, teens, young adults, older adults).

12. I feel (comfortable, uneasy, upset) when the subject of personal evangelism is discussed.

13. It is (easy, difficult, impossible) for me to speak about my faith with another member of the church.

14. It is (easy, difficult, impossible) for me to talk about my faith with a nonchurch member.

15. Our pastoral leadership is (completely, somewhat, not at all) "sold" on personal evangelism.

Ministry of Care

1. The ministry of care is (very important, important, not important) in the life of our congregation.

2. (All, many, some, few) of our members know each other on a first-name basis.

3. If I am hurting or in trouble, I know that I will receive (much, some, little) care and support from the membership.

4. When people are in the hospital, we expect (the pastor, deacons or deaconesses, other members, only relatives) to visit them.

5. We (do, do not) have an effective visitation program.

6. Members of our congregation are (often, sometimes, never) visited by other members.

7. We (quickly, sometimes, never) respond to personal crises in the lives of members.

8. We (quickly, sometimes, never) respond to personal crises in the lives of people in the community.

9. We offer (many, quite a few, some, very few) fellowship activities for the members of the church.

10. Our fellowship activities are (very well, somewhat, poorly) attended.

11. (Most, some, little) of our ministry of care takes place in small groups.

12. Our ministry of care is (a very large, a large, an average, a small) factor in influencing new people to become a part of our fellowship.

13. Our members are (very good, average, poor) listeners to other people.

14. Visitors are (very much, somewhat, not at all, negatively) impressed with our ministry of care.

Ministry of Worship

1. Those who attend our worship services are mostly (children, youth, young adults, middle-age adults, older adults, a mix of all ages).

2. We (often, sometimes, rarely, never) have new persons with us in our worship service.

3. My general impression of our worship service is (great, positive, neutral, poor, negative).

4. Our worship services are always (very well, well, poorly) prepared.

5. Our worship services are (filled with variety, sometimes varied, always the same).

6. We (often, sometimes, rarely, never) have lay participants in worship services, besides ushers and choir members.

7. Our facilities (enhance, somewhat help, hinder) our worship experience.

8. Music is (very meaningful, effective, not very helpful, negative) as a part of the worship services of our church.

9. Prayer is (very meaningful, effective, not helpful) as a part of the worship services.

10. The use of Scripture is (very meaningful, effective, not helpful, negative) in our worship services.

11. The announcements are (helpful, not helpful) to the atmosphere of worship.

12. The sermon is usually (challenging, helpful, unimportant).

13. We (always, sometimes, rarely, never) give an invitation for persons to accept Jesus Christ as Savior or to join the church.

14. When I leave a worship service, I usually feel (very good, good, okay, blah, disturbed).

15. The primary responsibility for what happens in worship belongs to the (pastor, deacons, worship committee). *You may circle more than one.*

Ministry of Education

1. The ministry of education is viewed as (very important, of average importance, not very important) in the life of our church.

2. It is (very easy, easy, difficult, almost impossible) to recruit enough teachers and leaders for our educational ministries.

3. On the average, the members of our congregation have (very good, average, poor) knowledge and understanding of the Bible.

4. Most of our members know (a great deal, something, little) about our denomination.

5. Most of our members are (very, somewhat, not at all) able to relate their beliefs to their daily lives.

6. We (fully expect, would like, don't expect) our teachers and leaders to be trained.

7. Our educational ministries focus mostly on (children, youth, young adults, middle-age adults, older adults, a mix of all ages).

8. In the eyes of the congregation, the Sunday church school is (very important, important, something we have to do, not important).

9. It's (exciting, okay, a bore) to attend Sunday church school.

10. Over the past *ten years* our church school has (grown, stayed the same, declined) in attendance.

11. During the last *two years* our church school has (grown, stayed the same, declined) in attendance.

12. We (strongly, sort of, do not) believe that people of all ages need to grow constantly in their knowledge of Jesus Christ and in a way of living that reflects more and more the presence of Christ in their lives.

13. Our ministry of education can be described as (creative and appealing, ordinary and average, the same as last year).

14. I feel (very good, good, ambivalent, negative) about our ministry of education.

Ministry of Service to the World

1. Our church is (heavily, somewhat, rarely, never) involved in the life of our neighborhood.

2. The people who live in our neighborhood are (very much, much, somewhat, not at all) aware of our church and its ministry.

3. Our church has a (positive, neutral, negative) image in the community.

4. Our church has (very good plans, a few plans, no plans) for our ministry of service.

5. (Most, some, few, none) of our members feel ministry of service to the world is important.

6. The membership of our church is (very much the same as, a mixture of, not at all like) our community.

7. We make (many, some, few, no) efforts to involve people from the community in our church's programs.

8. We are (very much, somewhat, a little, not at all) aware of our denomination's mission programs in this country and around the world.

9. We (strongly, somewhat, don't) support our denominational missions.

10. We have responded to (more than ten, five, at least one, no) community need(s) this past year.

11. We have responded to (five or more, four, three, two, one, no) worldwide need(s) this past year.

12. We are (strongly, somewhat, not) convinced that our faith calls us to try to meet the needs in our community and world.

13. There are (many, some, few, no) needs in our community to which we can respond.

14. Because we are there, our church makes (a great, a small, an insignificant) difference in our community.

15. I am (excited, satisfied, content, dissatisfied) with our church's service to the community and the world.

Ministry of Church Administration

1. In terms of our total ministry, we are (very effective, somewhat effective, ineffective).

2. Our members feel (very good, good, neutral, not so good, bad, very bad) about our church and its total ministry.

3. Our church has (a very strong, a strong, an average, a weak, a very weak) sense of purpose.

4. Our church's leaders, overall, have a (very positive, positive, neutral, negative) attitude about our church's goals and ministries.

5. Our church (does, does not) anticipate a future role as God's servant in this community.

6. Our church's boards and committees are (very, somewhat, not) effective in carrying out the tasks of ministries.

7. Our church is (definitely, perhaps, definitely not) located where it ought to be for an effective ministry to its community.

8. Our church's buildings are (very, somewhat, not) adequate.

9. We (like, put up with, can't stand) the community in which we are located.

10. The majority of our members are (very, somewhat, not) glad to be members.

11. Our people come to church with (great, some, little, no) anticipation and enthusiasm.

12. We are (very much, somewhat, a little, not at all) desirous of bringing in new people.

13. We (very much, somewhat, do not) want to grow in size.

14. We are (highly, firmly, somewhat, not very much) committed to the growth of individual Christians in their faith.

15. We are (strongly, somewhat, minimally) committed to support our church financially.

OBSERVATIONS OF THE COMMUNITY

Windshield Survey Information

Area to be surveyed: _____

Survey to be conducted by (names): _____

Completed survey to be returned to the Church Growth Committee by (date): _____

Read over the following questions before you survey.

a. What is the GENERAL LAYOUT of the community? What is observed in the layout of the streets and the traffic patterns for vehicles and pedestrians? What gives identity to the community? Are there physical features such as rivers, railroads, major highways, or industrial zones that divide the area geographically? Where are the schools, clubs, churches, civic buildings, shopping areas, industrial zones, and recreational areas? Where are the residential areas?

b. What are the HOUSING PATTERNS of the community? Are the houses old or new, single, multiple. or mobile dwellings? Are there apparent clusters of housing separated by race or economic status? What is the aesthetic impression from the general appearance of the houses and community? Are there signs of deterioration and abandonment or of growth and development? Do houses have porches that are used? Do fences separate houses? What kinds of cars are parked and where? Are there out-of-town license plates? Are there sidewalks that encourage pedestrian movement?

c. What are the patterns of INTERRELATIONSHIPS? Are there signs of people relating to each other? Are children playing? Where? What are the approximate ages of the people you see? Which sex predominates? What signs do you see posted? What kinds of bumper stickers?

Compile this information on the next page as you survey.

Windshield Survey Information Sheet

AREA COVERED _____

GENERAL LAYOUT

Street and traffic patterns _____

_____

Physical boundaries _____

_____

Identifying marks _____

_____

Characteristics of the area _____

_____

_____

HOUSING PATTERNS

Kinds of housing _____

_____

Clustering of housing _____

_____

General appearance _____

_____

_____

_____

_____

INTERRELATIONSHIPS

Signs of people relating _____

_____

General impressions of population (age, activity) _____

_____

_____

STATISTICS: OUR CHURCH HISTORY

The Purpose of the History

The beginning of growth for a congregation is knowing who you are as a church. Your history is part of the answer to that question. The other part is "Who are you going to be?" That can be answered by planning and the realization of those plans.

The history will be a part of the statement of who the church is. It should be an essential part of initiating any new members so that they can become members in the fullest sense of that word. The congregation can be free to try new things when it realizes that the church exists because someone once tried something radically new to establish the congregation. There were many new things in those years of development that brought the church to its present situation. Knowing this, the church can realize that trying something new is simply continuing the tradition on which it was founded.

Record Your History

Every congregation has history. Ask your pastor, church clerk, or secretary if a written record exists. If it does, be sure it is up to date. This written history can be made much more attractive with a scrapbook of pictures and articles about notable events of each year.

If the history has only been kept in the minds of some of the longtime members, one of the first things to do is to get it into print by interviewing those persons and recording their recollections. Here is some of the information which should be included in your history:

- when and how the church began;
- its original purpose;
- its meeting place, indicating when any building and remodeling was done;
- a list (with dates) of the pastors;
- a list of charter members;
- a list of those who have gone into church-related vocations or those who have become active lay workers;
- notations about any churches that were begun by your church including names, dates, places, and situations precipitating their origin, such as mission, splits, etc.;
- the current statement of purpose of the church, and when it was adopted;
- significant ministries the church carried out in its community and when.

The data for the rest of this section (listed below) would be available through the church clerk or secretary, the Sunday church school superintendent or secretary, and the church treasurer. If your church does not have any of these records, begin keeping them now.

Instructions to Record and Graph Statistics

The pages that follow will help you transfer data from record books onto charts and graphs. Particular charts or graphs may be made into transparencies or copied onto posterboard or newsprint for presentation.to the congregation, so make working copies of each page. Also keep a clean original for future planning purposes.

Time Span

The charts and graphs on pages 145-149 have space for thirteen years. This is intended to allow you to picture the current year with its past and future. Collect information from the past ten years and establish goals for two or three years ahead or use the data from only five years and plan farther into the future. Place the earliest year you chose in the left column on each of these sheets. If you have no records, start with the current year and build from there.

The Need for Percentages

Some of the charts have a space for percentage of increase or decline. Percentages raise questions that help to clarify problems and begin to suggest some workable solutions. Suppose your active membership was forty last year and currently is fifty. An increase of ten members this year indicates twenty-five percent growth. However, if you kept adding only ten members each year for the next ten years the increase that tenth year would be only seven percent. Does this indicate a decline in the vitality of the church? Is the congregation losing its interest and desire to reach out to new people? Or, is this decline in percentage due to a tremendous turnover in the population of the community?

Calculating Percentages

Some of the charts have a space for percentage of increase or decline. To determine that percentage, follow these steps using as an example the "Church Membership and Worship Attendance" chart on page 145.
   a. Always work with membership figures for two successive years: For example: 1980-1981 or 1981-1982.
   b. Subtract the lower membership figure from the higher.
   c. Divide that answer by the membership figure for the first year of the two years being calculated.
   d. Multiply that answer by 100 for the percentage. Enter the percentage on the chart under the membership figure for the second year of the two years being calculated.
   e. If the answer represents a decline because the figure for the first year was larger than the figure for the second year, put it between parentheses.

Preparing Graphs

It is difficult to analyze from numbers alone. Graphs put the numbers into a visual relationship with one another. Now that the data is charted, follow these steps. You will find it easy to make a graph.
1. Transcribe the years from the top of the chart to the bottom of the graph.
2. Follow the steps below to establish the vertical scale for each graph (pages 145, 147 and 149). You will be plotting more than one set of statistics per graph.
   a. Determine the highest number of all the charted data (excluding percentages).
   b. Divide that number by 10, and round the answer up to the nearest 5 or 10.
   c. Write that number on the first line above zero and its multiples on each successive line of the scale. Because there are 13 horizontal lines, each graph allows for recording future growth.

Church Membership and Worship Attendance

Purpose

To show the growth or decline of our church and how active our membership is in the worship program of our church.

Instructions—Refer to page 144.

1. Determine the years to be covered and record them at the top of the chart and below the graph.
2. Record the statistics and calculate the percentages.
3. Follow the instructions for building the graph.

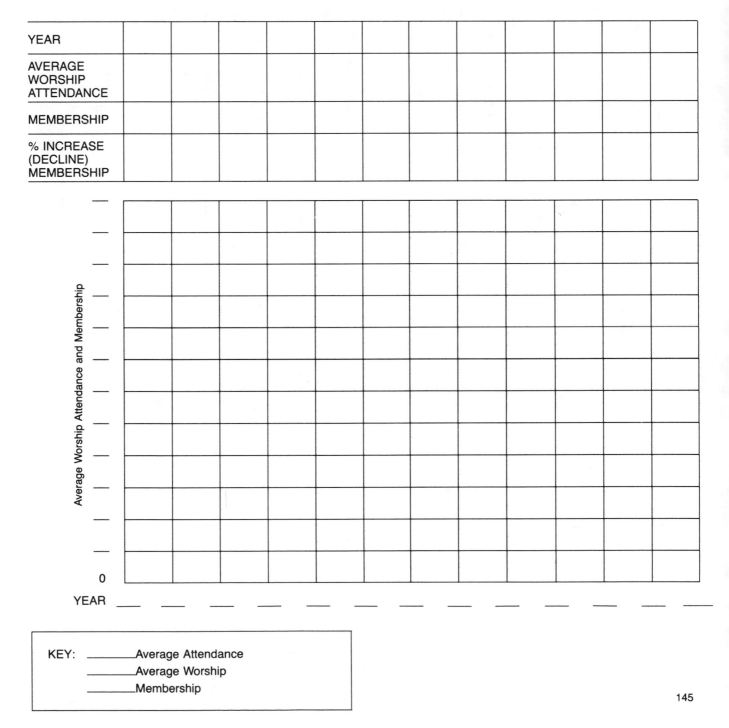

YEAR													
AVERAGE WORSHIP ATTENDANCE													
MEMBERSHIP													
% INCREASE (DECLINE) MEMBERSHIP													

Average Worship Attendance and Membership

0

YEAR

KEY: _____ Average Attendance
_____ Average Worship
_____ Membership

Membership Additions and Losses

Purpose

To show the ways in which our church membership has grown or declined.

Instructions

Complete only the information available from your church records.

ADDITIONS

Baptism										
Transfer In										
Other										

LOSSES

Death and Other										
Transfer Out										
Became Inactive										
Year										

Sunday Church School Enrollment and Attendance

Purpose

To discover what has happened in our Sunday church school over the last ten years.

Instructions—Refer to page 144.

1. Determine the years to be covered and record them at the top of the chart and below the graph.
2. Record the statistics from Sunday church school records and calculate the percentage.
3. Build the graph following the steps on page 144.

YEAR													
ENROLLMENT													
AVERAGE ATTENDANCE													
% INCREASE (DECLINE) ENROLLMENT													

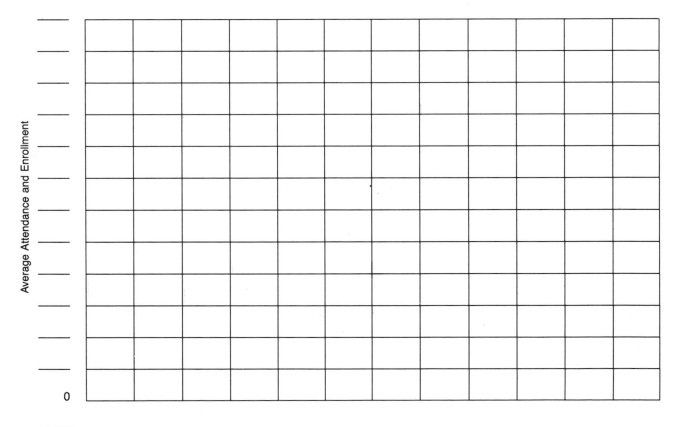

YEAR

KEY: _____ Enrollment
_____ Average Attendance

Our Church Record of Giving

Purpose

To show how our church has given to ministry in and beyond our own congregation.

Instructions

1. Determine what years you will study and record them at the top of the chart and below the graph.
2. Ask the treasurer to record the statistics for those years.
3. Follow the directions on page 144 to build the graph. The numerical scale may have to be built in hundreds or thousands instead of in fives or tens.

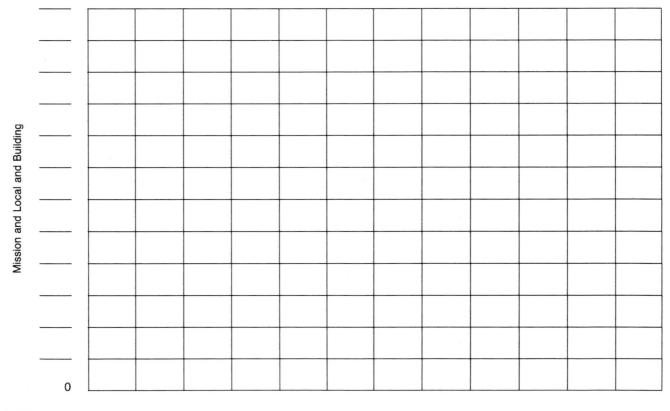

YEAR											
BUILDING											
LOCAL PROGRAM											
MISSION BENEVOLENCE											

KEY: _____ Building

_____ Local Program

_____ Mission and Benevolence

149

STATISTICS: OUR COMMUNITY HISTORY AND SURVEY

Purpose

To identify our community and those areas where it needs the strengths of our church's ministry. This section provides guides for obtaining information on the community in two ways:

Learn the community's identity and history — page 151
Gather census data — page 152

Identity and History

1. Identify the community.

Many congregations fail to make an impact on their community because they have never defined its limits. This is especially true in those congregations that have a scattered membership. It is most important for those churches to define their areas of mission as a group or as a number of small groups. Mission areas can either be around the building or the area or areas in which most of the members live.

2. Find the history of the community.

Check with the Chamber of Commerce, the Realtors Association, or the Historical Society to see if a written history of your community exists. If it does, be sure it is up to date. If not, interview some longtime residents. Here are some items that are very important to look for or to include.

a. Who were the settlers and the migrants? Where are they today? Has a new type of "settler" taken over?

b. What has been the growth pattern of the community? What are the projections for the future?

c. What has been and is the political structure of the community? Who made and makes decisions, and *how* were and are they implemented? Has the leadership been representative of the entire community or dominated by one part of it?

d. How has the economic structure of the community developed? What keeps it running? How is it serviced for food, clothing, housing, furnishings, utilities, banking, transportation, business, and industry?

e. How have the housing patterns developed over the years? What has attracted new people to the area? What has caused people to go elsewhere? Do certain classes or ethnic groups live in certain areas of the community?

f. What services are available to meet the physical, emotional, and economic needs of the residents? Are these services known by most of the residents and readily obtained? Is there a Council of Social Service Agencies in your community? Are they advertised by the Chamber of Commerce or the city?

g. Do volunteers work in community projects, such as hospitals, the school system, or county human services? Does the community coordinate the work of volunteers? Are there opportunities for youth and children to do volunteer work?

h. What is the school system like? Are there opportunities for adult continuing education? Does the educational system make heavy extracurricular demands on students?

i. What is the health care system of the community? How broad are its services? Does it work with the religious community in the healing process? What specialized care is offered for the handicapped, the aging, the addicted, the needy?

j. How safe do the residents feel in the community? What is the relationship between the community and the police? Are certain segments of the population viewed and treated as problems in the community?

k. Is there a local newspaper? Do the editors interact with community structures? Do investigative reporters who probe areas of community life live and work in the community? What influence does TV or radio have locally?

l. What is the role of religious organizations in the community?

Community Survey Through Census Data

When you have identified the community you consider as your mission responsibility, you can find numerical data about that community very easily. The County Planning Commission has a map showing the geographical limits of tracts. You can obtain the census data you desire by researching the census volumes or simply asking the County Planning Commission Office for a copy.

If you decide to do your own research, here is some information to gather which will be useful to your analysis.

a. Population totals from 1930 to the last census year.

b. Marital status of population.

c. Households, both family and nonfamily. "Family" means a group of two or more persons living together who are related by birth, marriage, or adoption. "Nonfamily" includes people living alone or sharing housing, people in institutions or college dormitories, nursing homes, and so forth. The information you are looking for in this category is numbers of married couples with and without children under age 18; male- and female-headed (single parent) families with or without children under age 18; people living alone or sharing housing.

d. Racial/ethnic characteristics of the community.

e. Age/sex categories are given in the following groupings:

0-5	18-24	55-64
6-9	25-34	65-74
10-14	35-44	over 75
15-17	45-54	

f. Housing characteristics include:

number who own or rent
number of dwelling units by kind
median value or rent
residents less than five years before census
new house since last census

STATISTICS: OUR CHURCH TODAY

Draw on data from the Membership Information Survey in this section (pages 155-156) to complete the following charts and graphs:

1. Age/Sex Profiles   pages 157-158
   This information is basic to any system of record keeping. Transfer it to cards in the church office. The age and sex information should also be transferred to the appropriate chart(s) on page 157. Some individuals will appear on both profiles; others on only one. The community age/sex profile on page 158 can be compiled from the census data.

2. First Contacts   page 159

3. Length of Membership   page 161

4. How Members Joined the Church   page 161

5. Distance Members Live from the Church Building   page 162

6. Activity of Members in the Community   page 163

7. Activity of Members in the Church   page 164

8. Family Status of Church and Community   page 165

   (See census data discussed on page 152, for community statistics.)

9. Racial Composition of our Church and Community   page 167

   (See census data discussed on page 152, for community statistics.)

Membership Information Survey

Name _____ ☐ ☐ Birthday _____ _____ _____
                                      M F   month   day   year

Address _____
                    (street)

_____
(city)   (zip code)

_____ _____
(home phone)   (work phone)

_____
(occupation)

(In the following statements, mark as many responses as apply.)

	very important	somewhat important	not important
I *first came to this church* because			
1. I grew up in it.	_____	_____	_____
2. it was close to my home.	_____	_____	_____
3. the building attracted me.	_____	_____	_____
4. I saw or heard an advertisement in/on _____ .	_____	_____	_____
5. a friend invited me.	_____	_____	_____
6. the pastor contacted me.	_____	_____	_____
7. I wanted my children educated in the Christian faith.	_____	_____	_____
8. I preferred the denomination.	_____	_____	_____
9. Other _____	_____	_____	_____
I *joined this church* because of			
1. a pastor's class.	_____	_____	_____
2. the denomination.	_____	_____	_____
3. the worship service.	_____	_____	_____
4. the Christian education program.	_____	_____	_____
5. a teacher's interest in me.	_____	_____	_____
6. a friend's invitation.	_____	_____	_____
7. the friendliness of the people.	_____	_____	_____
8. someone who joined with me.	_____	_____	_____
9. opportunities for service in the community.	_____	_____	_____
10. Other _____	_____	_____	_____

I joined this church in _____ as a new convert, but not related to anyone in the
                    (year)   church.   _____
                                   as a new convert whose family was part of the church.   _____
                                   by transferring from another church.   _____

I now live _____ mile(s) from the church.

I belong to or serve in the following community or social organizations:

_____ Lodge or auxiliary   _____ Veterans organization
_____ Farm organization   _____ Parent-Teacher Association
_____ Labor union   _____ Local political organization
_____ Professional organization   _____ Youth program _____
_____ Service club   Other _____
Other _____   Other _____

I am presently involved in the following church activities:

(List any office you hold or organization of which you are a member. Under "A" note how many *hours per month* you spend with that activity in meetings, work, or preparation. Under "B" put the number of those hours which you spend with nonchurch members.

For example: a deacon may work 12 hours a month, of which 3 are spent visiting nonchurch members. The deacon would put 12 under "A" and 3 under "B". A Sunday church school teacher may spend 24 hours preparing, teaching, and visiting but spend 2 of those visiting nonmembers. A choir member could put in 12 hours each month rehearsing and singing. All of the choir member's time would be under "A".)

Activity	A	B
_____	____	____
_____	____	____
_____	____	____
_____	____	____

My family status is (remember "child" means a person under 18 years) (check one of the following):

_____ married with no children at home.
_____ married with _____ children at home.
_____ separated/divorced with no children at home.
_____ female head of family with _____ children at home.
_____ male head of family with _____ children at home.
_____ widowed living alone.
_____ widowed living with children.
_____ single adult not living with parents.
_____ single adult living with parent(s).
_____ under 18

I am white _____, black _____, Asian _____, Hispanic/Latino _____, Native American _____, Other _____.

Age/Sex Profile of Church Membership

Age Group	% Female	# Female	TOTAL	# Male	% Male	Age Group
over 75						over 75
65-75						65-75
55-64						55-64
45-54						45-54
35-44						35-44
25-34						25-34
18-24						18-24
15-17						15-17
10-14						10-14
6-9						6-9
up to 5						up to 5

GRAND TOTAL
MEMBERS

Age/Sex Profile of Sunday Church School Enrollment

Age Group	% Female	# Female	TOTAL	# Male	% Male	Age Group
over 75						over 75
65-75						65-75
55-64						55-64
45-54						45-54
35-44						35-44
25-34						25-34
18-24						18-24
15-17						15-17
10-14						10-14
6-9						6-9
up to 5						up to 5

GRAND TOTAL
ENROLLMENT

Age/Sex Profile of Community

Age Group	% Female	# Female	TOTAL	# Male	% Male	Age Group
over 75						over 75
65-75						65-75
55-64						55-64
45-54						45-54
35-44						35-44
25-34						25-34
18-24						18-24
15-17						15-17
10-14						10-14
6-9						6-9
up to 5						up to 5

GRAND TOTAL
POPULATION

First Contacts

(From the Membership Information Survey, add the number of responses for each item. Place that number on the matching line. Total the number of responses. Divide the total for each response by the grand total of its section to get the percentage.)

Number of members responding _____

I first *came to this church* because	very important	%	somewhat important	%	not important	%
1. I grew up in it.						
2. it was close to my home.						
3. the building attracted me						
4. I saw or heard an advertisement in/on _____.						
5. a friend invited me.						
6. the pastor contacted me.						
7. I wanted my children educated in the Christian faith.						
8. I preferred the denomination.						
9. Other						
TOTALS						
GRAND TOTAL						

I *joined this church* because of						
1. a pastor's class.						
2. the denomination.						
3. the worship service.						
4. the Christian education program.						
5. a teacher's interest in me.						
6. a friend's invitation.						
7. the friendliness of the people.						
8. someone who joined with me.						
9. opportunities for service in the community.						
10. Other						
TOTALS						
GRAND TOTAL						

Length of Membership (in years)

Instructions:
1. On the first line, record how many members have belonged to the church for the number of years listed.
2. Divide that total by the number of years in each time period to get a yearly average. (Remember that 5-7 years is three years, not two, and 11-20 is ten years, not nine.) For the last time period (over 50 years), determine the longest membership. Then determine the number of years between 50 and the year of the longest membership. Divide the number of years by the total members in that category.
3. Starting at the left, add the "gross" number of members across the chart. Draw a line where half of the members have joined.

Less than 1 year	1-2 years	3-4 years	5-7 years	8-10 years	11-20 years	21-30 years	31-40 years	41-50 years	over 50 years
GROSS									
AVERAGE									

How Members Joined the Church

Joined by:	Number
New convert not church-related	
New convert with church relations	
Transfer of membership	

Distance Members Live from the Church Building

Distance	Number
Up to 1 mile	
1 - 2 miles	
3 - 5 miles	
6 - 9 miles	
10 - 15 miles	
over 15 miles	

Activity of Members in the Community

Number of
members

Involved in

_____   Lodge or auxiliary

_____   Farm organization

_____   Labor union

_____   Professional organization

_____   Service club

_____   Veterans organization

_____   Parent-Teacher Association

_____   Local political organization

_____   Youth program

_____   _____

_____   _____

_____   _____

_____   _____

_____   _____

_____   _____

_____   _____

Activity of Members in the Church

Activities	In Church Number of Members' Hours	Outside Church Number of Members' Hours

Family Status of Church and Community

Instructions: To determine the percentages for these charts, divide the number of persons in each category by the total for the entire column.

	CHURCH #	CHURCH %	COMMUNITY #	COMMUNITY %
Married with no children at home				
Married with children at home				
Separated/divorced no children home				
Female head of family				
Male head of family				
Widowed living alone				
Widowed living with children				
Single adult not living with parents				
Single adult with parents				
Under 18				

TOTAL   _____   _____

Racial Composition of Church and Community

	CHURCH		COMMUNITY	
	#	%	#	%
White				
Black				
Asian				
Hispanic/Latino				
Native American				
TOTAL	_____		_____	

LISTENING TO OUR CHURCH AND COMMUNITY

Listening data is obtained through the use of survey instruments or through personal interviews with individuals or groups. What people feel, say, or think should be added to the other data already compiled as the Church Growth Committee builds a base for growth in the church.

In face-to-face contacts with people, listen for both facts and feelings. In most cases those interviewed will gladly supply factual answers to questions, but they will also provide "feeling" data of which you should be aware. The tone of voice, the level of intensity, the facial and hand gestures, the look of the eye—these and other communication gestures provide messages of feeling. In many cases, how people feel about something is more important than the facts they can provide.

As a committee, decide how many interviews you need to make and who will be interviewed. Determine whether members of the committee will do the interviewing or whether you need to enlist others to aid you in the listening process.

In most cases a personal interview should last no longer than fifteen minutes. Interviews with groups should not last longer than thirty minutes.

More questions than you can (or should) use are included here. Your committee should choose the most appropriate questions and add any others that seem necessary. Be sure that all interviewers use the same questions so that there is consistency in the material your committee receives for analysis.

You may want to make copies of the "Data Analysis Summary" sheet on page 181 as a summary sheet for the interviewers.

Ministry of Evangelism

For Members

1. Do you regularly invite friends, neighbors, relatives, co-workers, and others to attend your church? If not, are you aware of persons whom you could invite?

2. Would you be willing to provide the names of persons to be placed on a contact list to be visited?

3. Is the ministry of evangelism a high priority for you and for your church? If it isn't, should it be?

4. Are you able to witness to someone outside of the church?

5. Does your church train its members to be witnessing Christians?

6. Is your church vitally interested in bringing new people into its fellowship?

7. Are you glad when visitors attend? Do you invite them to come back? Do you encourage them to attend activities other than the worship service?

8. Are you convinced that evangelism is the responsibility of the pastor, the deacons, or all the members of the congregation?

9. Are you ready and willing to be trained to witness?

10. Does your church regularly contact visitors soon after they have been present in a worship service?

For Visitors

Survey visitors to discover what they are feeling and experiencing. Check with each visitor *the day after* that person attends a service and ask the following questions:

1. Were you greeted by someone when you entered the building?

2. Were you given directions for hanging up your coat, putting children in the nursery, locating the rest rooms if necessary?

3. Were you introduced to other persons present, either before or after the service?

4. Were you ushered to a seat, provided with a hymnal and bulletin, and generally helped to be comfortable?

5. Were you invited to attend a refreshment time before or after the service?

6. Were you invited to a Sunday church school class? If you attended, how did you feel?

7. Were you invited to come back?

(This type of survey should be made over a three- to six-month period to provide sufficient information concerning what visitors actually experience when worshiping with your congregation.)

Ministry of Care

For Members

1. Is the ministry of caring basically the work of the pastor or should the laity be involved in this ministry?

2. What response and support systems exist for those in our fellowship who experience a crisis, illness, or tragedy?

3. Whose responsibility is it to organize the ministry of caring?

4. What efforts are made to involve all members in the fellowship activities of the church?

5. How many Sundays must a person be absent from worship or Sunday church school before some type of follow-up is made?

6. Are you aware of any unmet needs of members? Are there resources within the congregation to meet these needs?

7. How does the friendship of those present in worship experiences affect the visitors?

8. Are shut-ins, those with long-term illness, and inactive persons visited regularly and remembered in other ways?

9. Is our church known to the community as a caring church? Are there times when you reach out into the community and care for those in need?

10. Do the adults express love, care, and concern to children, youth, and young adults? Are the young people "wanted?" Do the adults make younger people feel they "belong?"

Ministry of Worship

For Members

1. Are you enthusiastic about your services of worship? Do you approach a worship service with anticipation?

2. How do you feel after a typical worship service?

3. Do you, or would you, invite friends, neighbors, relatives, and casual acquaintances to attend your services of worship?

4. Is the ministry of music varied and "alive?"

5. Is the congregational singing enthusiastic?

6. Are the sermons helpful? Do they relate the Bible to everyday life?

7. Does something worthwhile happen to people who attend your worship services?

8. Are those who lead your worship services always well prepared?

9. Are members "regular" in their attendance?

10. Do variety and different approaches to worship provide freshness and vitality?

Ministry of Education

For Members

1. Are the members satisfied with the program of Christian education? If not, why not?

2. Does your church's ministry of education address all age levels?

3. Is the Bible an integral part of your ministry of education? Are attempts made to relate it to everyday living for all ages?

4. Are those who teach and counsel trained? Do they regularly receive additional training?

5. Is the Sunday church school important to your worshiping congregation? Is it "owned" by most of the members or is it "owned" primarily by the board of Christian education?

6. Is it difficult or easy to secure teachers, youth advisers, and other leaders?

7. Do the members of your board of Christian education plan? Do they have clear goals and objectives toward which they are working?

8. Are the development and growth of your church's leaders important? Does some group have this responsibility for all of the church leaders?

9. Are there numerical growth targets for the Sunday church school, for youth groups, for music programs? Are these kinds of targets important?

For Teachers and Advisers or Other Workers

1. Why are you a teacher or youth adviser?

2. What training have you received that was beneficial in your role?

3. What type of training would you like to receive in the future?

4. Do you enjoy teaching or advising?

5. Do you feel there is an effective support system for you in your teaching role?

6. Do you regularly visit in the homes of your students? Do you feel that this is important?

7. Do you have enough time to prepare your lessons?

8. Do you have enough space, equipment, materials, resources, ideas, and budget?

For Students

1. What do you like best about Sunday church school?

2. What have you learned recently that you feel is very important to you?

3. Do you like the material currently being used? Can you understand it?

4. Have you ever invited a friend or relative to come to Sunday church school?

5. Do you have some friends who you think might come to Sunday church school?

6. What would you like to see happen in Sunday church school that isn't happening?

7. (For children) Do your parents attend Sunday church school?

8. Why do you think Sunday church school is important?

For Drop-outs or Infrequent Attenders

1. How long has it been since you attended Sunday church school?

2. Did you attend regularly before then?

3. Why did you drop out? (Or why do you not attend?)

4. Did you learn anything which was helpful to you at the time you attended?

5. What do you understand the purpose of the Sunday church school to be?

6. Do you feel any need for instruction, fellowship, and growth that can be provided by the Sunday church school?

7. What would it take to attract you to membership in a class or program?

Ministry of Service to the World

1. How many activities can you name in which your church or its members are involved in serving the community or the world? (Examples are PTA, Meals On Wheels, prison ministry, youth club, scouting, politics.)

2. How is your church involved in ministries which serve or assist persons outside of the church?

3. How is your church the presence of Jesus Christ in your community?

4. Are you aware of persons in need in your community to whom your church can minister? If so, are there channels through which you can communicate and meet this need?

5. Does your church spend most of its time and energy on programs and projects for persons on the "inside" rather than for those who are outside of the church? Is the opposite true? Or is there a balance?

6. Does your church respond to appeals which have a worldwide base, such as a hurricane in Haiti, earthquake in Nicaragua, hunger in Pakistan?

7. Does your church cooperate with other churches in serving the community? If not, should it? How?

8. Does your church have any contact with community social agencies? If so, which ones?

9. Is there any way members of your congregation could assist these social agencies?

10. Is the concept of ministry of service to the world the subject of Bible studies, announcements, sermons, or other group presentations?

Ministry of Church Administration

1. What is your church's "reason for being?" (Why does it exist? What is its purpose?)

2. What is your church trying to do with, through, and for its members?

3. What is your church trying to accomplish in the community?

4. What is your church's self-image?

5. How do people feel about belonging to your church—glad, happy, joyful, excited, okay, ambivalent, sorry, sad?

6. What are your dreams for your church?

7. What community needs are being met by your church that no other group or church is meeting?

8. Is your church planning for its future?

9. Is your church growing? Why or why not?

10. Are you satisfied with your ministry of evangelism?

11. Are you satisfied with your ministry of worship?

12. Are you satisfied with your ministry of care?

13. Are you satisfied with your ministry of education?

14. Are you satisfied with your ministry of service to the world?

15. Are you satisfied with the work and ministry of your professional staff?

16. Do the members adequately support your church's budget?

17. Is your church located in the right place for effective ministry?

18. Are your buildings adequate for the ministry in which you are currently engaged?

19. What do you wish your church were doing now that it is not doing?

20. In one word, describe the future of your church.

Appendix C

Worksheets for Analysis and Planning

CONGREGATIONAL ANALYSIS

The statistical data which you have gathered includes numbers of people, activities, and relationships in which they are involved. The charts and graphs which you have completed organized these numbers so that they tell a "story" about your church and its community. The story will unfold as you analyze the data from the charts and graphs. Your church will need to adapt the data you have gathered and the questions you ask to your own situation. What is provided here is only a guide. Just because the manual suggests that certain data be collected, it does not mean that your church must have it all to plan for growth.

On the pages that follow there are questions suggested. The answers to these questions will reveal part of the story of your church's growth in the past and its potential for the future. These questions will seek to draw out of the data those things that will help or hinder your growth.

Ministry of Evangelism

1. Refer to the census data and the "Church Membership and Worship Attendance" chart in Appendix B. Compare the number of people who moved into the community in the last five years and the number of people added to your church in the same time span.

2. Refer to "How Members Joined the Church," page 161.
   a. How many members were new converts not related to members of the congregation?
   b. How many were converts related to church members?

3. Drawing on the answers to the first two questions and the "Activity of Members in the Church and Community," pages 163-164, answer the following question:
   ● How would you describe the church's outreach to new converts?

4. Look again at the statistics on additions and losses (page 146). Make a list of all those who joined your church over the last five years. Review their "Membership Information Survey" forms. Then ask the following questions to discover for what reasons and in what ways people are attracted to your church:
   a. Is there a dominant age, economic level, social status, or family status?
   b. Why did they join your church?
   c. How are they sharing in the ministries of your church now?

5. What programs and characteristics aid recruitment and incorporation of new members? (See "First Contacts," page 159.) Which do not? Why?

6. Study the "Profiles on Age/Sex for Church and Community" on pages 157-158 and the "Family Status and Racial Composition of Community and Church" on pages 165 and 167, and answer the following questions:
   a. In which groupings does our church have strength?
   b. In which groupings in the community is there an opportunity for mission and evangelism?
   c. What training, motivation, or other preparation will be needed to take advantage of this opportunity?

7. Refer to "Length of Membership," page 161. How long have most of your congregation been members? It is a general rule that the older the membership is, the more intentional a congregation must be about inviting people to attend and about winning them to faith in Christ.

8. What types of evangelism have your church promoted? Refer to the "Activity of Members in the Church" on page 164. When was the last time your church undertook visitation in the community? Does the church have an annual time of evangelistic emphasis, such as a crusade? Are tracts available for members to use? Are they used by members? How?

Ministry of Care

1. Refer to "Church Membership and Worship Attendance" on page 145.
   a. Define the active, inactive, and nonresident membership. What other types of members do you have? (Shut-ins, students at school, students from another area living in your community, people in the military service, and so forth.)
   b. What percentages of the present membership are active and inactive members?
   c. What attempts have been made over the past few years to minister to the inactive members? What efforts are being made to bring them back into the fellowship of the church?
   d. Has there been a training program for people who will visit the inactive members?
   e. How many nonmembers attend worship regularly?
   f. How long do nonmembers attend before they are encouraged to join or to make a profession of faith in Christ and join?

2. Refer to the chart on page 161 entitled "Length of Membership."
   a. How many of the members who joined in the last ten years (see "Membership Additions and Losses," page 146) are still members (page 161)? What percentage of new members become dropouts within one, two, three, five, seven, and ten years? What does this imply about the nurture of new members?
   b. Is there a pastor's class for new members? How often does it meet? Is every new member required to take it before joining?
   c. How quickly are new members incorporated into a class or other small group? How soon are they allowed and invited to take on responsibilities and leadership?

3. Refer to "Distance Members Live from the Church Building" (page 162).
   a. If the congregation is scattered over a wide area, what do you do to build a sense of belonging and fellowship?
   b. Is there a regular time for social gatherings of the members?
   c. Is there a regular schedule for mixing visitors with members in social settings? Does it make them feel welcome?

4. In what way(s) does the present church program meet the needs of the various kinds of family groupings that make up the membership of the church? Look at "Family Status of Church and Community" on page 165.

5. Refer to "Activity of Members in the Church" (page 164).
   a. Compare the time spent in "in church" activity. What is the quality of fellowship resulting from time spent "in church?" (Use observation data already recorded on the Summary sheet.) How could fellowship be improved?
   b. What kinds of training are given ushers and greeters? How many have been trained in the past three years? How many serve in each capacity? How effective is their work?

6. How welcome do people of other races and nationalities feel in the church? (Refer to "Racial Composition of Church and Community" on page 167.)

Ministry of Worship

1. Refer to "Church Membership and Worship Attendance" (page 145).
   a. How do you account for the "ups and downs" or plateaus in worship attendance over the years?
   b. What percentage of your membership attends worship regularly?
   c. Are certain age groups or categories of persons absent from worship on a regular basis? Does the age/sex profile (pages 157-158) provide any answers to this question? Does a dominant age group affect the type of music and style of preaching as well as the degree of spontaneity in the services?

    d. Does worship attract or not attract visitors to the church? What could make it more meaningful to them?

2. Refer to "Our Church Record of Giving" (page 149). Consult your church treasurer or financial secretary to determine the following information.

    a. How many members support the budget of your church?

    b. What was last year's per-member giving for local program and for mission? Has there ever been training in stewardship? Is there an emphasis on denominational mission programs?

    c. Over the past ten years, what factors account for the level of giving to local program and benevolence and mission?

Ministry of Education

1. Refer to "Sunday Church School Enrollment and Attendance" on page 147 and the "Age/Sex Profiles of Sunday Church School, Church Membership, and Community" on pages 157-158.

    a. How does Sunday church school enrollment compare to attendance? When persons are absent, does follow-up take place? Are teachers trained to follow up on absentees? Are they encouraged to visit? How many times must a person be absent before a contact is made? Which method is most used: a postcard, a telephone call, a personal visit? Which is most appropriate for your church?

    b. Look at the age/sex profiles. Which are the largest and smallest groups in the Sunday church school? How does this compare to the age groupings of the membership of the church? Who is responsible for and what is being done to promote Sunday church school for adults?

    c. How does the age/sex distribution in Sunday church school compare with the community age/sex profile? What age groups do you attract? What age groups have not been attracted?

2. From "Activity of Members in the Church," page 164, what do Sunday church school teachers say about their commitment to Christian education in the church? How much time do they give to preparation? How much time is given to the students outside of class? How much is given to nonmembers?

3. Refer to "Family Status of Church and Community" on page 165.

    a. What educational opportunities does your church have for children, youth, young adults, adults, or senior citizens? Are the opportunities appropriate to the existing groupings?

    b. What are the possibilities for growth?

    c. When was the last time a new class or small group was formed for education or training purposes? Who is responsible for forming new groups?

4. Do you have a vacation church school? If not, when was the last time there was one in the church? Why was it discontinued? Do community statistics suggest the possibility of having one?

5. Did the responses to "Questions Regarding the Role of the Holy Spirit in Your Church" (page 117) suggest any needs to be met?

Ministry of Service to the World

1. Use a map, the "Windshield Survey," community history, and census data from Appendix B to help define the community in which your church carries out its ministry.

2. How does your church compare to the community in terms of its distribution by age/sex (pages 157 to 158), family status, and racial composition (pages 165 and 167)?

3. What is your church's present involvement in community affairs? Refer to "Activity of Members in the Community" on page 163.

4. What community needs has your church responded to over the past ten years? What changes took place as a result of that work? (See the written church and community histories from Appendix B.)

5. What issues of importance in the life of the community were studied by your congregation in some way during the last three years?

6. What issues of importance to the nation and world were studied by your congregation during the last three years?

7. In what ways has your church related to the work of social agencies in your community? (See your community history.) Is there a committee responsible for this work?

8. What education takes place in your church to make it more aware of the mission outreach of the denomination? What has been the congregation's financial and prayer support for mission over the past ten years? Refer to "Our Church Record of Giving" on page 149. What is your per capita giving to missions? Ask the treasurer or financial secretary to determine the percentage of members who contribute to special mission offerings.

9. In what way is the building used by the community? How is the congregation involved in activities that take place? Have these activities provided opportunities for witness and evangelism in the community?

Ministry of Church Administration

1. Does your church have an up-to-date history? Refer to page 143.

2. Does it have a statement of purpose? Is it owned by the congregation? Does it state clearly your "reason(s) for being?"

3. What is the organizational structure of your congregation? It will help to make a list of boards and committees. A diagram could show the relationship between various groups.
   a. Does each group have a sense of purpose? Are jobs clearly defined? Are job descriptions used for recruiting new workers and leaders? What is the motivation for people to accept leadership responsibility in the church? Use the "Activity of Members in the Church" on page 164 to help answer these questions.
   b. Is there effective communication between the various groups in your organization? Does the "right hand know what the left hand is doing"?
   c. Does your present organizational structure provide possibilities for growth or does it work best at maintaining the status quo?
   d. What "Qualities That Contribute to Growth" (page 121) need to be considered?

4. Is your building attractive to those who pass by? Does it need major or minor repairs? What changes may be needed to make the building fit the needs of the people? Do you need ramps, railings, signs, lights, and so forth? How is your building's space being utilized at present? Is more space needed? Is there extra space that can be used? By whom? For what?

5. What actions express your church's relationship to the denomination? to other Christian organizations? to the community?

DATA ANALYSIS SUMMARY

for the Ministry of _____

		Data Source
To Be Affirmed		
New Directions		
Needs for Pastoral Care		

HORIZONS

From the analysis of both our church and community, we have learned the following:

Strengths/Resources:

Opportunities/Challenges:

Potential for growth:

Needs:

Problems (a difficulty or need that is already well defined and understood):

Issues (a difficulty or need that is not yet clearly focused and to which you cannot yet apply specific actions):

FOCUS

The top five concerns for growth in the arena of _____ are:

_____

_____

_____

_____

_____

THE VISION

_____

_____

_____

_____

_____

_____

_____

_____

_____

GROWTH GOALS

(Do a worksheet for each part of the vision on page 185.)

Part _____ of Our Vision: _____

Possible Growth Goals:

_____

_____

_____

_____

_____

_____

_____

_____

_____

_____

_____

_____

_____

_____

_____

_____

_____

_____

_____

_____

_____

_____

_____

GROWTH OBJECTIVES

Written on: _____
(date)

GROWTH GOAL _____

GROWTH OBJECTIVES   PRIORITY

#1 _____

_____

#2 _____

_____

#3 _____

_____

#4 _____

_____

#5 _____

_____

#6 _____

_____

#7 _____

_____

WORKSHEET
for
GROWTH PROGRAM PLANS

OBJECTIVE: _____

_____

	What is to be done?	Who is responsible?	Completed by? (date)	What resources or training will be given?
#1	_____	_____	_____	_____
	_____			_____
	_____			_____
#2	_____	_____	_____	_____
	_____			_____
	_____			_____
#3	_____	_____	_____	_____
	_____			_____
	_____			_____
#4	_____	_____	_____	_____
	_____			_____
	_____			_____
#5	_____	_____	_____	_____
	_____			_____
	_____			_____
#6	_____	_____	_____	_____
	_____			_____
	_____			_____

What is the cost? _____

How will this program be evaluated? _____

_____

_____

A MODEL FOR TELE-SURVEY

Identify yourself by name clearly. Identify your church by name and location. Identify your purpose in calling very briefly. Excuse this unarranged call and ask if it is convenient to talk. If it is a phone call, you may state that it will take two minutes to ask a few questions. If you are calling in person, assure the person that you will not stay more than ten or fifteen minutes. If your call is inconvenient, arrange for another time and be sure the time is understood. In returning the call, remind the person of the prior arrangement. Thank him or her for the opportunity and begin the conversation. A conversation may go as follows:

"Hello, I'm _____, from the _____ Church on _____ street. My church wants to get acquainted with its neighbors and see if there is any way we can be of help. That's why I'm calling and I hope it isn't an inconvenient time for you. I have a few questions I'd like to ask you. Do you have about two or three minutes to talk right now?

If the answer is "no," ask for another time that would be convenient. Be sure it is mutually agreed on. Remind the person of the time you'll call back.

If the answer is "yes," continue the conversation but be aware of the person. He or she may not want to answer your questions but only to talk to someone who will listen. Be flexible. While you want to gather information, you want to make a friend, if possible, by listening and witnessing. Start by getting acquainted.

"As I said, my name is _____ and is your name _____?" If you have used a directory, you will have a name for that address and phone number. Don't take for granted that it is correct.

"How long have you lived here?" This question may open up some spontaneous conversation. If the family moved recently, you may ask where they came from and if they move frequently. Here you may get some expressions of frustration and fatigue or a sense of excitement at being in new places. Remember that listening takes priority over information gathering.

"Are you a member of a church?" Whether the answer is "yes" or "no," ask the next question.

"How frequently do you attend?"

"Does all your family attend with you?"

If the answer is "regularly," you may want to express how glad you are that they have found meaning in the church, for you, too, have found that. . . . Go on to leave a word of witness and let them know that your church is willing to be of help in any way possible for them at any time. Invite them to call the church whose number is in the yellow pages under Churches, _____, and in the white pages under _____. This will give you another opportunity to identify yourself and the church. Wish them a pleasant day and God's blessing. Your object is not to do "sheep-stealing." But if the person shows a desire to talk, listen and move with the conversation.

If the answer to the attendance question is "hardly ever" or "never," invite the person to open up by asking a few more questions such as . . .

"Even though you don't attend church regularly, I'm sure that you have an idea of what a church should be or do in its community. Would you share with me some ways you think we could be that kind of church in our community?"

The response could be one of three:

1. A negative response such as, "I have no ideas and I don't care about the church at all."

2. A courteous response that gives information but implies the desire that you stay at a distance.

3. An eager response that wants the relationship you offer. This will lead into extended conversation beyond the time limit you set at the beginning of the call. Let the person know that it is more time than you had mentioned at the beginning of the call but that you are willing to take the time to talk if it is convenient. If not, you would be willing to call back. Agree on a specific time. If you continue talking, be a listener and be ready to meet some needs even if you must refer them to another person in the church. You are saying the church cares enough to listen; you may have to care enough to act as well.

Appendix D

Leader's Guide

FIRST STEPS
ORGANIZING FOR GROWTH IN YOUR CHURCH

The agenda included here is to be used in an introductory session and is designed for a 90-minute meeting. All other sessions are designed for two and one-half hours.

1. Begin your session with prayer, asking God's guidance and blessing on your work together.   10 min.

2. If members are not well acquainted, be sure names and some pertinent information about all are shared. Spend a few minutes sharing answers to questions such as: What was the biggest event or activity you've ever planned? What was the most enjoyable event you've ever planned?

3. You will need a secretary or recorder for your Church Growth Committee. Elect or select someone from the group to serve.

4. Give a copy of this to each committee member. If copies are not available, tell the members when they may expect their copies. Review pages 17-20 in the following manner: 10 min.

   a. Select four or five of the key thoughts or sentences on page 17 and read them to the group. Select one of the Scripture passages mentioned and read it.

   b. Using the information at the bottom of page 17 and top of page 18, guide the group through the description of the chapters in the book.   5 min.

   c. Assuming that Steps 1 and 2 (on page 18), have been completed, or are at least in process, point out Step 3 (on page 18), and remind the group again of the criteria for committee membership found on page 19. Ask for questions or comments.   5 min.

   d. Point out the options in Step 4 on page 19 for number and length of sessions. Set dates for your future meetings and activities. Among those activities are sermons about the church's purpose prior to the writing of the statement of purpose which will be done in chapter 3. Put the dates on pages 13-15 in the column marked "To Be Done By." Use this chart as your checklist for progress.   25 min.

   e. Briefly mention the importance of Step 5 (see page 19). Determine when you will report to the congregation how you have organized your meeting pattern, and how long you expect to be involved in the process.   10 min.

   f. In conclusion, share some of the content on pages 19 and 20. Challenge the group to be a thorough, effective committee.   10 min.

5. Introduce chapter 1 briefly and show the group the options for building a covenant at your next meeting. Ask all committee members to read chapter 1 before the next meeting.   10 min.

6. Answer any questions that may remain. Close with prayer.   5 min.

SESSION ONE—
AND GOD SAID . . . GROW?
(CHAPTER 1)

Here is a suggested outline for the first meeting of your Church Growth Committee. Use whatever you can and make adjustments where you feel they are necessary. This agenda is designed for a two and one-half hour meeting.

1. Have the pastor lead the devotional based on the second chapter of Acts. Perhaps a few minutes could be used to share some "moments of awareness" from committee members. Have prayer together.   15 min.

2. Ask committee members to share with each other their answers to the two questions on page 23. Consider the material in the opening section of the chapter.   20 min.

3. Refer to the definition of church growth on page 25. Be sure it is fully understood by all members of your committee before proceeding further.   15 min.

4. Briefly deal with the section on attitudes beginning on page 25. Do any of the dialogues reflect your church situation? How would your committee members describe your church's attitude toward church growth right now?   15 min.

5. Take a break. Perhaps a light snack and/or something to drink would be enjoyed by the committee members.   15 min.

6. Point out the paragraphs in "Why Churches Fail to Grow," beginning on page 26, that you feel are significant to your local situation. Ask committee members to share some of their ideas why churches in your community, and perhaps your own church, are not growing. Poll the group, using the "Church Member Perception Questionnaire" (page 115). Does the group think much the same? Are there any significant differences? Decide how this questionnaire should be used with members of the congregation. Determine how many should be surveyed, by whom, and by when.   40 min.

7. Discuss the "costs" of church growth. Which can be applied to your church? How "expensive" will the task of growing your church be? Challenge committee members to invest themselves in the task, whatever the cost.   15 min.

8. Conclude your meeting by signing the suggested covenant or by praying together as a form of covenant. Whichever form is used, close the meeting by joining hands and praying.   10 min.

Looking Ahead   5 min.

- At the end of chapter 3 you will be asked to write a statement of purpose for your church. You must decide whether that will be the responsibility of the growth committee, the deacons, or a special group. If another group is to write the statement, then that group should read the materials on the biblical background for the meaning and mission of the church and take part in the study of chapter 3.

- Look at pages 53 and 54. Make plans for these steps now, noting the dates you have set up for these stages (pages 13-15). Plan to have the results of the "Church Member Perception Questionnaire" for Session Three.

- Remind all committee members to read chapter 2 and complete pages 117 to 121, Appendix A, before the next meeting.

SESSION TWO—
THE LABORERS AND THEIR TASKS
(CHAPTER 2)

Six roles are identified in chapter 2. Each should be dealt with to clarify and underline its importance.

1. Begin the session by reading the Isaiah and Acts passages mentioned in the devotional. 10 min.

2. Ask your pastor to guide your thinking about who the Holy Spirit is and who the Spirit could be in the life of your congregation. 15 min.

3. Guide the committee in sharing responses to "Questions Regarding the Role of the Holy Spirit in Your Church." Tabulate the exercise. Then decide how to use the questionnaire with members of the congregation. These findings will be valuable to your committee and other groups later in planning. 20 min.

4. As a committee, discuss pertinent thoughts and deal with questions raised by members concerning the role of the pastor. Ask your pastor to comment. 10 min.

5. Take a break. 15 min.

6. Now discuss the roles of lay leaders and the congregation. Share thoughts and comments regarding any of the text material. Conclude by sharing responses to "Questions About Your Congregation." 10 min.

7. Discuss briefly comments about the important role of your Church Growth Committee. Complete the Summary Sheet for "Qualities That Contribute to Growth" in Appendix A. Decide if you wish to use this evaluation instrument with other members of the congregation. If you do, decide who will do it and who will be surveyed. 20 min.

8. Prayer Support Persons (PSPs) are very important to your church growth effort. Recruiting suggestions can be found on page 39. You may want to assign a small task force of two or three persons to do this for your committee. 15 min.

9. To conclude this meeting, deal with the material titled "In Preparation for Future Meetings." The data collection process needs to begin now, since you will want to use it starting with chapter 5. You will be wise to enlist other persons, as suggested, to assist you in gathering the data. If the task of making these decisions cannot be done quickly, you may need to form another small task force to deal with the data collection or schedule another meeting of the committee to handle the matter. 25 min.

10. Review your calendar (pages 13-15). Conclude your meeting with prayer. 5 min.

Looking Ahead 5 min.

● Be sure the Church Member Perception Questionnaire" is being completed and will be ready for your next committee meeting.

● In preparation for Session 5, set in motion the data collection in Appendix B (pages 141 to 173).

● Remind all committee members and any other persons who will help to write the statement of purpose to read chapter 3 before the next meeting.

SESSION THREE—
THE CHURCH THAT CHRIST BUILT
(CHAPTER 3)

It is possible to complete work on chapter 3 in one session of about two and one-half hours, unless you choose to write the statement of purpose as a committee. If you do, you will need an additional session to complete the task.

1.	Three questions are asked at the conclusion of the devotional. Share your answers with one other person. Then pray.	15 min.
2.	Ask your pastor to guide the committee through the content on the three images of the church on pages 44 to 48.	25 min.
3.	Under the section titled "The Life and Character of the Church," on page 48, there are four categories: gathered, sent out, faithful, and united. At the end of each there are questions for discussion, and in one case an exercise to complete. Guide your committee through these steps.	20 min.
4.	Ask each person to share where he or she placed the mark on the line in the diagram on page 52. Is your church a "yesterday," "today," or "tomorrow" church? Pose several of the questions related to the diagram on page 52.	15 min.
5.	Take a break.	15 min.
6.	Make every effort to help your committee understand the definition and meaning of a church's statement of purpose. Teach them if they still do not know what it is and does. Review responses to question 15 of the "Church Member Perception Questionnaire."	15 min.
7.	Review your approach to developing a statement of purpose. Develop your statement of purpose.	40 min.

Looking Ahead

● Decide what concerns should be sent on to prayer support persons.

● Check on progress of data collection which is to be done before Session 5. (See Step 8 on page 14.)

● If necessary, allow time to finish or rewrite the statement of purpose. You may need to revise your calendar for taking the statement to the board and congregation (Step 6, page 14). The church vote must be taken before Step 10 can happen.

● Remind all committee members to read chapter 4 before the next meeting.

SESSION FOUR—
THE ARENAS FOR VISION
(CHAPTER 4)

1.	Use the Scripture passages suggested in the devotional and discuss the questions.	10 min.
2.	Six arenas of ministry are dealt with in this chapter. Highlight each and respond to the questions and exercises related to each ministry. In advance you might ask other members of your committee to lead the discussion about the various arenas of ministry. The following time schedule is suggested:	
	Evangelism	15 min.
	Care	15 min.
	Worship	15 min.
	Take a break	15 min.
	Education	15 min.
	Service in the World	15 min.

Administration	10 min.
3. Ask each person to share a dream that he or she has for your church in each arena of ministry.	15 min.
4. Close with a brief time of prayer.	5 min.

Looking Ahead   20 min.

● Talk with your committee about chapter 5. On your calendar (page 14) you set aside two meetings to do the analysis. Is this still realistic? Should changes be made?

● Make six copies of the "Data Analysis Summary" sheet (page 181) for each member before the next meeting.

● Determine who else needs to be involved at the Program Stage (chapters 6-8). Consider the chairpersons of all program boards and committees and the church's elected officers. (See pages 74-75.)

● Look ahead to chapter 8. You will find a large number of resources listed. Some of them will need to be obtained for use by those who write growth program plans. Duplicate the "Ideas and Resources" sections from chapter 8. Give each section to those responsible for that arena of ministry. Have them order material needed for the work of chapter 8. Remind all committee members to read chapter 5 (up to "Synthesis") before the next meeting.

● Ask the prayer support persons to pray for God to guide your committee as you analyze the data.

● Check on the progress of collecting the data you will need for the next meeting.

● Check on the status of the statement of purpose. Are changes needed before it goes to the congregation or is it ready for presentation?

SESSIONS FIVE AND SIX—
AN EYE TO THE FUTURE
(CHAPTER 5)

Before you conduct the sessions dealing with this chapter, you need to have gathered all the data. You will no doubt need to spend two meetings on chapter 5. The time breakdown here includes two sessions of two and one-half hours each.

Session 5

1. Use the devotional in the text or create another which deals with the search for vision.   15 min.

2. Explain the three categories on the "Data Analysis Summary" (Appendix C, page 181). Be sure the committee understands what you are looking for (see page 65).   15 min.

3. The time you need to deal with each of the three categories will depend on the amount of data you have collected for each, the intensity with which you study the data, and whether the data is easy or difficult to interpret. (See pages 65-66.) Because you have scheduled two meetings to complete the task, don't assume you have excess time. Try to keep within the time frame suggested.

Observation Analysis	40 min.
Statistical Analysis	40 min.
Listening Analysis	35 min.

Looking Ahead   5 min.

● Remind the committee to read the rest of chapter 5 before the next meeting.

● Give each member six copies each of the "horizons" and "focus" worksheets from Appendix C, pages 183 and 184, respectively. Have them work on the forms for each arena of ministry prior to the next meeting.

Session 6

Here is a suggested devotional with which to begin this session.   10 min.

Pray, seeking God's guidance and support for this very important work. Take as much time as necessary to make yourselves aware of the presence of God as a significant influence in your process.

Consider the story recorded in Luke 13:10-17. A crippled woman, bent double for so many years, was not a pleasant sight. She was always in the background, stooped and huddling in the corners of the synagogue. Those who came to worship in the synagogue avoided her. After all, she didn't look right! She wasn't like the rest of them; she didn't fit in. Jesus not only noticed her, but called her and then touched her. Healing took place.

Then consider this bit of wisdom from the past:

The energizing, dynamic center is not in us but in the Divine Presence in which we share. Religion is not our concern; it is God's concern. The sooner we stop thinking that we are the energetic operators of religion and discover that God is at work, as the Aggressor, the Invader, the Initiator, so much the sooner do we discover that our task is to call men to be still and know, listen, hearken in quiet invitation to the subtle promptings of the Divine. Our task is to encourage others first to let go, to cease striving, to give over this fevered effort of the self-sufficient religionist trying to please an external diety.

. . . I am persuaded that religious people do not with sufficient seriousness count on God as an active factor in the affairs of the world. "Behold, I stand at the door and knock," but too many well-intentioned people are so preoccupied with the clatter of effort to do something for God that they don't hear Him asking that He might do something through them.[1]

Most churches tend to shout the gospel at people from a distance rather than to involve themselves deeply in the life, activities, structure, and needs of the community. Is that true of your congregation? If so, will you continue with "business as usual" or will you seek to change your approach to ministry?

You are God's people. What is it that God would like to do through your church? This is a question related to your church's purpose which you discussed in chapter 3. It is a critical question as you bring the analysis into focus as your vision.

What should be the shape of the vision of your church? Who will it include? Where will it take place? Will all of your people be ministers? Will people be changed? Will people be healed?

This is one of the most critical points in planning for growth. There are messages for your congregation hidden in all of the data you have analyzed.

1. Discuss your church's place in its life cycle (page 68).   20 min.
2. Review the "horizon" worksheets for each ministry. If necessary, complete a new   40 min.
   worksheet for each ministry combining the comments of all committee members.
3. Break.   15 min.
4. Now, complete chapter 5 by creating your vision (page 185).   50 min.
5. Close with prayer and instructions for the next session.   15 min.

Looking Ahead   15 min.

● Remind your committee that new persons will be joining them for the rest of your planning sessions to plan programs for growth. Also remind those persons to come.

● Select graphs or charts of church and Sunday church school attendance and giving patterns that you may want to share with the congregation. Decide how this sharing will be done.

● Are you using the purpose statement in worship periods and newsletters?

● Remind all persons attending the next session to read chapter 6.

---

[1]Thomas, R. Kelly, A Testament of Devotion (New York: Harper and Row, Publishers Inc., 1941), pp. 96-97.

SESSION SEVEN—
GOALS FOR THE GROWING CHURCH
(CHAPTER 6)

The new persons joining you for the Program Stage will not have experienced what you have been through as a committee. There will be times when you need to explain, clarify, summarize, and point out certain things for the new persons. During this session be sure to ask them often if they understand things or if they need assistance in "catching on." You, the coordinator, hold the key to bringing these persons into your planning process effectively.

1. Summarize the devotional from Jonah. Lead the group in reading Jonah's prayer in chapter 2. Talk about verse 7. Then ask God's guidance for the group as you write growth goals.   15 min.

2. Briefly highlight the importance of growth goals as presented on pages 73-74.   10 min.

3. Take time to read about the ingredients in growth goals (page 73).   10 min.

4. Present the vision that has been identified by your committee. Place it on newsprint or a chalkboard. Be sure that all new members understand each element of the vision. Give them time to ask questions.   15 min.

5. Assign each part of the vision to those who are responsible for that arena of ministry. Give each group a copy of page 187 to record its growth goals. The Church Growth Committee may take the responsibility to develop goals for the ministry of administration. If another group has that task, the committee members may divide up among the other goal-writing groups.   5 min.

6. Take a break.   15 min.

7. Follow the steps for developing growth goals found on page 75. Give groups a time limit for their work. It might be helpful if you, the coordinator, moved from group to group from time to time to check on progress and to answer questions. If needed, the pastor could be asked to assume a similar role.   70 min.

8. If after 30 minutes, several groups have something to offer to the total group, you may want to reconvene. However, this is probably unlikely to happen; you will most likely discover you need more time. If no goals have been completed at the end of an hour, decide if the group wishes to continue for a specified length of time or if you should set another date for a meeting to complete the process. Remember that this step is not completed until the total group has placed its stamp of approval on all the growth goals. When the goals are submitted to the congregation, it is important that they be presented with the complete agreement and approval of the expanded Church Growth Committee.

9. Close with prayer for God's continued guidance in this process.

Looking Ahead
    10 min.

● When you have completed developing your growth goal statements, they should be submitted to the congregation for discussion, modification (if necessary), and approval. Do not develop objectives until the goals have been approved by the congregation. Discuss with the moderator and pastor what would be the most appropriate time for consideration by the congregation. If the next church business meeting is many weeks away, it would be wise to schedule a special meeting of the congregation for this purpose. Do not go on to Session Eight until the goals have been approved.

- Be sure all the persons who participated in this step are invited to the next meeting.

- Send copies of the growth goals to your prayer support persons. Ask them to pray for your church as it considers these growth goals and for the next steps in planning as well.

- Are resources for Session 9 available or at least anticipated? When they arrive, distribute them for study in preparation for that session.

- Have everyone prepare for the next session by reading chapter 7.

SESSION EIGHT—
OBJECTIVES FOR THE GROWING CHURCH
(CHAPTER 7)

The length of time your committee needs to deal with chapter 7 will be determined by the way you choose to develop objectives. Your committee is now composed of the original members as well as those persons you have invited to write growth goals. Study "How to Develop Growth Objectives" (page 81), in advance of your meeting and be prepared to explain the process to your group.

1. Ask your pastor to provide the devotional on John 14:12. Pray together.   15 min.
2. Highlight the key points on pages 79 and 80.   15 min.
3. Carefully describe the process for developing objectives. Refer to page 81. Be sure   15 min.
   the participants understand what objectives are and how they are developed.
4. Refer to the illustrations of growth objectives found on pages 81 and 82.   10 min.
5. Take a break.   15 min.
6. Now it is time to write the growth objectives. Determine which persons should   60 min.
   work on particular growth goals, including those which are the responsibility of
   the Church Growth Committee. In some cases it would be possible to bring together
   two committees or boards to develop the objectives for a common goal.

   Distribute adequate copies of page 189, titled "Growth Objectives," on which
   groups can record the growth objectives they develop. Begin writing.
7. Discuss what to do with the growth objectives when they have been completed.   5 min.
   Refer to page 82. If you do not finish by the closing time you have set, be sure
   the boards and committees understand when the growth objectives are to be completed. Work on program plans cannot begin until objectives have been finalized.
8. Close with prayer.   5 min.

Looking Ahead   10 min.

- Discuss with the moderator and pastor the steps you will need to take to present the growth objectives to the congregation.

- Materials should have been ordered some time ago for those who will have the task of writing growth program plans. Check on the availability of these resources. If some have not arrived, find out why.

- Remind the enlarged committee to read the introduction to chapter 8 before the next meeting.

SESSION NINE—
PROGRAMS FOR THE GROWING CHURCH
(CHAPTER 8)

The purpose of this session is to create program plans for the growth objectives. Be certain committee members fully understand growth program plans. Then make assignments for writing them.

1. Begin with the devotional focusing on John 10:22-30 and with an opening prayer. 10 min.
2. Discuss the definition and content of a growth program plan. (See page 83.) Be sure everyone understands what needs to be done at this stage of planning. 10 min.
3. Discuss the process for developing growth program plans, beginning on page 83. 10 min.
4. Discuss the illustrations printed on page 84. Be sure everyone understands them, as well as how they are to be used by groups. 10 min.
5. Distribute the recording form for growth program plans (page 191). Discuss plans for program plan writing. 15 min.
6. Take a break. 15 min.
7. If the Church Growth Committee is creating growth program plans for the administrative church growth objectives, you may wish to begin now. If not, join others in writing their program plans. 50 min.
8. Confirm the date to receive the program plans. If boards and committees are not finished, give them a reasonable, but short, deadline. It would be wise for your committee to review the program plans. 5 min.
9. Close with a time of prayer. If this is your final working session for some time, a closing celebration or meaningful worship experience would be appropriate. 20 min.

Looking Ahead
5 min.

- When you have received the program plans, alert your prayer support persons about this step; supply them with copies; and ask them to pray for each of the programs and projects over the next six to twelve months.

- The work of your Church Growth Committee is not yet completed. Ahead of you lie the tasks of monitoring what is happening, encouraging groups to keep deadlines, reminding groups of tasks that may not yet be completed, and, finally, the task of evaluation. Don't forget your next meeting at which time you will want to review program plans and make a calendar for the activities mentioned in chapter 9.